THE STORY OF THE 29TH DIVISION

A RECORD OF GALLANT DEEDS

BY

Captain STAIR GILLON

(LATE KING'S OWN SCOTTISH BORDERERS, 29TH DIVISION)

Compiled from Narratives supplied by the Three Divisional Commanders and Others

πέμπε δέ μ' ἐς Τροίην, καί μοι μάλα πόλλ' ἐπέτελλεν
αἰὲν ἀριστεύειν καὶ ὑπείροχον ἔμμεναι ἄλλων.

—HOMER, *Iliad, Book VI.*, *lines 207-8.*

THOMAS NELSON AND SONS, LTD.
LONDON, EDINBURGH, AND NEW YORK

First impression October 1925

Printed and bound by Antony Rowe Ltd, Eastbourne

TO THE MEMORY OF
THE OFFICERS
NON-COMMISSIONED OFFICERS
AND MEN

WHO SERVED IN THE TWENTY-NINTH DIVISION
AND FELL IN THE GREAT WAR

Nulla dies unquam memori vos eximet aevo
VIRGIL

INTRODUCTION

By the Editor

A MARKED feature of the British army in the Great War was the growth of divisional *esprit de corps*. In some instances divisional self-consciousness was fostered by nationality, as in the case of the Australian, New Zealand, Canadian, and Scottish Divisions. In the case of the Guards Division the spirit was there from the date of formation, which merely intensified an already existing *esprit de corps d'élite*. This was by no means the first war in which the Brigade of Guards had fought; but in most divisions, whether Regular, Territorial, or New Army, the spirit had to be born. It was in such cases, invariably, the product of hard knocks shared under the same leadership; it was engendered by the sense of solidarity in success and failure.

The 29th Division was one of the last kind. Accident and the War Office brought its component parts together and launched it against the Turk labelled with the distinguishing number " 29," which was a puzzle to all but the initiated. When it started its career, it was to all intents and purposes a " regular " division as regards infantry and artillery. Its territorial units—*i.e.*, field companies of Royal Engineers, pioneers, signals, R.A.M.C., and the 5th Royal Scots—were as good as any. Its *moral* was high, but it was the *moral* of eleven superb battalions brought home from stations overseas. Colonel Wolley-Dod has pointed out that, apart from the scattered stations and unsuitable country, in which the division trained in Warwickshire on assembly before embarkation, there were two factors which tended to retard divisional sense. One was the employment of the troops, when in Egypt, on heavy fatigues, with the result that no brigade—much less divisional—training was done. The other was that the division was not tested as such until April 28, 1915, under unfavourable conditions, when below half strength and inadequately supported by artillery. The landing was, as the *Times* pointed out this year in an article which appeared on 25th April, a " soldiers' battle." It was the achievement of regimental gallantry on the part of the very finest officers and men. The divisional spirit was not long in coming. When, early in June, General Hunter-Weston handed over the division, or all that was left of it, to his successor, he handed over an undaunted although wearied remnant, fully conscious of the fame of the 29th, and prepared to maintain it inviolate, *et famam extendere factis.* The brilliant operation on 28th June and the gallant struggle at Suvla in August, to say nothing of the two evacuations in December 1915 and January 1916, were good team work and served to intensify *esprit de division.*

It was with high hopes that the division sailed for France in March 1916 and prepared for the impending battle of the Somme. The blow received on 1st July was such as to incapacitate the 29th from further participation in offensive warfare till the middle of October 1916, by which time fresh reinforcements had been absorbed. Indeed, it was not until the battle of Arras that the 29th took the field as a whole or in anything approaching war on a grand scale. From that moment there is no looking back. The sanguinary fights east of Monchy in April and May 1917 proved that the 29th Division of April 1917 was worthy of—in fact *was* —the 29th Division of April 1915. Arras was followed by the Third Battle of Ypres, from the exacting trials of which the division emerged in mid-October with an almost higher *moral* than when it entered. But a still greater trial was in store. In a sense it is true, apropos of the battle of Cambrai, for a writer to say that the 29th " had won an almost fabulous reputation in Gallipoli, although few of its original rank and file were left." But the greater truth seems to be contained in the inspiring words spoken by Sir Ian Hamilton on April 25, 1917 :—" But the division is more than a memory—it is alive, it marches on, it fights to-day in France. A blood akin to that which reddened the waters of Helles runs still in the veins of their successors in France. Even during the Gallipoli campaign the *personnel* of the division passed away and was thrice renewed, but in each case those who fell out bequeathed their spirit to those who took their places." " At the end (of that campaign) they were materially the youngest of all the formations, but morally they were still the 29th Division." The tenacity and pugnacious valour shown by the 29th Division in repelling the massed counter-attacks of the Germans at the tip of our great salient round Masnières from November 30 to December 5, 1917, was perhaps the most signal achievement of the 29th since the landing on the Gallipoli Peninsula. Nor in the severe trial of the defensive fighting on the Lys in April could any falling-off be detected from the standard set up in the battle of Cambrai. The performances of the 88th Brigade in the battle of Bailleul when attached to the 34th Division, and of the 86th and 87th Brigades in the battle of Estaires under their own commander, General Cayley, did much to save the Western Front from disaster.

It was a fitting termination to the work and sufferings of the division that it was chosen to be the first infantry division to cross the Rhine by the Hohenzollern Bridge and garrison the bridgehead on the right bank until disbandment. Sufferings were mentioned advisedly. The total casualties of the 29th Division amounted to something like 94,000. Gallipoli alone accounted for 34,000. This must be, if not a record, among the highest totals in any division. It saw as much actual fighting as, if not more than, any other division engaged. No recommendation for a Victoria Cross was ever submitted by a G.O.C. 29th Division and refused. At least one was awarded by the Commander-in-Chief where a lesser decoration had been recommended. The number of Victoria Crosses won by members of the division was 27. This constitutes a record. And where V.C.s are won, death and his attendant horrors stalk. These astonishing figures by themselves alone would justify a chronicle of the events, during which they were rolling up.

But there are other considerations which invest the doings of this division with peculiar interest. In the first place, the 29th Division is indissolubly associated with the attempt to force the Dardanelles by landing troops on the Gallipoli Peninsula. That tale has often been told and well told, but a good tale will bear repetition, the more so, if it is told from a different point of view from that taken by such brilliant writers as John Masefield, Winston Churchill, H. W. Nevinson, John Buchan, and Sir Ian Hamilton —to select a few out of many to whom grateful acknowledgment is made. The exploits of the British, Australasian, and Indian troops along with our gallant allies, the French and their Senegalese comrades, constitute one of the grand, heroic, Homeric episodes of the world's history. The 29th Division was in the thick of it from start till finish.

In the second place, the 29th retained the characteristics of a regular division in spite of the decimation of its cadres and the untrained or partially trained material sent to replace casualties.

The loss in officers started at once, and was always severe : 1,100 became casualties between the landing and the evacuation. Yet the remnant, seconded by N.C.O.s of the real pre-war brands— sterling, stout-hearted soldiers—managed to keep alive the old discipline and the old fighting spirit. There was a " professional touch " about the 29th that caught the eye and took the fancy the moment one came in contact with it. This was true of all units. There were plenty of regular divisions, and each no doubt had its own individuality. The 29th had a very strong individuality. It literally butted its personality at one.

It is obvious that the *rôle* played by the generals commanding it, by the commanders of brigades and battalions, and by the staff, must have been of paramount importance. It will be seen from the story that the division owed its efficiency largely to the outstanding ability of the three men who commanded it during its existence, and particularly to General de Lisle, who had had two and a half years in which to make or mar the troops under his command. If General Hunter-Weston might fairly be termed the inspiration of the 29th and General Cayley its embodiment, General de Lisle was, emphatically, its re-creator. For by June 4, 1915, even the iron constitution of the 29th was undermined after the stunning blows and steady drain of seven weeks' incessant fighting. Something amounting to a re-birth was necessary. The three commanders in turn would be the first to pay tribute to the efficiency and loyal service of their immediate subordinates.

In the third place, the men, round whom the real interest and romance of the tale centre—I mean, the infantrymen of the line, who dug and swore and laughed, and bled and died of wounds, pestilence, poison, heat, and cold—showed under the discipline and training of the 29th the characteristic qualities of the British soldier. Mainly English, and representative of all parts of England from Carlisle to Cowes, the division contained also men from Wales, Ireland, Scotland, Guernsey, and Newfoundland. New Zealand and South Africa made small but distinguished contributions. From all parts of the Empire, India, Africa, Ceylon, came eager British volunteers. The ties which bound these heterogeneous elements together were patriotism and membership of the 29th Division. Patriotism requires a home and society. The zeal to die for the homeland evaporates in an unhappy atmosphere. But those who came to the 29th found a spirit which was simply patriotism in action. After the war, one who knew it well wrote that the spirit which pervaded it was closely paralleled by the feeling which the Australians had for Australia. " They took the pride in their country that the members of the 29th Division took in the division." The 29th was at no time composed of picked troops. It drew upon the regimental depots, when it could, and upon what it could get elsewhere when that channel of supply failed. Its achievements were, therefore, those of everyday ordinary Britons turned into soldiers, mostly in the 29th. The story, then, is like the 29th's operations in many cases, one with limited objectives. This has always been at the back of the minds of the moving spirits in the publication of the present volume. " The idea," wrote General Cayley in 1923, on behalf of himself as well as Sir Aylmer Hunter-Weston and Sir Beauvoir de Lisle, " is not to write a military history, but to make the book a human document, containing accounts of gallant deeds, collective or individual, and also accounts of incidents behind the line, amusing or otherwise, which would bring to the minds of readers the kind of life they led during the war."

Nevertheless, if the book fails to give an accurate and intelligible account of the battles through which the 29th won undying fame, it will have missed its purpose signally. It is, of course, impossible in an unofficial history of 280 pages to do justice to the 29th Divisional Artillery. Fortunately the attempt is unnecessary. There is already in print an admirable compilation entitled *The Twenty-ninth Divisional Artillery War Record and Honours Book*, compiled and written by Lieutenant-Colonel (since publication, Brigadier-General) R. Marr-Johnson, C.M.G., D.S.O., sometime C.R.A. 29th Division. From that well of information I have freely drawn, and I can only recommend readers of this story, who want to know more about the Royal Artillery, to study that book. Little more than a passing mention can be made of the Royal Engineers, the Signals, the R.A.M.C., the machine gunners, the train, the amusements, and, finally, that indispensable but modest adjunct of the soldier's life—the chaplain's department. But they are not forgotten, although they do not figure in special chapters or bulky appendices. Training will be more in evidence. It bears directly on *moral*, and the *moral* of the division is just the division itself. But the nature of the subject only admits of very light handling, for the purpose of indicating the way they had of doing things in the 29th. The fact is, that all these technical services and matters are already treated elsewhere at all sorts of lengths, to suit any taste, and, no matter what division is concerned, the specialists have a strong family resemblance. To give one instance, if any

one thinks I have been unfair to the R.A.M.C., he can solace himself with the eleven ponderous volumes entitled *Official History of the War : Medical Services.*
Divisional spirit has found vent in many interesting and valuable publications. These histories frequently have an official character. They are based on divisional, brigade, and battalion records, official diaries, and on personal contributions, wherever possible, from the largest available source, and are garnished with handsome and elaborate maps and illustrations. A history of the 29th on these detailed lines is beyond the aims of this modest essay. Its purpose is to enable those, who can find interest in the deeds of men who saved the Empire, to follow the fortunes of the 29th Division from formation to disbandment, and to remind those who served in it of the divisional life and of incidents in which they played a part. Omissions are inevitable. It is not only those, who win Victoria Crosses, who show the highest bravery. But time and space and lack of funds exclude the possibility of a detailed story, and restrict the scope of the tale to the division itself and what was typical of it.

The names that occur are those which fit into the incidents, about which information was available to the editor, and those, like the G.O.C.s' and higher commanders', which necessarily appear again and again. The official history of the 29th Division has yet to be written ; the secret history of the 29th will never be written. Nor need it be. The main characteristics of the 29th were loyalty to authority, comradeship, and healthy emulation. Inside each battalion there was company rivalry, and inside each company platoon rivalry. Battalion vied with battalion and brigade with brigade. Before July 1, 1916, every one in the division believed it to be the best in France. Their faith was rudely shaken, but by the end of the following February completely restored as the result of hard work, rigid discipline, and three successful brigade operations. That faith remained unshaken to the end of the war. The recuperative power resulting from the three cardinal soldierly virtues manifested itself not only after the Somme, but again and again till peace came. Faith calls for works, and the works of the 29th were their training, travels, fights, and frolics. The realistic details of battlefields have been deliberately omitted. It is a very feeble imagination that cannot realize what lies behind " shrapnel," " machine-gun fire," " we got home with the bayonet," " battle casualties were unusually heavy," " it was impossible to advance through the wire." Moreover, the 29th was not the only division, and the horrors of war have found pens, which make any efforts on the part of the editor superfluous. Mr. Rudyard Kipling's *History of the Irish Guards* and Mr. Masefield's *Gallipoli* are masterpieces of awe-inspiring description, to which the uninitiated can turn, if in danger of supposing that a battle is not such a bad thing after all. None of those who took part in the Great War will desiderate the lurid touch. So all that the book aims to be is a plain tale, which, if not free from editorial shortcomings, and possibly errors in information supplied, but for which he is responsible, must in the main be true. No effort has been spared to arrive at the truth, and it is thought that by the facts of this story the 29th will stand out as a unit with a will to victory, which played a material part in the ultimate triumph of the Allies. The book is, frankly, from the point of view of the Higher Command. Book I. is, for the first six months of the division's existence, the result of the most careful researches of Brigadier-General Wolley-Dod, G.S.O. 1., of the 29th in its early ordeal, in that most friendly and helpful of Government departments, the Historical Section of the Committee of Imperial Defence. General Sir Aylmer Hunter-Weston has placed his official and private papers at the disposal of the editor and given him the benefit of his counsel in writing and by word of mouth. Generals de Lisle, Lucas, and Cayley have been unwearied in helping the editor with the part subsequent to June 4, 1915.

As regards Book II., it has been built round the framework of a very compact but complete synopsis of events prepared by General de Lisle from his voluminous store of documents. The " building material " is based on the official reports sent in by the 29th Division, supplemented by contributions elicited either by personal letter or by voluntary offers, or as the result of appeals printed on the back of the divisional monthly calendar. Such supplementary information is invariably that of an eye-witness. Among those who assisted in this section, Colonel Fuller, Generals Lucas, Cayley, and Cheape, and the editor's old friend Captain Nickalls, M.C., A.D.C., were the most indefatigable helpers.

Part II. of Book II. is, to all intents and purposes, the work of General Cayley and covers the period of his command—*i.e.*, from March 1918 to the close of the war. This was the first part of the story to be completed, and on it the style and scope of the remainder of the narrative have been largely modelled.

The editor has never discovered that there exists any other point of view than that of the Higher Command. Broadly speaking, commanders and commanded have seen eye to eye. This little book is therefore confidently put before the public as revealing something of the real 29th, and so far as the editor is concerned, it is a tribute of admiration to the discipline and traditions of the regular army.

It only remains to thank the contributors on behalf of General Cayley and the editor. The General wishes to acknowledge with much gratitude the receipt of a great deal of information from the following officers, whose names have in many cases been given in the text : Brigadier-Generals Jackson and Cheape, Lieutenant-Colonels Murray, R.A., Macaulay, R.E., Wilson, Royal Fusiliers, Modera, Lancashire Fusiliers, Meiklejohn, 29th Machine-Gun Battalion, and the late Lieutenant-Colonel Weldon, Leinster Regiment ; Captains Healy, Royal Dublin Fusiliers, and Ogilvie, R.A.M.C. The editor is under a special debt of gratitude to Captain E. A. James, 48th (South Midland) Divisional Signals, T.A., for the statistical information placed so generously at his disposal and embodied in Appendices II. and III., as well as for many hints which would have been followed had space and time permitted. The Rev. Kenelm Swallow, M.C., Captain K. M. Moir, late adjutant of the 29th Machine-Gun Battalion, Major W. J. Rice, late quartermaster of the divisional F.A.—and with an unbroken record of service with the division from its start to its finish—Lieutenant-Colonel E. T. Wright, D.S.O., in spite of his arduous labours in connection with the Association, Major W. H. S. McAlester, and Captain C. S. Stirling-Cookson, D.S.O., M.C., both of the K.O.S.B., and, once again, Captain Maurice Healy, have all contributed information of interest and value. Lieutenant-Colonel T. Nangle, R.N.F.L.D., placed at the disposal of the editor numerous records and printed matter, of which liberal use has been made. Among printed books the *History of the 1st Essex Battalion* has been of the greatest use. A lecture by Captain Millar on the Cambrai fighting on November 20, 1917, has been gratefully utilized. Typed accounts of actions by Captain James Oliphant, K.O.S.B., have been of much help.

Both General Cayley and the editor are specially indebted to Brigadier-General Johnson for the movements and actions of the 29th Divisional Artillery recorded in the *War Record and Honours Book* already mentioned.

CONTENTS

BOOK I—GALLIPOLI

BOOK II—THE WESTERN FRONT

PART I—THE INFERNO

PART II—THROUGH TRIBULATION TO VICTORY

APPENDICES

LIST OF ILLUSTRATIONS

LIST OF MAPS

BOOK I

GALLIPOLI

THE STORY OF THE
29TH DIVISION

—◆—

CHAPTER I

THE BIRTH OF THE DIVISION

BY the end of 1914 there were ten regular infantry divisions
of the British army engaged in the life and death struggle on
the Western Front. There were, however, eleven infantry battalions of the finest quality still available, and early in January 1915
the formation of the last possible regular division was ordered. Its
two immediate predecessors were the 27th and 28th Divisions. It
therefore received the number 29, the ordinal of which has become
a household word throughout the British Empire. As is well known,
the gap between the 8th and 27th Divisions was filled up by the
eighteen divisions of the New Armies. But for this circumstance,
the three junior divisions composed of regular troops would have
been the Ninth, Tenth, and Eleventh respectively.

Major-General F. C. Shaw, C.B., home on leave, in order to
recover from a wound received in France, was appointed to
command the 29th. By 18th January he and his staff had
established their headquarters in the Manor House Hotel at
Leamington. Troops began to pour in, and billets were allotted
to them in Leamington, Warwick, Stratford-on-Avon, Banbury,
Southam, Kineton, Rugby, Coventry, and Nuneaton. Thus the
troops, nearly all of whom had come from afar, and all of whom
were destined for the grimmest enterprise in a distant theatre of
war, drew their patriotic inspiration and enthusiasm from contact
with the kindly folk of the very heart of Old England. The troops
were nearly all strangers to the district, but in a short time they

were, and remained, on the best terms with their entertainers. They were much missed when they went away.

Order of battle is a somewhat forbidding expression, but it is necessary to know a little about the component elements of the 29th before the tale begins. The principal staff-officer on operations' side (G.S.O. I.) was Colonel O. C. Wolley-Dod, D.S.O., along with Major H. E. Street, R.A., and Captain C. A. Milward of the 53rd Sikhs as G.S.O. II. and III. respectively. Taking the three infantry brigades in order, the 86th was under the command of Brigadier-General Hare, afterwards Sir Steuart W. Hare, K C.M.G., C.B., with Captain T. H. C. Frankland of the 1st Dublin Fusiliers as his brigade-major. The 2nd Battalion Royal Fusiliers (the City of London Regiment) had returned from Calcutta, and were under the command of Lieutenant-Colonel H. E. B. Newenham. The 1st Battalion Lancashire Fusiliers (the 20th Regiment) had just returned from Karachi. Their commanding officer was Lieutenant-Colonel H. V. S. Ormond. Both of these battalions were destined to immortalize themselves in the names " Lancashire Landing " and " Fusilier Bluff." The 1st Battalion Royal Munster Fusiliers (the 101st Regiment), under Lieutenant-Colonel H. E. Tizard, and the 1st Battalion Royal Dublin Fusiliers (the 102nd Regiment—Neill's Blue Caps), under Lieutenant-Colonel R. A. Rooth, were both crack Irish regiments, recently returned from a long term of service in Rangoon and Madras respectively. It will be seen that the 86th Brigade was a fusilier brigade.

The 87th—the Union Brigade—was composed of (1) a Welsh battalion, the 2nd South Wales Borderers (in future " S.W.B."), with the exception of L Battery R.H.A. the only unit with actual experience of the Great War, home from fighting alongside our Japanese allies at Tientsin, then and now, at the opening of this story, under command of Lieutenant-Colonel H. G. Casson ; (2) a Scottish battalion, the 1st Battalion King's Own Scottish Borderers (K.O.S.B.), under Lieutenant-Colonel A. S. Koe, returned from Lucknow ; (3) an Irish battalion, the 1st Royal Inniskilling Fusiliers (R.I.F.), under Lieutenant-Colonel F. G. Jones, returned from Trimulgherry ; and (4) an English battalion, the 1st Border Regiment (the Borders), under Lieutenant-Colonel R. O. C. Hume, returned from Maymyo.

The 87th was commanded by one of the distinguished soldiers of the war, Sir William Marshall, G.C.M.G., K.C.B., K.C.S.I., then Brigadier-General W. R. Marshall. His brigade-major was Captain C. H. T. Lucas of the Berkshire Regiment, a trained staff-officer, with five months' experience of the Western Front in the trenches and on the staff. Captain Lucas was a born soldier, and when his immediate chief was promoted to command a division in the summer of 1915, he replaced him as commander of the 87th, a position which he retained (with the exception of one short interval) until January 1918, when he was appointed, after three weeks' command of the machine-gun training centre in England, to be inspector of machine-gun units at G.H.Q., France, until, in October 1918, appointed to command the 4th Division.

The 88th Brigade was commanded by Brigadier-General H. E. Napier, of the Royal Irish Rifles, who, along with his trusted brigade-major, Captain J. H. D. Costeker, D.S.O., of the Royal Warwickshire Regiment, fell, alas ! at the very outset of the campaign. Captain A. E. M. Sinclair Thomson of the Essex Regiment was staff-captain. The brigade consisted of three regular battalions —(1) the 4th Battalion Worcestershire Regiment (the Worcesters), back from Burma and, incidentally, the only near neighbours of the area of concentration. Their commanding officer has left his mark on the story of the 29th. Practically the whole of his service in the war was seen in the 29th. On two occasions in 1917 he was invalided home as the result of gas-poisoning. But these short absences are trifles in a record of service from the inception of the Dardanelles campaign to the Armistice. Besides commanding the Worcesters at the landing and during the subsequent combats on the peninsula, Lieutenant-Colonel D. E. Cayley was in command of the 86th Brigade for a short time. Early in June 1915 he became brigade-commander of the 88th, until September 1917. On March 12, 1918, he became G.O.C. 29th Division, and thus the final phases of this story, as well as many episodes and details in the earlier portions, are told by one who shared the roughs and smooths through which the division passed, until his troops crossed the Hohenzollern bridge and taught the Germans that there was a " Wacht am Rhein " with a somewhat different, if not altogether novel, signification from that which they were accustomed to attribute to these words.

But to return to the Worcesters. The old " 29th " Regiment of Foot was worthy of its numeral and always maintained a name for steadiness and reliability. (2) The 2nd Battalion Hampshire Regiment (Hants for brevity), home from Mhow, under command of Lieutenant-Colonel H. Carrington-Smith. (3) The 1st Battalion Essex Regiment (henceforth Essex)—the old 44th—had been stationed in Mauritius. It arrived in England under command of

Lieutenant-Colonel O. G. Godfrey-Faussett. It has found an admirable historian, and the many mentions in the ensuing pages can be supplemented by those who choose to read its story. And now for the last battalion ! The 1st Middlesex Regiment had at one time figured in the scheme, but just as the 1st Borders, intended first for the 27th, and then for the 28th Division, ended up by joining the 29th, so the 1st Middlesex, intended for the 29th, vanished elsewhere. A bold experiment was tried, and succeeded. The 5th Royal Scots, the " Queen's," an Edinburgh Territorial unit of good repute, was ordered to fill the gap. It had had the good fortune to possess for three years, and to take with it to Gallipoli, in Captain W. D. Hepburn of the Seaforths, an adjutant second to none in Britain, who, curiously enough, came of the same (Monkrig) branch of the Hepburns which produced Sir John " Hébron," tutelary father of the Royal Scots, and one of the most brilliant of Scottish soldiers of fortune ! In the 88th it made rapid strides. It was brought skilfully into the mêlée by General Hunter-Weston, who realized to the full that young troops have to be initiated to battle gradually, but that nothing is more catching for the right raw material in the right military atmosphere than the true soldierly spirit. The 5th had one defect : their speedy and heavy losses were not made good, and they only lasted till September 1915. One wonders why such a fine cadre was not kept up to strength. They arrived at Leamington Spa in the second week of March under command of Lieutenant-Colonel J. T. R. Wilson (afterwards D.S.O.).

Three regular brigades of Field or Horse Artillery—the 15th R.H.A., the 17th R.F.A., and the 147th R.F.A.—all armed with the 18-pounder and all with recent service in India, were attached to the division under command of Brigadier-General H. N. Breeks.

On 1st February the 460th Howitzer Battery R.F.A., with a special ammunition column of its own, was allotted to the division, and remained with it till the end of the war. It was, however, not until 13th March that its commanding officer, Major J. H. Gibbon, R.A., an old Cambridge rowing " Blue," learned, to his delight, from Colonel Malcolm Peake (afterwards C.R.A. 29th Divisional Artillery), that his fine new guns, his excellent horses, and most promising material in men and officers were for the Dardanelles. The battery trained direct from Stowmarket, Suffolk, to Avonmouth, and embarked on the *Campanello*, the officer commanding being on the *Arcadian*.

On 10th March the following additional units were added :—

90th Heavy Battery R.G.A. (four 60-pounder guns).
14th Siege Battery (four 6-inch howitzers).
1/4th Highland Mountain Brigade R.G.A. (T.F.).

The signal company allotted to the 29th really belonged to the Second London Division, the units of which, even before the end of 1914, were broken up for attachment to regular brigades at the front. It was in this way that the London Scottish received their baptism of fire. The London divisional troops thus became available, and it so happened that the signallers were assigned to the 29th. Thus, also, it came about that when the 2nd London Division was re-formed as the 56th Division, a new signal company had to be provided for it.

The life of a regular division prior to embarkation has little interest for the general reader. It will have been noted that the area was large, and the country unsuited to manœuvres. Practically no divisional, and next to no brigade training, could be accomplished before embarkation.

Two incidents call for mention. One speaks for sanity (not to speak of sanitation) and discipline, the other of inspiration. Over 99 per cent. of the force submitted to inoculation against enteric, a record which was all but equalled at the second inoculation on the peninsula, when General de Lisle set the example. So much for the first. The second was the inspection by His Majesty, King George V., held, in the words of an existing monument, " here in the centre of England, where Telford's coaching-road from London to Holyhead is crossed by the Roman Fosse Way, on the 12th March 1915." The 29th received its send-off amid the best associations : Thomas Telford, once a herd laddie in Dumfriesshire, and afterwards the foremost engineer of his time, the martial Romans, and the King-Emperor of the British Realm.

Early in the morning of March 12, 1915, units began to move towards the rendezvous. So little did the local people suspect what was going on, that the troops were not followed. Later on, however, quite a number of people assembled in Stoneleigh Park, a rumour having got into circulation that the review was taking place there.

When the royal train arrived at Dunchurch Station, the artillery and infantry of the division, with representative parties of the other units, were drawn up in line, facing west, with the left of the line just clear of the railway bridge on the main road.

His Majesty and staff rode along the line from left to right, and were then conducted to the cross-roads where Ermine Street crossed Telford's Holyhead Road. Then the march past commenced, the artillery in column of route, followed by the infantry in double fours (eight abreast). It sounds quite simple, but in actual practice the infantry did not attain this formation, with proper distances between battalions, without some severe strain being thrown on the brigade originally on the left of the line (the 88th). It must be remembered that to get into the " double four " formation, properly closed up, the extreme left battalion had to gain about 2,500 yards.

A more effective sight than the march past of the infantry it would be hard to imagine. Twelve splendid battalions, each at war strength in personnel, with fixed bayonets, filling the broad roadway from edge to edge and constantly flowing onward under the canopy of gigantic elm trees, was a splendid spectacle, and His Majesty was obviously greatly impressed by it. As they got clear of the saluting point, units proceeded, by prearranged routes, back to their billeting areas.

When all was over, His Majesty, ignoring the cars waiting for the royal entourage, turned his horse, the handsome " Delhi," on to the grass border under the elm trees, and rode back the three miles to Dunchurch Station at a smart canter.

His message to the division, as follows, was, by order, not issued to the troops till after their embarkation.

BUCKINGHAM PALACE

Message from the King to the 29th Division
March 12, 1915

I was much struck with the steadiness under arms and marching powers of the splendid body of men composing the 29th Division.

The combination of so many experienced officers and seasoned soldiers, whom I particularly noticed on parade, will, I feel confident, prove of inestimable value on the field of battle.

That the 29th Division, wherever employed, will uphold the high reputation already won by my army in France and Belgium, I have no doubt.

Rest assured that your movements and welfare will ever be in my thoughts.

A few years afterwards that splendid double avenue of elms was cut down, on the ground that they had become unsafe, as old elms are prone to do.

At the spot where the King saw the division march past, a fine monument has been erected by the people of Warwickshire, and the open space at the cross-roads has been rounded off and planted with shrubs. The fine avenue has been replanted, and those who like to look will find that it has been replanted in honour of the immortal 29th Division.

Even before the formation of the division, its use when formed had been the subject of controversy. As late as the end of February, a decision had not been reached, whether it was to help to "kill Germans" on the West or sail East, to put a short and sharp end to the war. Mr. Churchill's *The World Crisis in 1915* contains much of interest on this point. But here it is enough to note that before the end of February it was definitely decided, and the Government committed thereto, that the 29th were to sail to the Dardanelles.

Early in March sun helmets were issued and mules largely substituted for horses. The 29th were to form the "backbone," to use the commander-in-chief's own word, of a force of British and French to be employed under command of General Sir Ian Hamilton in assisting the fleet to force the Dardanelles. They were to embark immediately, but not under their original commander. Their new commander, who took over from General Shaw on 13th March, was Major-General A. Hunter-Weston, C.B., happily hit off by his commander-in-chief as "a slashing man of action, an acute theorist." There was no hyperbole in thus describing the man who, practically single-handed, cut the railway behind Bloemfontein, while the British forces were still facing that important and defended city. Born at Hunterston on the Ayrshire coast, the home of his maternal ancestors, in full view of the noble outline of Arran, Aylmer Hunter-Weston carried lightly his fifty years. In build he was a powerful athlete, active, a bold horseman, and hard as nails. On both sides he traced a long line in Staffordshire and Ayrshire, and in his case a long pedigree produced chivalrous instincts and an iron resolution. His past, which stands in shorthand in *Who's Who*, indicated a keen sportsman and soldier. And so it turned out. He spared neither himself nor others when work had to be done. Yet in "out of school" hours the natural geniality of the man found vent in kindly greetings to those whom he felt to be his comrades as well as his subordinates.

For, like Cæsar in the Ayrshireman's poem, " the fient a pride,
nae pride had he." Snobbery was as foreign to him as slacking
an abomination. Indeed, comradeship was the keynote to the
general's conception of discipline, for of it is born cohesion and
confidence and the solidarity that commands achievement, even
where success is unattainable. He spoke French with ease, which
helped to render him *persona gratissima* to our Allies on the contracted terrain which they shared. All ranks lamented his sun-
stroke, which occurred on 17th July, and missed his capacity, his
personality, and his abounding vitality. It takes energy as well
as resolution to plan the execution and carry it out of operations,
of which one doubts the practicability, but no originator of the
scheme for landing on the Gallipoli Peninsula could have directed
the dispositions with greater singleness of purpose than Hunter-
Weston, once the decision was taken by those in authority. It
would be difficult to overestimate the importance of what he did
for the expedition in its early days. He had foreseen, as his
masterly " appreciation," which can be read in Sir Ian Hamilton's
Diary, shows, the class of difficulty with which the invaders would
be confronted. He saw the need for heavy artillery and unstinted
ammunition. He knew that the Turk excelled in trench warfare
and had good siege troops, and he realized that it would be a long,
slow business. Always fit and cheery, knowing his own mind,
and keeping in touch with subordinates and colleagues, he kept
all in good heart and inspired confidence in his leadership from
G.H.Q. downwards. When he spoke at the final conference on
22nd April on the *Andania*, a pin could have been heard to drop.
" For three months," writes Mr. H. W. Nevinson in *The Dardanelles
Campaign*, " without cessation by day or night, this general, who
certainly never spared his troops, had himself endured all the
perils, anxieties, and sorrows of an officer directing a series of desperate actions, or rather one continuous desperate action, which
as the price of an unparalleled achievement had deprived him of
nearly all his most trusted subordinates, devastated devoted troops
with irreparable loss, and stretched his mind on the rack of ceaseless
apprehension how best to encounter imminent dangers with insufficient means."

In a word, he not only led his division, but inspired it from the
outset with faith in its destiny and confidence in its own prowess.

CHAPTER II

THE DEPARTURE

" And I maun leave my bonny Mary."
BURNS.

AVONMOUTH was the port of an embarkation which began on the 15th and ended on the 19th March. The G.O.C. and his staff sailed on the *Andania* late on the evening of the 17th. The seas were not so perilous as they afterwards became, and the division reached Alexandria intact, and the work of re-embarkation began on the 28th March. Malta, unfortunately, lacked the necessary anchorage. And this was the more regrettable because, quite apart from its comparative proximity to the theatre of war and its situation on the direct route from Gibraltar to the Dardanelles, it had as its governor Field-Marshal Lord Methuen, who showed the utmost practical sympathy with the requirements of the expedition. There was also on the spot Admiral Limpus, who knew Greek waters and the Greeks and Turks, and was ever ready to supplement with ingenious improvisations the somewhat deficient equipment of the expedition.

At Alexandria the troops had to be reshuffled into the transports, so as to conform to the general plan of invasion, which had been worked out during the voyage. As much material for the construction of piers, derricks for landing the material, and as many other appliances for landing stores as could be spared, were procured from the arsenal at Alexandria and loaded on board. With a wise forethought 10,000 new kerosene tins were filled with drinking water, and packed by twos into wooden crates and put on board. Besides these, 250 " fantesses " and 100 skins were procured from Cairo. Then there was the replenishment of the usual tank supply on board the transports. This caused delay, and the limits of quay space were responsible for still further delay in putting

11

to sea. Meanwhile, almost simultaneously with the 29th, the troops of the Corps Expéditionnaire Français d'Orient began to arrive at Alexandria. Such a concentration of troops told its own tale, and in the absence of effective control over the Egyptian press, the Turks had ample warning that an attack in force was likely to be made against their territory on one or other side of the Dardanelles. It must be observed, however, that the naval failure to force the straits in March had eliminated the possibility of surprise. The Turks, with the help of the German General von der Goltz, had fortified the peninsula and the Asiatic coast, and garrisoned both with regular troops. Moreover, the unsettled state of the weather, with the probability of its continuance, made an immediate landing very difficult. It is therefore a matter of opinion how far the Alexandria episode marred whatever chances Sir Ian Hamilton's forces had of gaining their objective, but it certainly was a factor militating against success. Hospital ships were conspicuous by their absence, and it is to the credit of the authorities both in Egypt and Malta that the alarming congestion in the respective base hospitals was successfully coped with.

Owing to the causes mentioned, it was not till 7th April that the troops were able to embark. On the 6th the commander-in-chief had inspected the Franco-British troops under his command. He has told us in so many words that what converted him from a feeling of hopelessness in regard to the enterprise to one of determination to carry out his desperate and thankless task, was the inspection of the 29th. With men like these, what was impossible ? A full account of the inspection and some admirable photographs are to be found in the fifth volume of the *Times' History of the War.* On 8th April General Hunter-Weston and his headquarters staff left Alexandria, and safely reached the bay of Mudros in the island of Lemnos. The rest of the division followed, the only unit to suffer loss being the 147th Brigade R.F.A. as the result of a sensational incident. The brigade embarked on the 15th on the *Manitou,* a vessel of some 7,000 tons. The guns were stowed in the hold, and the small ammunition was in the magazine. So great was the confidence that the seas had been swept of hostile craft other than submarines, which had not yet appeared in the Mediterranean, that no preparations had been made to meet an attack. The astonishment of all can be well imagined when, on the morning of the 17th, ten miles off Skyros, a Turkish torpedo-boat signalled the *Manitou* to stop. An officer, apparently a German, gave those on board three minutes (afterwards extended to eight) in which to leave the ship. Somewhat inconsistently, he thereupon fired a torpedo, before the expiry of three minutes, which missed. Meanwhile boats were being lowered, and men were going over the side in large numbers. In one case the davits were strained to breaking point, and with a crash the occupants of the boat were hurled into the sea. To add to the excitement, the enemy loosed a second torpedo, which also missed, whereupon, possibly to make sure of his range, the torpedo-boat retired for at least half a mile, only to wheel about and return to the *Manitou*. From short range the third and last torpedo was fired. It struck but did not explode, or else did not strike, and the destroyer made off with all speed for Asia ; and it was afterwards ascertained that she was run ashore on Chios, and blown up after an unsuccessful attempt to escape the pursuit of British destroyers. This tragi-comic incident was witnessed by Major (now Lieutenant-Colonel) A. F. Thomson, R.F.A. What might have been the destruction of an entire brigade of artillery resulted in a regrettable but comparatively small number of casualties by drowning and bruises.

Leaving the infantry and artillery on their transports in the animated harbour of Mudros to throw off the effects of the voyage and to practise exercises, begun when under canvas at Mex near Alexandria, in disembarking in open boats with full pack, horses, guns, etc., we may now consider the task before the 29th. None but those who enjoyed the valour of ignorance doubted its formidable nature. The Turk and the German had loudly proclaimed its impossibility. It was—to land in force in full sight of an expectant enemy, who had had plenty of time to fortify commanding positions, to strew barbed wire entanglements, and to make his dispositions out of ample troops at his disposal. For a parallel a search had to be made for more than a hundred years back to Abercromby's landing at Aboukir in 1801. But Abercromby's was a very different task from that presented to a leader fighting under modern conditions. It may therefore be regarded as an unprecedented attempt. It is little short of a miracle that it succeeded—so far, at least, that the strategic goal was never regarded as unattainable until the Suvla fiasco. It is unnecessary to consider the task before the Australians at Gaba Tepe, some fifteen miles from the scene of action of our division, much less to consider Sir Ian Hamilton's operations as a whole. Everything hung on what the 29th could do, and total failure on their part would have led to an indefinite abandonment of the entire enterprise.

On account of its concavity the southern end of the peninsula of Gallipoli has been compared to a spoon and to a saucer with a bit out of the left-hand side looking towards the tip. On the west there are a line of high bluffs falling steeply to the sea. At the very tip above and due east of Cape Tekke there is quite an eminence. The British military name given to it was Hill 114. From Cape Tekke the coast takes a right-angle turn south-east, and the character of the coast here is a beach for a quarter of a mile, followed by more cliffs all the way to Cape Helles, above which stood a lighthouse. North of the lighthouse is the highest ground at the tip, and it was named Hill 138. The coast turns east at Cape Helles, and for three furlongs consists of cliffs, but thereafter comes the best of the beaches at and around the tip of the peninsula. It curves south towards the southernmost point of the peninsula, Sedd-el-Bahr, upon which was an old castle backed by what was known as Hill 141. This high ground, the principal heights of which are Hills 114, 138, and 141, overlooks all the country between the western bluffs, the Achi Baba range and Morto Bay on the straits, which was the name of the " bit out of the saucer." It was obvious that the Turks from Achi Baba must have ideal observation of every movement of troops north-east of the hills at the tip, for Achi Baba stood 709 feet above sea-level. At the eastern end of Morto Bay cliffs succeed, and at Eski Hissarlik—in future called Eski—was an old battery known as " de Tott's."

All the beaches were given military names. That at de Tott's Battery was lettered S. Morto Bay can be ignored. The beach between Sedd-el-Bahr and Cape Helles was lettered V; that immediately south of Cape Tekke, W. North of the corner and facing the Ægean there was a feasible landing lettered X. Finally, more than two miles to the north of X, and nearly a mile north of the opening of a long and sinuous ravine (called Zighin or Zaghir Dere, and named by the invaders Gully ravine) on to a sort of beach called Gully Beach, came Y beach at the foot of a steep but scalable line of cliffs. It may be added that W beach is also known as Lancashire Landing and X as Implacable Landing, for reasons which the sequel will show. The assault of this veritable fortress had been planned as follows : A large covering force was to make five separate landings. The 1st K.O.S.B. and one company of the 2nd South Wales Borderers, along with the Plymouth battalion of the Marines from the Naval Division, were to land at Y and scale the cliffs, with the object, *inter alia*, of getting into touch with those landing at X. Right opposite Y the remainder of the S.W.B.

were to land at S, *alias* Eski. Two flank positions, one on the Ægean and one on the straits, would thus be secured. The most perilous task fell to the principal covering force, namely, the whole of the 86th Brigade, who were to land at X, W, and V, and push up to join hands with the forces at Y and S in the course of the day, and the final objective included Achi Baba.

The animated scenes at Lemnos, the splendid tune in which one and all of the battalions of the 29th were found to be, the mighty cheers of the crowds on the transports as they steamed out of harbour on the great adventure, have been depicted by Mr. John Masefield in inimitable cadences of English prose. Suffice it to state here that the wild weather which began on the 20th caused a postponement of the attack until Sunday, 25th April. On the evening of the 23rd the wind had dropped. The great decision was taken. To the strains of "Tipperary," played by a French naval band, the greater part of the covering force of the 29th steamed slowly out of the harbour of Mudros and headed for Tenedos, an island lying close to Asia and about fifteen statute miles from Cape Helles. One of the many problems that beset an amphibious operation is how the sailors are to land the soldiers and, if necessary, get them off again. The solution arrived at on this occasion was suggested by the presence of H.M.S. *Euryalus*, *Cornwallis*, and *Implacable* ; the collier steamer, the *River Clyde*, *alias* " the wooden horse," which was to hold 2,100 men, and a kite-tail of small craft in tow. Tenedos was reached, as scheduled, on the morning of the 24th. The wind was troublesome for much of the day, and the transhipment of the G.O.C. and his staff to the *Euryalus*, their battle headquarters, made demands on the agility and intrepidity of all. The *Euryalus* was the flagship of Rear-Admiral Rosslyn Wemyss (now Lord Wester-Wemyss), one of the many famous sailors who participated in the, to them, somewhat unsatisfactory side-show at the Dardanelles, and afterwards rose to great distinction in the war.

Fortunately for the men the wind fell rapidly towards evening, and all were transferred without hitch or mishap on to their respective floating destinations.

Meanwhile the Y detachment of the covering force remained at Mudros until the 24th, when the K.O.S.B. were transferred from their transport *Southlands* by half-battalions to H.M.S. *Amethyst* and *Sapphire*. The S.W.B. company and the Plymouth battalion of the Royal Naval Division were on the *Braemar Castle*, and H.M.S. *Goliath* and *Dublin* were the escort. Long before dawn they were lying off the Ægean coast of the peninsula, in readiness to land by means of trawlers and rowing boats.

As for the main body, which consisted of half the 87th Brigade, the 88th Brigade, the Royal Artillery, the balance of Royal Engineers not already with the covering force, the transport of all kinds, food, ammunition, etc., proceeded on the 24th direct from Mudros to Cape Helles in their transports and awaited with breathless excitement the march of events in which their comrades of the 86th Brigade were to have first say. General Napier and the head-quarters staff of the 88th Brigade along with the 4th Worcesters and two companies of the Hants, were on the *Aragon*, a vessel which later arrivals associated with pay, lunches, confusion, and red tape rather than with participation in the heroic happenings of the 25th. The 1st Essex were on the *Dongola*, save one company on the *Caledonia*. It was from the *Aragon* that Brigadier-General Napier and his staff began the short and tragic episode to be shortly narrated. There was also diverted one company to the 4th Worcesters under Major Carr, so that, in connection with the doings of that battalion on the 25th, it has to be kept in mind that they were short by one company. A tow took them, shortly after the attack opened, to the *River Clyde*. This is not surprising when it is realized that the *Aragon's* complement were originally allocated to V beach, and were only diverted to W by the march of events.

It is probable that no troops ever were in finer heart or more " in tune " than the 29th as the battle hour drew near. Not that these men underrated the dangers or privations ahead of them. They were no novices. Those who had not seen a shot fired in war had associated with scarred veterans of all ranks. Furthermore, they believed in their cause. Without hatred of the Turk they felt that when they killed a Turk they were injuring Germany's chance of success. The feeling against Germany and Germans was intense. The average Briton hates insolence, and that unpardonable defect of character and breeding was personified for him in the spring of 1915 by the typical Prussian officer with pickelhaube, bullet head, glasses, long greatcoat buttoned across a convex front, and tubular legs, with whom the illustrated papers had made him familiar. He summed up his distaste for " German-entum " by invariably alluding to a German as a " Hun," with or without an epithet.

Consequently the troops were ripe for the final touches—*i.e.*, the spirited and inspiring messages of their G.O.C. and of the Commander-in-Chief.

General Hunter-Weston's ran thus :—

PERSONAL NOTE
from
Major-General AYLMER HUNTER-WESTON, C.B., D.S.O.,
to EACH MAN of the 29th Division
on the occasion of their first
going into action together.

The Major-General Commanding congratulates the Division on being selected for an enterprise the success of which will have a decisive effect on the war.

The eyes of the world are upon us, and your deeds will live in history.

To us now is given an opportunity of avenging our friends and relatives who have fallen in France and Flanders. Our comrades there willingly gave their lives in thousands and tens of thousands for our King and Country, and by their glorious courage and dogged tenacity they defeated the invaders and broke the German offensive.

We also must be prepared to suffer hardships, privations, thirst, and heavy losses by bullets, by shells, by mines, by drowning. But if each man feels, as is true, that on him individually, however small or however great his task, rests the success or failure of the expedition, and therefore the honour of the Empire and the welfare of his own folk at home, we are certain to win through to a glorious victory.

In Nelson's time it was England, now it is the whole British Empire, which expects that each man of us will do his duty.

A. H.-W.

Sir Ian Hamilton's was in these terms :—

FORCE ORDER.
(SPECIAL.)

GENERAL HEADQUARTERS.
April 21, 1915.

Soldiers of France and of the King !

Before us lies an adventure unprecedented in modern war. Together with our comrades of the fleet we are about to force a landing upon an open beach in face of positions which have been vaunted by our enemies as impregnable.

(2,655)   3

The landing will be made good, by the help of God and the navy ; the positions will be stormed, and the war brought one step nearer to a glorious close.

" Remember," said Lord Kitchener when bidding adieu to your commander, " remember, once you set foot upon the Gallipoli Peninsula, you must fight the thing through to a finish."

The whole world will be watching our progress. Let us prove ourselves worthy of the great feat of arms entrusted to us.

IAN HAMILTON,
General.

FORCE ORDER.
(SPECIAL.)

GENERAL HEADQUARTERS,
April 22, 1915.

The following message has been received to-day by the General Commanding, and is published for information :—

" The King wishes you and your army every success, and you are all constantly in His Majesty's thoughts and prayers."

CHAPTER III

" Juvenum manus emicat ardens."
VIRGIL.

AT dawn on April 25, 1915, a Sunday, the air was still. A hazy mist hung about, but it was soon dispelled, and a perfect Ægean spring day broke. So far as the eye could see, the whole of the Helles region was lifeless. Not a sound was heard. The naval bombardment opened with a roar at five a.m. The combatants were soon to get to grips. The first party ashore was the Ægean flanking force at Y under command of Lieutenant-Colonel Matthews, officer commanding Plymouth battalion, who was the senior officer at this point. The troops were transferred from the warships and transports to lighters, and from these again to boats rowed by bluejackets. At first in the dim light nothing could be seen but the great wall of the bluffs close on 200 feet high. But as the boats drew nearer, a narrow strip of beach some few yards wide came into view, and the apparently vertical cliffs modified into steep slopes or red clay, thickly covered with scrub. It was at this moment that the sudden burst of fire announced the battle hour. It was a tense moment for the men in the boats. Were the bluffs guarded? Were there entrenchments? The K.O.S.B. were the first on shore. Some jumped into the sea, and waded up to the breast in water to the shore. Others leapt on to rocks, and escaped with a slight splashing of the lower limbs. The company of S.W.B. followed closely, and after them the Plymouth battalion of the Royal Naval Division. Not a sound of opposition! It was a surprise. Up the slope through the scrub streamed the invaders right on to the ridge at the top. The work of dragging water, ammunition, and food was arduous in the extreme. Patrols soon came in contact with perturbed Turks, who vanished hurriedly.

The Turks were well warned. They had plenty of good troops in Krithia, and between Krithia and Achi Baba, and they had sent a party to Gully beach. But they could not be ubiquitous nor reckon on the luck of the calm, which alone enabled two battalions and more to land on an inhospitable shore. The British force proceeded to throw out one flank to the left, another to the right, and dig a position of defence. We shall leave them there meantime; the regulars on the right, with the S.W.B. on the extreme right, and the R.N.D. battalion on the left or north. The first landing had come off up to time, and, but for two casualties by a shot from the *Goliath*, bloodlessly. The sequel will follow in the next chapter.

The other flanking party were held up by that strange phenomenon, the out-running Dardanelles current. Signals were actually sent to divert it to V beach. They failed to get through, and the three companies of the S.W.B. under Lieutenant-Colonel Casson, thanks to the skilful covering fire of Captain Davidson, R.N., of H.M.S. *Cornwallis*, reached S beach about 7.30 a.m., according to plan and without casualties. In their first rush for the hostile trenches they were assisted by the gallant captain and his blue-jackets and marines. Them, too, we can leave making their position sure in de Tott's Battery, to hang on doggedly until they got contact with French troops on their left through the combined operations of the 27th April. It was a precarious isolation. Neither as regards land nor water was it a healthy spot. Mines, submarines, and guns from behind Achi Baba, from the Narrows, and from Asia! Their fate depended largely on what happened at X, at W, and V. To them we now turn. We know that the assault at V failed as a daylight operation, but the wonderful work done under fire by both arms of the service enabled full advantage to be taken of the stupendous feat of arms performed at X and W, regarded, as they must be, if the situation is to be properly understood, as one operation.

As already pointed out, X lies one mile north of the right angle at Cape Tekke. If troops could land on the narrow sandy beach and scale the 100-foot cliff confronting them they would be in a position to assist their comrades on the right in the still more formidable task of landing at W, which is just east, and no more, of the cape itself.

At 6 a.m. the 2nd Royal Fusiliers landed half their strength under cover of a withering bombardment by the guns of the *Implacable* (Captain H. C. Lockyear, R.N.). The remainder followed with all speed, the whole battalion being landed in two successive tows of six boats each. Small wonder that the scene of this successful and brilliantly executed landing was ever afterwards known as Implacable Landing. The Royal Fusiliers speedily became involved with the enemy, and the full details of its long ordeal on the 25th can be read in *The Royal Fusiliers in the Great War*. Their immediate objective was Hill 114, the capture of which was essential to the support of the Lancashire Fusiliers at W. This important tactical movement was executed with great determination, and by 11 a.m. Hill 114 was ours. But a company was detached with the view, if possible, of joining hands with the Y party. This company, under Captain Leslie, became involved in a sanguinary combat, and its leader was killed. Meanwhile the 87th Brigade were landing between 8 and 9 a.m. under cover of the Royal Fusiliers at X. With these troops were Brigadier-General Marshall and his staff. Of this landing Colonel Lucas (then brigade-major) has written : " The landing of the 87th Brigade Headquarters differs from some others. I recollect a bright sunny morning, dead calm sea, not a shot fired. I had a bag in one hand, a coat over my arm, and was assisted down a plank from the boat by an obliging sailor, so that I should not wet my boots. The only thing missing was the hotel." Of the 87th the R.I.F. were on the right and the 1st Border Regiment (Borders) on the left. Hard times were in store for all of these, but especially for the Royal Fusiliers, but the land fighting has to be postponed to the tale of the landings.

In the whole story of the 29th's fighting there is nothing quite so stirring as the landing of the 1st Lancashire Fusiliers at W. It is one of the most astounding exploits in history.

On board H.M.S. *Euryalus* were three companies of the Lancashire Fusiliers. On a mine-sweeper was the fourth company and the headquarters staff of the 86th Brigade. At 6.30 a.m., somewhat after scheduled time, the tows left the *Euryalus*, and a few minutes later the smaller party pulled away from the sweeper. All headed for W beach. It was, of course, broad daylight. There on the sand stretched a formidable entanglement of undamaged, heavily barbed wire. A sinister play of little ripples indicated more wire in the water. Land mines were to be discovered on the beach. The packed boats presented an ideal target. The only question was : When would the shooting begin ? Not a man of these veterans did not know the murderous efficiency of machine guns, magazine rifles, and pom-poms. It is matter of controversy whether the Turks were right in so long withholding their fire. That must be left to the pundits. It is equally disputed, whether they didn't

keep their heads down by reason of the naval fire, the moral effect
of which must have been tremendous, until the sense of a more
imminent danger brought them up. Suffice it to say that the
ominous silence ended with a sudden blaze of fire directed on the
boats from three different points just as the leading boats touched
the beach. As Colonel Wolley-Dod tells us : " It appeared as if
the whole battalion must be wiped out. The wire on the beach
was intact, and to those watching anxiously from the *Euryalus*
the situation appeared hopeless. It looked as if each man was shot
down as he left his boat." It was t so bad as this, though bad
enough, as here and there men were seen to press on to the wire
and cut as if possessed. Some of these would crumple up in the wire,
but others would be there to take their places. Here, as always in
times of strain, work was the panacea. It was work on which the
fate of the whole expedition hung, and but for a diversion on the
left even this superhuman valour might have been in vain. By
good luck the boats on the left of what was an échelon rather than
a line of boats struck the beach with relatively fewer casualties.
Indeed some landed on the rocks beyond. Here there was no wire,
and under Major G. S. Adams a band of warriors dashed like lightning
to the shore and up the cliffs. The British soldier is a terror *in rixa*,
and not a Turk in the machine-gun teams on the hillside escaped
the butt or the bayonet. Many of the rifles were too foul with water,
sand, and soil to be fit for firing. The effect of this daring dash was
to bring immediate relief to the heroes on the beach. Better still,
General Hare and his staff at the head of the fourth company in the
second party from the sweeper landed on the cliffs still farther west
and dashed up to the top, dislodging the enemy. It was a bitter
counterstroke of fate that the brigadier was badly wounded in the
leg at the moment of triumph, so that he became a casualty and
had to be removed to the *Euryalus*. It was indeed a triumph.
Deep lanes were now cut through the wire on the beach. The
enemy had been cleared out of the whole amphitheatre, and W was
British until after 4.30 a.m. on January 9, 1916.

 " There is no fighting man in the world like the British Tommy,"
was a favourite saying of a Mutiny veteran. So reliable are British
troops that estimates have been made as to the average amount of
punishment they can be expected to stand, calculated as percentages
of casualties. The losses incurred by the Lancashire Fusiliers far
exceed the highest estimate of what the best-disciplined British
infantry are expected to face. The G.O.C. wrote home : " In the
face of severe opposition, from defences that were apparently

impregnable, we have managed it—we have achieved the impossible. We are established at the end of the GALLIPOLI PENINSULA. Wonderful gallantry on the part of regimental officers and men has done it. On the 25th the Lancashire Fusiliers did under my eyes the most marvellous feat in landing in open boats on an open beach, which was covered with a broad belt of barbed wire and fired on by machine guns from both flanks and by riflemen from deep trenches dominating it all round." Six Victoria Crosses were won for the 29th on this great day by officers and other ranks of the 1st L.F. (see Appendix I.). The Commander-in-Chief—as good a judge of gallantry as any man living—has testified in no cold words to what he saw. His dispatches and his Gallipoli Diary leave nothing more to be said in this story. As the news reached home a gasp of wonder went up. The national *moral* was strengthened. Hopes revived.

The result of the Lancashire landing was the acquisition of a terrain for what turned out to be a war of attrition. What it might have been has nothing to do with the 29th. The 29th's Christmas card of 1915 with the British bulldog hanging on like grim death to the toe of a Turkish boot representing the peninsula contains the kernel of the matter. It was the storming and retention of W that made possible the subsequent campaign. Without W, V would have been a complete disaster. Without W the forces at S and X would have evaporated under the pressure of Turkish reinforcements like those at Y. Everything, in short, hinged on W, and, terrible and heartrending as the casualties were, W was a triumphant success, and for once the luck of the weather had been a substantial contributor to this success. On the brine " Sleek Panope with all her sisters played," and in consequence of the dead calm whole boat-loads had leapt direct on to the rocks. Away out on the wings, at S and Y, surprise had had its easily won reward. Far otherwise was it at V.

The visit to Tenedos was fully explained by the sight that met the eye shortly before 7 a.m. Three companies of the 1st Dublin Fusiliers were distributed into boat tows, and tugged slowly against the five-mile current by picket boats. Hovering about in the offing under her own steam was the *River Clyde* under Commander Unwin (afterwards V.C.), literally swarming with troops ready to burst from the wide ports in her side. Besides the fourth company of the Dublins, there were cooped up inside her the whole of the 1st Royal Munster Fusiliers under Lieutenant-Colonel H. E. Tizard, and two companies of the Hampshire Regiment, with their commanding officer, Colonel Carrington-Smith, a field company of the West Riding Royal Engineers—the divisional engineers, like the heavy artillery and the mountain batteries, were Territorials —with signallers, stretcher-bearers; and a platoon of handy men from the Anson battalion of the R.N.D. made up the complement. At seven o'clock a signal was sent to Commander Unwin, R.N., to run the *River Clyde* ashore. Headed in a north-easterly direction for the right end of the belt of wire where it impinges on the old castle of Sedd-el-Bahr, the collier took the ground with her bows about a hundred yards from dry land. There she stuck, and there she stayed throughout the entire Dardanelles campaign. To connect her with the shore there were a hopper under her own steam and lighters to be towed into position and moored. At the critical moment the engines of the hopper elected to stop, and for a time she was useless and at the mercy of the westward-flowing current. Sunk rocks complicated matters further. The sailors from the water strove to pull the lighters into position with their hands. Once again the Turks reserved their fire for the khaki-clad. At the first sight of a gallant sally of the Munsters there opened, in the words of Colonel Wolley-Dod, " a terrific fire of pom-poms, machine guns, and rifles," concentrated on the Munsters from the half circumference of a circle. Scarcely a man escaped. Meanwhile the Dublins in the boats, pulled by the most intrepid boatmen in history, had followed in the wake of the *River Clyde*.

As they cleared the cover of the collier's hulk a similar murderous fire from front and flanks produced a shambles. Whole boat-loads swung silent with the stream, not a living soul on board. Strange to tell, some two to three hundred did escape death, and took cover under a steep ridge of sand formed by the combined action of the current and the winter storms in a tideless sea. Colonel Rooth, the commanding officer, was among the killed. With the exception of the remnant on the shore and two platoons heading for a tiny cove or landing-place, known as the " Camber," on the eastern or Morto Bay side of the promontory, on which the old castle and fort of Sedd-el-Bahr stood, and the one remaining company on board the *River Clyde*, this gallant regiment was *hors de combat*. Their very chaplain, Father W. Finn, was killed while in the discharge of his priestly duty. Some were shot dead, some cruelly wounded, some drowned. The waters of the bay were tinged red. The bursts of fire made silver lines on the surface of the sea. But misfortune still pursued every attempt, although these were courageously persisted in. Towards 11 a.m. two companies of the Hants, and with them Brigadier-General Napier, commanding the 88th Brigade, were being towed in accordance with the original plan to V beach. An attempt by the G.O.C. to divert them to W failed, and when the picket boats cast off by the side of the *River Clyde* and it was time for the oars, the enemy fire was turned on to them. Two boat-loads under Captains Spencer-Smith and Wymer landed with surprisingly and comparatively small loss, and joined the Dublins under the shelter of the sandbank, which afforded nearly six feet of cover. Some of the other boats got out of control, and that which contained brigade headquarters drifted against a lighter. The general leaped into the lighter, and from the lighter on to the hopper earlier mentioned. But, alas! there was a gulf of deep water between him and the shore. There was nothing for it but to lie down on the hopper's deck and wait. There he was killed, along with his brigade-major, Captain John H. D. Costeker, both sorely missed. Captain Sinclair Thomson, the staff-captain, alone escaped on to the *River Clyde*. Presently the survivors of the two platoons of the Dublins who had landed at the Camber were rowed back to the *River Clyde*. They had failed to hold their own. Nothing more was attempted at V, and before we turn our eyes elsewhere we can see that the situation was grave in the extreme. The small force on the shore, now numbering about 400, could scarcely move a limb. Only the machine guns in the bow of the *River Clyde*, ably controlled by Lieutenant G. A. Rosser of the 2nd Hants and Commander Josiah Wedgwood, M.P., of the R.N.D., the moral effect of the naval guns, and possibly the barrier of wire, prevented the Turks from counter-attacking and annihilating the party at the water's edge. The *River Clyde* was in a position of dire peril. She was a target for every high-angle gun within range. Asia constituted a special danger. Four times was the old steamer struck direct, and four times the fuses failed to explode the shells. That the troops inside, in spite of casualties, in spite of the din of the naval salvoes, of the rattle of the machine-guns and the irregular sputter of musketry, kept their heads, speaks worlds for their *moral*. Another commanding officer had fallen in the person of Lieutenant-Colonel Carrington-Smith, killed while reconnoitring on the bridge of the *River Clyde*. Hour after hour, penned in their precarious shelters, they waited for the dark. And when darkness came, thanks to its cloak and to events farther west, nearly the whole force landed without further casualties, and prepared for the strenuous work, that daylight would inevitably bring. The wounded on the gangways and on the beach were evacuated. So much for the landing. Now for the fighting on shore.

By 10 a.m. on the 25th the general situation was much like this : At Y and S we were on the shore, but on the defensive ; at V advance appeared to be definitely held up ; at X and W there was life and movement. It was a long, long way to Achi Baba, and formidably placed on the right flank of the line of advance of the 2nd Royal Fusiliers and the R.I.F., and the Borders behind them in support, was, as already pointed out, Hill 141. It had to be captured. Similarly the 1st Lancashire Fusiliers, and the 1st Essex of the 88th Brigade under Colonel Godfrey-Faussett, along with the remaining half of the 2nd Hants under Major Leigh, all of whom landed after 10 a.m., could not advance against Hill 138 (see Chapter II.), upon which was a formidable redoubt, without the assurance that Hill 114 was in our hands. It was not the least of the services of the Lancashire Fusiliers that the parties at the Tekke bluffs had pressed on to Hill 114. The Turks made efforts to dislodge them, but with the support of the Essex and the Hampshire contingent the ground was held. Perhaps the result might have been secured with fewer troops, but higher direction had suffered another loss in the death of Major Frankland, brigade-major of the 86th Brigade, who was shot near the lighthouse. He was reconnoitring alone far in advance of the brigade. In fact, he was nearly as far as the ruined barracks and fort at Helles. Lieutenant-Colonel Cayley of the Worcesters was the first to come upon his body after the advance shortly to be narrated. As soon as possible—i.e., shortly after noon—G.S.O. 1., Colonel Wolley-Dod, was sent on shore to organize the next important step—i.e., the attack on Hill 138. That height was the key to Hill 141 at Sedd-el-Bahr. Its possession would ease the situation on V beach and on the River Clyde. Colonel Wolley-Dod at once arranged with Colonel (afterwards Major-General) Cayley, who had landed about 11 a.m. at W with the first loads of his three-company-strong battalion, the famous 4th Worcesters of the 88th Brigade, for an attack upon Hill 138. Some time must necessarily elapse before the battalion was in attack formation, and opportunity was taken reverently to bury the 120 corpses of what had once been the stoutest-hearted warriors in the British army. By 2 p.m. all was ready, and the assault was launched. Its detail belongs to battalion rather than divisional history. It has been frequently stated that the 4th Worcesters took part in the capture of Hill 114. This was not the case. They entered the fight in the following way, according to their commanding officer: " We had nothing to do with Hill 114. The Essex and two companies of the Hants were working on our left. We passed over some men of the Lancashire Fusiliers above the lighthouse, and after a hard tussle, owing chiefly to uncut wire, we got the redoubt on Hill 138, and extended our right to the destroyed fort and barracks on the cliffs just short of V beach. By this time it was evening, and we dug in. Our casualties were about 60 for the day. Our advance was slow owing to the masses of barbed wire. The fire was not very severe. By the time my right company reached the demolished fort just short of the cliff above V beach we could look down on the beach from one point. It was an awesome sight. Simply rows of dead men."

By 4 p.m., after hard fighting and a superb bull's eye by H.M.S. *Queen Elizabeth*, observed by Major J. H. Gibbon, R.A., the height and redoubt were won, and the G.O.C. reported that the Worcesters had done " an excellent piece of work." To this the troops on their left—*i.e.*, the Essex and Hants—had naturally contributed in no small degree. In result, a line was dug from a point 400 yards north of X beach through Hills 114 and 138 with a bend back to the barracks and ruined fort well in advance of the lighthouse. It must not be imagined that the 2nd Royal Fusiliers and the two battalions of the 87th Brigade had had things their own way. The first-named battalion in particular had had to fight for every inch of the ground on Hill 114 and to repel attacks from the direction of Gully Beach. Contact had been established with the Lancashire Fusiliers on Hill 114, but they had been heavily attacked by superior numbers, and for long were hampered by a battery near Krithia, which was eventually silenced by H.M.S. *Implacable*. Lieutenant-Colonel Newenham, who won the C.B. for his ability and gallantry on this day, was wounded and a casualty. So was Major Brandreth, the second in command.

Thus the memorable day ended. A foothold had been gained on the fateful peninsula. Two workable beaches had been covered by an advance on to dominant heights. With any luck the morrow would see V beach and Sedd-el-Bahr in our hands and the French installed there and at Sedd-el-Bahr. But the gains had been got at a heavy cost. The rifle strength of the 29th was estimated by the Commander-in-Chief at 13,000. About 24 per cent. of these were casualties. One brigadier-general was dead, another a casualty, three commanding officers and two brigade-majors were killed, besides a long list of valuable officers and N.C.O.s *hors de combat*. General Marshall had been shot in the leg above the knee by a bullet, but refused to go sick, or even rest his leg. Every regiment had been in action except the 5th Royal Scots, and at 9 p.m. one company of them was brought into the line to fill a gap. From right to left it ran thus : Worcesters, some Lancashire Fusiliers, two companies of the Hampshires, one company of the Royal Scots, most of the Essex, more Lancashire Fusiliers, some Royal Fusiliers, the R.I.F., the Borders, and some more Royal Fusiliers. Units had become somewhat mixed, and extrication could not begin till the line was dug. Besides, at 10 p.m. the Turks attacked Hills 114 and 138, covered by heavy rifle fire. For a short time there was anxiety in regard to ammunition supply. Colonel Cayley spent most of the night organizing further consignments. They were hard to find, and hard to carry in the dark over the awkward terrain. The consumption was more rapid than it afterwards became. But this anxiety soon terminated, and long before dawn the Turks had given up their first attempt to drive the British into the sea. After one of the noisiest nights on record the mutual casualties were found to be trifling. What was more surprising was the comparative quiet which prevailed at V, where the troops landed from the *River Clyde* were being organized for an attack at dawn on Sedd-el-Bahr fort. Possibly the continuous rifle fire had puzzled the Turks. Possibly also the absence of the autocratic will of their Higher Command, which afterwards sacrificed them in swarms, may account for a certain degree of passivity.

CHAPTER IV

"MAKING GOOD"

APRIL 26, 1915, brought no anti-climax to the titanic deeds of the 25th. Before resuming the tale of the toe of the peninsula, it is necessary to narrate, and in doing so go back in time, the experiences of the old 25th—the K.O.S.B.—and the company of S.W.B. who composed the 29th's contribution to the force under Colonel Matthews' command at Y. Things had gone hard with them. The general plan was that if the landing was successful the force should fan out to either flank—to the left to meet attacks from the north-east, to the right to assist and establish touch with the force landed at X. Under Captain Cooper a K.O.S.B. company moved inland and slightly to the right—i.e., southwards. It has been stated that between X and Y there was fixed a far greater gulf than we had dreamed—namely, the Zighin or Saghir Dere marked on the War Office map, but without hint as to its character as a formidable military obstacle. Its upper reaches were never reached by our troops. Except in spates its water was a trickle, but the cleft in which it flowed was about a hundred yards wide and flanked on either side by steep cliffs.

Captain Cooper's party crossed this ravine without opposition. There were plenty of Turks nearer the sea who had been detailed to meet a feared landing at Gully beach, but it was not from them but from shrapnel fire from the direction of Achi Baba that the probing troops advancing over the open suffered. It must be kept in view that the Turks in this area were much concerned by the demonstration made by a company of the Royal Fusiliers. The affair developed into quite a battle, and as the bulk of the sounds of fire, naval and military alike, was coming from the Cape it was natural that the Turks should pay most attention to the danger from that quarter.

From whatever cause, it was plain that contact with X was out of the question, and the small force retired upon the position, where the main body of regulars and the Plymouth battalion were trying to scrape some sort of shallow trenches with their entrenching tools. What would they not have given for picks and shovels to cope with these tough scrub roots ? The original plan had been that the brigade was to re-form here under its own commander at a fixed time in accordance with a scheduled time-table. In the light of that plan a somewhat more extended line was laid out than was required by the troops then on the spot. The morning and early afternoon passed away without any hostile demonstration beyond sniping of a desultory kind. About 4 p.m. a battery of artillery trotted down the slopes of Achi Baba, and fighting in earnest began. A second probing party on the left—*i.e.*, in the direction of Krithia—also retired upon the position held on the left by the Plymouth, in the centre by the K.O.S.B., on the right by the S.W.B. company. The position was vigorously shelled, but most shots were overs into the sea.

The hostile infantry began to develop an attack, chiefly on the left company of the K.O.S.B., then under command of Major Welch (afterwards O.C. K.O.S.B.). Colonel Koe, the original O.C. K.O.S.B., was in the centre. Commander Adrian Keyes was naval liaison officer, and a timely message through him brought most effective flanking fire on the advancing lines.

Night fell, and there was a lull in the fighting ; but when the moon rose, with rifle, bomb, and bayonet the Turk delivered attack after attack. They were all repulsed, but the ranks of the defenders were thinned and had to be filled by the S.W.B., hitherto intact, and by the K.O.S.B. probing party. Thus the right flank came to be guarded only by the K.O.S.B. machine guns under Lieutenant Paterson. These persistent and impetuous attacks lasted till 4.30 a.m., when they suddenly ceased at the very moment when a final and supreme effort seemed to be on the point of being made. Now, the curious thing is that that was the end of the battle of Y beach, so the state of matters can be reviewed without delay. Colonel Koe had received a mortal wound while gallantly restoring a bent bit of the line. The adjutant, Captain Marrow, was shot through the head by one of the last shots fired. Altogether, the K.O.S.B. lost half their men and more than half their officers. The S.W.B. suffered in much the same proportion. To the actual horrors of war was added the nerve-stretching din of unceasing rapid rifle fire, much of which must have been sheer waste. The dawn found a sorely tried but undaunted remnant of 29th. The situation was anything but bright. Ammunition was none too plentiful, and there was thought to be less of it than in fact there was. There were no supports or sign of support. Indeed, none were available. Retreat was impossible in the event of an attack in force. The difficulties of evacuating wounded and of bringing up stores and ammunition were great. It is neither uncharitable nor untrue to point out that the young untrained troops of the Naval Division were out of their military depth, and had had a terrible experience.

Major McAlester, *pro tem.* O.C. K.O.S.B., received orders to withdraw his force. A company of K.O.S.B., skilled in scrub warfare, as that battalion was after years of Indian fighting, was told off to act as rearguard. As a job it was a sinecure. There was no molestation of any kind. Not a Turk was in sight when the O.C. K.O.S.B. and the liaison officer—the last to leave the position—took their departure. By 11 a.m. all were afloat on the *Amethyst, Sapphire, Dublin,* and *Goliath,* and taken round to the anchorage off Cape Helles. On the following morning, at 11 a.m., the K.O.S.B. and S.W.B. rejoined their own brigade. The thought of bravery ending in failure is bitter. The K.O.S.B. had held on the left an awkward piece of ground where a nullah drained the water down to the shore. Attacks had concentrated against them. But if shaken at moments, they had held firmly to their ground, and there were many displays of gallantry all through the night. All were agreed that Lieutenant Miller had been conspicuous in this respect. The wounded had been evacuated with the utmost care—a task of magnitude. At Y, as elsewhere, this detachment of the 29th had been tried and had responded. That they were ready to participate in the advance of the 27th April was due to the gallantry of regimental officers and men who took part in the highly speculative, trying, and ultimately discouraging episode of Y beach. The inertia of the Turks is one of the puzzles of a somewhat puzzling expedition. It was a sort of foretaste of the final evacuation on January 9, 1916. One simple explanation suggests itself : they had trod on a thistle and found it could sting. They had suffered from naval guns' indirect fire enough to have a wholesome dread of what would greet them if they showed their noses above the cliff wall.

To return to the principal operations. As soon as daybreak came, the men beneath the fort at Sedd-el-Bahr were withdrawn to V beach, while the ships bombarded fort and village. " After the bombardment our troops were able to advance. They met with a stubborn resistance, but gained the village at 10 a.m., and had occupied the old castle and Hill 141 by 2 p.m." Thus a student's text-book. Translated into human experience, this is what happened. Those of the Dublins, Munsters, and Hampshires who had escaped death or wounds, who had lain for a day and a night at the foot of a sand-ridge or sweltered in the black hole of the frail collier, who had seen the sea whipped white by the bullets of apparently limitless numbers of machine guns, who had seen their comrades fall dead or drown, and, worst of all, the gloomy procession of the badly wounded, perhaps dying, shipwards to the overcrowded wards—these men had to force their weary limbs to fresh scenes of carnage. Fortunately they did not lack leaders of exceptional ability fresh to the battle. Nor did the leaders lack valiant warriors, as the seventh V.C., won for the division by Corporal Cosgrove of the Munsters, proves (see Appendix I.). Colonels Doughty-Wylie and W. de L. Williams were on Sir Ian's staff. There were also Major Beckwith (afterwards Brigadier-General Beckwith and commander both of the Hants and of the 88th Brigade for a time) and Captain R. N. Walford, R.F.A., the brigade-major of the divisional artillery. Led by these officers, the troops mentioned and a company of Worcesters began cautiously but with determination that jumpy and exacting form of tactics known as village warfare. Shell fire is not to be expected unless the enemy have evacuated, and the empty stronghold is intended to become a target, a trap, and a graveyard. But a village is a sniper's paradise, and the Turkish sniper in the early days of the Gallipoli campaign, with the valour of faith in Allah plus the valour of ignorance, was *the* sniper *par excellence*. The Osmanli, and in particular the Anatolian, have always been brave, especially in defence. Advance meant clearing every house, and every room, cellar, and crevice of that house. Our mainstay was machine guns. Lance-Corporal Stone of the Hants earned the D.C.M. and the gratitude of his comrades by skilfully directed covering fire. It was sad that one of the triumvirate had fallen to a sniper during the assault. Captain Walford's posthumous V.C.—the eighth won for the division—marks the premature end of the most valuable form of gallantry—bravery, directed by brains toward a goal worth reaching.

It was at this juncture that the rest of the Worcesters joined in the attack made on the old fort at Sedd-el-Bahr, taking the trenches in flank and reverse until contact was reached with the left of the *River Clyde* troops. Their captures included some pom-

poms. It was the Dublins, in reserve up till now, who captured Hill 141 mentioned in Chapter II. The angle of attack enabled the navy to co-operate. The salvoes of the 15-inch guns of the *Queen Elizabeth* at short range were terrific. The Turks retired, the hill was ours, the old fort was ours. Sad to tell, Colonel Doughty-Wylie fell at the moment of achievement, shot through the head. But he still lives in the roll of the V.C. order and in literature. Sir Ian Hamilton's Diary contains a sketch that depicts the Happy Warrior. Colonel Williams the survivor, equally gallant, had a long and distinguished career in the 29th as commander of the 86th Brigade, which post he left during the battle of Arras to command the 30th Division. The army cannot be worked on the plan of the Dodo, " Everybody has won, and all must have prizes." At the same time, his comrades on that great day, who survived, felt a sense of omission when the list of V.C.s came out.

The work of consolidation began, and at a late hour the troops bivouacked on the cold ground. The net result of the day was that where the X troops touched the sea the situation was unchanged. But from that point the line had advanced and swung round northwards. On an average, a quarter of a mile all along the line had been gained, including Hill 141 and Sedd-el-Bahr *in toto*. From the Ægean to the Straits a hold had been taken. Three companies of the S.W.B. were still isolated, but the day of their relief was at hand.

At the end of the day General Hunter-Weston was able to report in these spirited words :—

> My line is thin, my men are tired, but we shall be ready to push forward as soon as the French are in line and we have weight enough for a further advance.

The 27th April brought a welcome change. The Turks began to retire and the French to arrive. They had accomplished the work of distracting the enemy from the peninsula by the brilliant landing in force at Kum Kale, and had successfully evacuated their Asiatic lodgment when their task was completed. They landed at V beach in the course of the morning.

About 11 a.m., on the extreme left of the X position a half-hearted attack on the Borders was easily repulsed. Its probable purpose was to cover the retirement of the force at Gully Beach. The morning passed in preparation for a general advance to a line from the Ægean to Eski more or less at right angles to the lie of the peninsula. A modest amount of artillery support

(2,655)

4

was now available. Brigadier-General Marshall was in command of all the British troops on shore and Colonel Wolley-Dod was chief staff-officer. The operations were directed by General Hunter-Weston. Colonels Cayley, Casson, and Faussett were appointed to command the 86th, 87th, and 88th Brigades respectively. Colonel Casson was, of course, still at de Tott's Battery, and not yet available. The advance started at 4 p.m., and was unopposed. On the extreme right was the French Regiment No. 175. It was the first to move and the first succour to reach the three companies of S.W.B. who had been isolated, and, so to speak, interned, since the early hours of the 25th. By 9 p.m. the right rested on a hill a quarter of a mile north-north-east of de Tott's, and the left on the mouth of Gully ravine. No more could be done that day, but a farther advance was ordered to start at 8 a.m. on the next day. This was hard on troops tired by the prodigious exertions of the preceding three days. There was a prospect of two more days of incessant fighting. But they well knew that it could not be otherwise, and that the hour had been fixed so as to give them as much rest as possible. If Krithia and Achi Baba were to be ours not a moment was to be lost. By this time the brigades had been sorted out. The left section was the 87th's, the right the 88th's. The 86th were in reserve. The French were on the right of the British. Little aid could be expected from the artillery, for it was still practically immobile.

The following morning (the 28th) the G.O.C. said farewell to the *Euryalus*, and came on shore for good. Neither he nor his staff could be said to wallow in the lap of luxury, for they had the clothes they stood up in and one change of underwear. Their shelter a tent! The site selected for the headquarters of the 29th was on the reverse or sea slope of Hill 138, captured by the Worcesters on the 25th. If a few steps were taken to the summit a view opened up the concave foreground and the swelling natural glacis towards Achi Baba which lay beyond the woods and fields. " Hunter-Weston " Hill accordingly displaced Hill 138 as a place-name in the story of the 29th, and it remained D.H.Q. till the G.O.C. was evacuated. On this morning he was early on the hill to watch the progress of the advance, which started at 8 a.m., with the almost detached interest of a commander who has thought his dispositions out and issued his orders. Possibly there may be question about reserves, but in the main he is a spectator.

The advance was soon held up. The Borders and R.I.F.

were the first to feel resistance, which gradually spread to the right and became general. Strong points were here and there encountered, and the enfeebled 29th lacked that weight behind the spear with which to surround and smother the resistance. A counter-attack on the left seemed to be developing, but it melted away before a terrific broadside of the *Queen Elizabeth* witnessed by the Commander-in-Chief. This was the first day on which the 29th moved as a formation, and it was handicapped. Everybody was tired. Men who should have added to the volume of rifle strength in the firing line were toiling backwards and forwards, doing the work of mules on the line of communication. There was a local and temporary shortage of ammunition. There had been no opportunity for an adequate reconnaissance. But in spite of rebuffs and set-backs, and possibly because the enemy too was tired, there was advance on the whole, and here and there considerable penetration of the hostile front. Parties actually reached Krithia, only to be hurled out by counter-attack. Out on the left the original scene of the Y party's fight was all but reached, and, of course, we had the Gully beach and a good slice of the ravine.

In spite of a repulse to the Senegalese which involved the Worcesters on their flank in a retirement and consequent losses, the French at the end of the day were nearly a thousand yards ahead of their position on the night before. But the centre had sagged, and from a tactical point of view the results were *nil*. Achi Baba was just as far away. It was not a favourable trial of the 29th. Their artillery were under strength ; the targets elusive. The losses to the infantry were heavy, and there was still confusion. Troops of the 86th called from reserve were found already to have been appropriated by the 88th. At the end of the day the 86th had only 1,900 men and 36 officers. The Dublins' officers were represented by one, Lieutenant H. D. O'Hara. The Royal Scots lost their adjutant, Captain Hepburn. The already formidable total of commanding officers killed was swelled by the deaths of Lieutenant-Colonels Jones of the R.I.F., and Hume of the Borders. In the whole division only four commanding officers were left who had taken part in the landing.

Fortunately the Turk had been hard hit. He was quiet at night, and a line fairly approximate to the famous Eski line was dug, never to be crossed by the Turks (except as prisoners) till the evacuation. So it was not all failure in spite of fatigue, rain, cold wind, and the absence of packs littering the battlefield as they had been cast off by the men in the sweltering heat of midday. Colonel Wolley-Dod sums up the day's doings thus :—

" The attack on an unreconnoitred Turkish position with tired troops, a shortage of artillery and of machine guns (many of which had been lost in the sea or knocked out at the landing), was as great an adventure as the landing itself. It very nearly came off. Probably the chief reason why it failed was, that at the critical times, when the Turks on our centre were on the run, we had no fresh troops to make good our success." The same observer also records the opinion that "with one fresh brigade we were clean through the Turks." Presumably in that event Achi Baba would have been won. This day is associated for the first time with Fir Tree Wood and Krithia. Pink Farm became General Marshall's headquarters. That night Lieutenant-Colonel W. de L. Williams took over command of the 88th Brigade, and Colonel Casson the 86th.

The 29th April was a quiet day. Some wounded prisoners were exchanged. So far as known, the Turks had not ill-treated our prisoners. Some they had treated to the doubtful pleasures of hashish. In the early hours of the 30th one section of 60-pounders (the only " heavies " that ever functioned on the Gallipoli Peninsula) and one section of 6-inch howitzers (14th Siege Battery) were landed. This completed the landing of the 29th Divisional Artillery. On the 30th the French, having landed more troops, took over the whole line between the Straits and the one road of the country, the Krithia road (from Krithia to Sedd-el-Bahr). This move enabled the 88th to go to reserve near Morto Bay (see Map). The next night was also quiet. On the 1st May the 29th (Indian) Brigade landed and went into reserve near Helles. The day passed off with what appeared to be desultory cannonading on the part of the enemy, which explained itself when a heavy fire opened on our trenches at 10 p.m. At 10.30 masses of Turks assaulted our front line. The first rush penetrated the trenches held by the Munsters, but a prompt counter-attack, in which the 5th Royal Scots and the Essex figured prominently, restored the situation. Elsewhere the enemy were repulsed and the British front held ; but the Senegalese on the right gave way, and our guns were in danger of capture. Thanks to the forethought of the O.C. Worcesters, and the initiative of Captain Daubuz, R.A., the situation was promptly appreciated and counter measures taken. With complete *sang-froid* Colonel Stockdale, R.A., organized a party of R.H.A. to man a trench not yet reached by the Turks, and they held it until relieved by the Worcesters. That battalion had been withdrawn on 30th April from the extreme right, from the very sector from which the Senegalese had just been ejected. Three companies were in reserve ; the fourth was posted in close support, under command of the gallant Captain G. C. Deans—who was fated to fall on 6th May—to watch the point of junction with our Allies. At once appreciating the situation, Captain Deans saw that his company filled up the gap caused by the withdrawal of the Senegalese, and incidentally snapped up a Turkish patrol consisting of an officer and four men. The line was held, and no reserve company was required in this sector. Gunner Allpress, one of a party of three Royal Artillery signallers, received the D.C.M. for his coolness in attending to the telephone when within close range of the enemy. The fatality which had hitherto pursued the higher grade of officer continued. That night we lost Colonel E. P. Smith, R.A., and Captain Morgan, his adjutant. Major Edward Leigh, who had done so well at Hill 114, and now commanded the Hants, was mortally wounded, as was his adjutant, Captain Reid. The Essex lost Lieutenant-Colonel Godfrey-Faussett, their distinguished C.O. It was a sterling bit of work to beat off a hard-pressed attack by what is generally accepted to have been a force of about 16,000 strong. We were to have been driven into the sea with the bayonet. A dreadful fate was to be meted out to the Turkish " slacker."

The two following days saw little change. The Turkish corpses now accumulated upon our front were removed by permission. The blows sustained by the 29th compelled the G.O.C. to take the drastic step of breaking up the 86th Brigade. The Dublins and Munsters were amalgamated into one battalion, which was incorporated into the 87th Brigade. The Royal Fusiliers and the Lancashire Fusiliers went to the 88th, which no longer was confined to the original four battalions, but had attached to it certain units of the Naval Division. These changes were made on 3rd and 4th May. The 86th recovered its separate existence early in June, when the whole division was reorganized.

Meanwhile at 11 a.m. on the 6th May a three-days' battle began by a general advance. The Commander-in-Chief, keenly alive to the risk of stationary warfare at the Helles end of the peninsula, had sent reinforcements from Anzac. Some Australasian batteries—e.g., the 3rd Battery New Zealand R.F.A.—landed on the 4th, were to assist the divisional artillery, and the depleted ranks of the infantry supplemented by the 2nd Australian and the

New Zealand Brigades ; besides these, the 125th Brigade of the recently landed 42nd (East Lancashire) Division of Territorials, and the 29th (Indian) Brigade, consisting of the 14th Sikhs, the 1/5th Ghurkas, and the 69th and 89th Punjabis. The last two were soon replaced by Ghurka battalions, one of which was commanded by " Everest " Bruce, the world-famed explorer and mountaineer, as it was considered undesirable to employ Mohammedan troops against the Turks. The Lancashire (Fusilier) Territorial Brigade of the 42nd Division was stationed on the bluffs on the left. On the right—*i.e.*, as far east as the ravine known as the Krithia nullah—were the 88th Brigade. It may be interpolated here that the Krithia nullah was the product of two short confluent nullahs, known as the East and West Krithia nullahs respectively, which originated on either side of, and close to, Krithia. After these joined, the course was a contorted but generally south-westerly one, past and enclosing Pink Farm. It then curved more than a right angle to the left, and drained into the centre of Morto Bay. On the right of the 88th was a composite naval brigade under Colonel Casson of the S.W.B. The attack was ordered for 6th May.

The fighting on Gallipoli had reached the stage when no advance was possible without artillery preparation. Naval guns co-operated in the bombardment. The Territorials were soon held up by machine-gun fire, and the 88th found themselves with their flanks exposed, for the French also had failed to get forward. Opposite the 88th was the strong point of Fir Tree Wood. The fight was abandoned.

On the 7th at 10 a.m. the advance was resumed. For a time, thanks to a good rush by the Royal Scots, we gained and held for some time Fir Tree Wood ; but the Turks kept counter-attacking, and by 1.30 they were back in it. The 87th then entered the firing-line, and the New Zealand Infantry Brigade was brought into immediate reserve. A heavy bombardment recommenced at 4.30, under cover of which the 88th recovered the wood. The Territorials were then withdrawn, and the 87th took over the left sector.

The third day's fighting was equally inconclusive. Australians participated with the composite brigade. Ghurka Bluff (see Map) was seized, but lost again. The battle died out, and a period of stagnation began.

It must, however, be kept in view that no great change in position had been intended. The most important consideration of all was to keep alive the offensive spirit, not by purposely frontal

attacks, but by supporting the efforts of our Allies to advance in
the area of the Kereves Dere near the Straits (see Map) to ground
which was of vital importance for observation and concealment.
It would have been easier to have exploited the tempting line of
advance along the bluffs and up Gully ravine.

At last the 29th were taken out of the line as far and for
as long as possible. By the 12th May the whole division was
at rest. The constant strain had lasted for close on three weeks.
Sir Ian Hamilton issued the following Special Order :—

SPECIAL ORDER

For the first time for eighteen days and nights it has been
possible to withdraw the 29th Division from the fire line.
During the whole period of unprecedented strain the division has held ground or gained it against the bullets and
bayonets of the constantly reinforced forces of the foe. During
the whole of the period they have been illuminating the pages
of military history with their blood. The losses have been
terrible ; but mingling with the deep sorrow for fallen comrades
arises a feeling of pride in the invincible spirit which has
enabled the survivors to triumph where ordinary troops must
inevitably have failed. I tender to Major-General Hunter-
Weston and to his division at the same time my profound
sympathy with their losses and my warmest congratulations
on their achievements.

The G.O.C. addressed a remnant of 90 officers and 4,810 other
ranks out of an original total of 312 officers and 12,000 other ranks.
Half the force had been put out of action at the landing and on
the succeeding day.

So much of the tale of Gallipoli is national rather than divisional that one feels justified in passing over food supply, water
supply, hospital ships, tobacco rations, barter of frogs for French
bread, etc., etc. Much of interest will be found in Major Gillam's
Gallipoli Diary. Similarly the graver causes for concern—namely,
the sinister activities of German submarines—are outside the scope
of this narrative.

Naval co-operation is a theme on which writers have naturally
dwelt from Sir Ian Hamilton downwards. The feelings between
the 29th and the men on the ships had never lost the warmth
of 25th April. In all sorts of ways good-will was shown.

Although much has been written about the scenery of Cape Helles, its possibilities as a winter health resort, and its spring colouring, the following description of Colonel Wolley-Dod has all the freshness of an eye-witness's account :—

" After the end of May the country dried up very quickly, and the water supply to the front trenches became a matter of great difficulty.

" On the 25th May what is frequently called a ' cloud burst ' broke over our front trenches. An observer on Hill 138 stated that it appeared as if a water-spout from the Ægean, west of the peninsula, had attempted to make a short cut across land to the Straits and had broken up in the attempt. One moment he saw our trenches, Achi Baba, etc., quite clearly, and the next the whole scene was blotted out by an inky cloud. The front trenches were flooded and had to be temporarily evacuated, and the gully became a raging torrent. Fortunately the Turks were also flooded out of their trenches, and, pending the subsidence of the waters, a sort of local armistice by mutual consent was maintained.

" No rain fell at Cape Helles, and for about one mile inland the country was bone dry. This was the last heavy rainstorm before summer really set in and the country became parched up. At the end of April, before the country became devastated by war, the peninsula was quite fair to look on. Round Sedd-el-Bahr were the remains of gardens in which roses bloomed in spite of the general destruction. Olive and fig trees abounded, and the lower ground held a fair crop of barley. Towards Krithia there were masses of scarlet poppies, and here and there the cornflowers grew so thick as to make distinct patches of blue. In the low ground beautiful irises were growing, and the banks of the gully were gay with clusters of tree lupins in bloom. Large trees were non-existent. The Turkish cemetery north of Sedd-el-Bahr held some funereal cypresses, and Fir Tree Wood near Krithia was the scene of much fighting. Stunted Levantine oaks were fairly common. The uncultivated land was covered with thick scrubby growth, of which perhaps the most conspicuous and unpopular was a dwarf holm oak with small leaves rather like holly. This was usually spoken of as gorse, presumably because of its prickliness. It had very tough, deeply penetrating roots, which greatly interfered with trench digging.

" The country produced nothing with any food value, and there were no means of catching fish, though occasionally an aeroplane bomb, or a high explosive shell, dropping in the sea, provided fresh fish for lucky bathers who chanced to be in the neighbourhood."

The remainder of May was a period of comparative quiet for the 29th. On the 26th, Brigadier-General W. Doran, C.B., took over command of the 88th Brigade, a position which he held until Colonel Cayley took over on 7th June, on the reconstruction of the 29th as a three-brigade division. It was not encouraging to witness the results of German submarine activity in the sinkings of the *Triumph* and *Majestic*. It was not conducive to health to be plagued with flies from sunrise to sundown. The climate had been delightful until the 20th May. It then became hot enough for sun-helmets. With the flies came a distressing and lowering sort of dysentery. When acute it would take the vitality and spirit out of its victims, and the young suffered specially. If it came with the flies, it left with the flies. But that belongs to a later chapter. Meanwhile it diminished still further the fighting value of the sorely tested 29th.

In a work of this size it is impossible to do justice to the R.A.M.C. In the 29th all the Field Ambulance were Territorials, and all the officers were in civilian practice before the war. Major W. J. Rice, R.A.M.C., has furnished the editor with the materials for this short notice.

Attached to every battalion and unit is a medical officer along with stretcher-bearers at the Regimental Aid Post. Behind the Regimental Aid Posts comes the Field Ambulance and its varying number of dressing stations, to which wounded are brought after collection at the Regimental Aid Posts. After imperative dressings the wounded are sent back by stretcher wagon or car to the main Dressing Station. From thence after further treatment the wounded are sent to the Casualty Clearing Station for dispersal. The Field Ambulance is, therefore, mobile, and is a link between the hospitals far behind and the battlefield itself. The dangers incurred, little less great than those of the fighting soldier, and the horrors witnessed and the suffering seen, and from which there is no escape, make the highest demands on the character of the corps. Aberdeen, Liverpool, and Ipswich supplied Field Ambulances to the three brigades of the 29th. They all landed on Gallipoli on the 26th April, and did splendid work at what was literally their baptism of fire. On that day of trial the beaches were too small for anything more elaborate than dressing stations. The wounded were sent off in boats and lighters to the very ships they had come off. Indeed, it sometimes happened that as troops were being discharged for action on the port side, wounded were being embarked on the starboard. Quite undaunted, the troops called out " Hurry up, and let's get at 'em ! " or " Are we downhearted ? " Even a little later on, when the usual posts and stations were established, the aim of the R.A.M.C. was still to convey the wounded or sick by trawlers to the hospital ships lying off the shore, whence they were taken to Alexandria or Mudros, as ordered. Casualty Clearing Stations were then established, and respected by the Turk. Red Cross wagons were safe if they didn't get mixed up with transport. Major Rice lived for three months at Suvla in full view of the Turks, and lights were increased when an aeroplane came over. The difficulties were due to the cramped space. There were thousands of men crowded round the beaches. The ground was in an insanitary condition. There were frequent dust storms—*e.g.*, one raged during the battle of the 4th June. The flies have been mentioned. There was no fresh fruit or vegetables. Fresh water was often scarce. Wounds that were mere scratches became septic ; dysentery was rife and deadly ; operations were avoided as almost impossible. Houses there were none ; therefore cases were hurried on board the ships as soon as possible. These were indeed adverse conditions, and culmination was reached in the famous blizzard to be narrated, when men froze as they walked, when every Advanced Dressing Station, Main Dressing Station, and Casualty Clearing Station was choked to overflowing with cases of frost-bite. Like Trojans, the staffs toiled to collect every tarpaulin and brazier to warm and shelter the sufferers. Cooks, orderlies, officers, all vied with one another in trying to cope with the rush. And this at a time when every R.A.M.C. unit was sadly understaffed.

The work of the R.A.M.C. in France was more ordinary, and calls for the less mention in that excellent accounts of the work done are extant. Such places as the prison at Ypres were shared in turn by most of the units of the British army. The 29th medical services were as efficiently organized as those of any other division. They had refitted in Egypt, and were ready for the work when it began in earnest on July 1, 1916. It may suffice to mention the new features for those from the East. Trench feet and " mud maladies," facilities for cleansing and bathing, scabies (treated by isolation), and rest camps were all new to the men from Gallipoli. Thanks also to the Red Cross Society and the generous donors behind it, much could be done in the way of furnishing sufferers with comforts hitherto undreamt of.

It was cheering to learn that His Majesty the King was delighted to hear of the gallant conduct of the 29th Division in effecting a landing in the face of such severe opposition, and that he was following the movements of the division with the keenest interest, and that he wished General Hunter-Weston and the division every success. On the 15th General Gouraud arrived to replace General d'Amade, who was recalled home upon an important military mission.

Attached to the division was the 127th (Manchester) Brigade, to which were loaned senior officers of the 87th Brigade. This was a fine fighting brigade. Indeed, with officers like the late Harold Cawley, M.P., to inspire and lead the men it could not be otherwise.

And now we come to the last of the early efforts to break through —namely, that of the 4th June. The bombardment began at 8 a.m. The shooting of the *Swiftsure* and the *Vengeance* was a wonderful sight. There was an abrupt pause at 11.20 a.m. At 11.30 the firing was resumed, and at noon the infantry left their trenches. As is well known, the day was not a success. The 5th Ghurkas on the left lost all their British officers. The steadiest advance all along the line was made by the 88th Brigade, reinforced by the K.O.S.B. and R.I.F. of the 87th, in the sector from the Gully to the Krithia nullah. The 4th Worcesters distinguished themselves by their tenacity and by their capture of a German naval officer and machine-gun crew from the *Goeben*. " These prisoners," says General Cayley, " were just being roped in as I came along with battalion headquarters, and they seemed quite content to be captured—one of them, who spoke perfect English, chaffing the men about him. Not so the officer. As he was being led to the rear he drew his Mauser pistol and shot himself in the chest within a yard or two of me. He did not kill himself, however, but was quickly put upon a stretcher. His mood seemed to change at once, and he accepted and contentedly smoked a cigarette handed to him by the nearest soldier, and was last seen by me being carried down the trench smoking away placidly."

The following day brought little change in the situation. There was an anxious moment during a vigorous counter-attack by the Turks, when it looked as if they had broken through at a particularly vulnerable point on our right at the junction of two battalions each commanded by a second lieutenant. One of these officers, Second Lieutenant R. G. Moor of the 2nd Hants, and then in command of his battalion, seeing the disorderly retirement in the sector of the battalion on his left, which amounted to panic for want of officers to control them, and realizing the dangers of his own battalion, with great presence of mind, and regardless of danger, rushed across the open, exposed to fire for 400 yards, and succeeded in heading the mob. He had to use severe measures to bring them to their senses, even shooting the leaders of the panic. He then collected the troops in a hollow, organized them, and led them to the counter-attack. He regained the lost trenches, driving out the Turks, organized the defences, and when reporting by telephone what had occurred he utterly collapsed from the strain. This was not surprising, when it is realized he had only left Cheltenham College the previous September. By this gallant action Lieutenant Moor gained the ninth Victoria Cross for the division. After a period at home recovering from his collapse, he became A.D.C. to Major-General W. de L. Williams, who commanded the 30th Division in France. There Lieutenant Moor distinguished himself on many occasions. When visiting the line with his general as A.D.C. he used to plan trench raids and lead them himself, receiving the Military Cross with a Bar for these dangerous enterprises. It is to be regretted that this gallant and promising young officer died from pneumonia in 1918 shortly after the Armistice—a great loss to the army.

The Turks made a vigorous counter-attack on the 6th. Mutual messages for help were sent from this or that sector. All reserves were in the line. In result, the line was held but for one or two trenches retaken by the Turks. The Turks lost many killed and 100 prisoners.

The fact had to be faced that the 29th needed rest and reorganization. It had been tried to the utmost. On 23rd May General Hunter-Weston had been promoted to command the VIII. Corps. He still was G.O.C. 29th Division, but, with all his other cares, it was impossible that he could devote that incessant and exclusive care to the concerns of the 29th that is essential to the welfare of a division in peace or war.

Fortunately it was realized at home that the 29th, with its wonderful record of achievement behind it, was worth keeping in life. What was needed was something amounting to a re-birth. Few remained of the heroes of the landing, and they were a dwindling band. If the character of the division was to be maintained, it would have to be taken in hand by one who knew what was required and how to get it done. The officer selected for this task was Major-General Beauvoir de Lisle, C.B., D.S.O., who had commanded the 1st Cavalry Division in France. He arrived at 7 p.m.

in the middle of the battle on 4th June, and he left in March 1918. He found the 29th famous but faint. He left it, if anything, more famous, and as efficient a fighting unit as any division in any army engaged in the war. Meanwhile the 29th had to go through much strenuous toil and fighting before it left the peninsula with which it is, and will always be, indissolubly associated.

CHAPTER V

THE new G.O.C. was eminently fitted for the command which he had just taken over.   His study of the military art had been long and laborious.   He had served for many years with the infantry before transferring to the cavalry.   He had commanded the 2nd Cavalry Brigade for the three years preceding the war, and he was with the original Expeditionary Force in 1914–15 in command of the 1st Cavalry Division until sent to command the 29th.   He had earned the D.S.O. in 1885, long before many of those who served under him in the 29th had seen the light.   He was famous as a horseman, horse-master, and polo player.   His relaxations had been of the kind that keep the muscles firm and preserve youth. The devotion which he gave to the welfare of the division during two and a half years was returned with interest.   But at the time of his arrival at Cape Helles all that was known to most was that they had got a G.O.C. of whom they could expect much and who would certainly expect a great deal from them.   It was known that he was a man of few words, who did not suffer fools gladly.   It was soon seen and felt that his will was iron, and that he had no concern about his personal safety.   His organizing power and thoroughness were soon expressed in improved trenches and communications.   He excelled as a leader, as a tactician, and as a trainer of troops.   He had a *flair* for a fighting man.   His own personality was strong.   It made for respect and confidence rather than popularity, for there was reserve and a certain abruptness of speech.   The pick and the shovel were wielded to some tune in the 29th, and it acquired and retained to the end of the war the reputation of a hard-working unit commanded by the hardest of hard workers.   The following entry in Sir Ian Hamilton's Gallipoli Diary on 22nd July brings out this trait of the general's in the clearest possible manner : " These Eski lines were first held about

LIEUT.-GENERAL SIR BEAUVOIR DE LISLE
K.C.B., K.C.M.G., D.S.O.

the 7/8th May, and have since been worked up, mainly by the energy of de Lisle, into fortifications humanly speaking impregnable." Quite so, one murmurs, if the gunning is on a Mediterranean Expeditionary Force scale.

The formation on May 24, 1915, of the VIII. Corps under General Hunter-Weston somewhat depleted the 29th of its staff-officers. Moreover, after the unsuccessful attack of 6th June, units were disorganized. The work of reorganization began at once. The 86th Brigade was once more called into being, and Colonel Wolley-Dod on 6th June appointed to command it. Brigadier-General D. E. Cayley was now in command of the 88th. The brigades had to have fresh officers on their staffs, because the Corps staff had been formed by transferring staff-officers from the 29th. The work of reorganizing a severely depleted unit is never easy. It could not have been carried out under more adverse conditions than those which prevailed at Cape Helles. There was no reserve area, no region of peace where the guns could only be heard faintly in favourable winds. There was no certainty of being out of the line for a definite period. The area was cramped and the division under fire at all times ; and, more than that, after the battle, it was still holding the line with troops of all three brigades.

The 87th Brigade had the advantage of being under the officer who had trained it from the first—Brigadier-General (afterwards Lieutenant-General) Sir William Marshall, of Mesopotamia fame. It had incurred practically no losses on 4th June. This brigade, therefore, served as a model ; and with the improvement of discipline there grew up in the other brigades that sense of order and confidence which soon developed into enthusiasm. There was pride in the care of person and arms. The dead were buried, and derelict packs and arms retrieved from No Man's Land.

Lieutenant-Colonel D. E. Cayley, officer commanding 4th Worcesters, was appointed to command the 88th Brigade, which post he retained, with short intervals spent in recovering from the effects of gas, till promoted to command the 29th when General de Lisle went to command first the XIII., and later, at the time of special stress, the XV. Corps. Lieutenant-Colonel C. Perceval succeeded Colonel Wolley-Dod as G.S.O. 1. Lieutenant-Colonel C. G. Fuller, R.E., transferred from G.H.Q., became the A.A. and Q.M.G. to the division. Soon afterwards he became G.S.O. 1., and in that capacity a tower of strength. A finished product of the Staff College, he was a rapid and accurate thinker, clarity itself on paper, and an indefatigable visitor of the forward positions. Meanwhile the division was absorbing considerable reinforcements. The men and N.C.O.s were relatively better than the officers, who lacked experience and thorough military grounding. The most useful type of officer was the man who had earned his living in the East, accustomed to wield authority, to live a practical out-door life, to engage in wild sports in jungle and foot-hills, and to understand business. They were never numerous, and the supply naturally ran dry ; but they were a great asset to our army, for they had in most cases served in Volunteer Corps. They had eagerly perilled their chance of future advance in life for the joy of fighting for their country. Most of them are gone. The 4th and 28th of June saw the death of at least two officers of great actual and greater potential value, who had come from India and Burma, only to fall in their first and second engagements respectively. An entry in the short *History of the 29th Divisional Artillery* for June 3, 1917, recording the great loss sustained by the 92nd Battery of the 17th Brigade R.F.A. in the death through wounds of Second Lieutenant H. I. Hilary, records a most conspicuous instance of the type of officer referred to. " He had been Chairman of the Calcutta Port Trust, and, though nearly forty-two years of age, gave up this important post to enter the ranks as a cadet." The juvenile recipients of hastily bestowed commissions, on the other hand, who formed the bulk of the subalterns drafted out at this time, had everything to learn, and not always the means whereby to learn it. Now that the trenches of the opposing forces were separated by a narrow No Man's Land, still further contracted in places by saps, bombs were a crying necessity. In May and June, there being no ready-made bombs at all, the Royal Engineers set to work to improvise bombs out of jam-tins. The later sneer at " the jam-pot artillery " when trench-mortars appeared in the front trenches had its foundation in actual fact. These primitive missiles were flung by hand or catapult. It was Mediterranean Expeditionary Force all over that when a box was sent from Egypt in response to an urgent wire for fuses, it was found, on examination, to contain small Bengal lights of different colours and intense brilliance. It did not diminish the risk of flinging a jam-pot bomb that the projectile surrounded the thrower with a halo of blue, green, or red light. The trenches left much to be desired. They were shallow, and they had no proper communications to the rear. The Turks frequently counter-attacked, the more so that they were familiar with the trenches in the Krithia sector, out of which they had just been ejected. It took time and the intervention of brigade authority, in the absence of senior officers in the battalions, to get the work of defence organization under way. It must not be supposed that the month of June was a period of peace and slippered ease. There were never-ending bickerings with bombs and bayonets, and much rifle fire at night. The smell from the corpses was awful. The chief discouragement was the meagre reply of our guns to those of the Turks. Shortage of guns and gun ammunition was all through the campaign a bar to complete success. On 18th and 19th June Turkish attacks followed fierce bombardments, with the result that our men were kept busy burying dead Turks and repairing parapets. In this fashion the time passed until the G.O.C. was able to report that the 29th were now capable of undertaking an operation. The 28th June was chosen by the Commander-in-Chief as the day for an advance with limited objectives, and an intensive bombardment as a prelude. If anything had been wanting to stimulate the spirit of the British troops, it was amply given by the brilliant action of the French on 21st June under General Gouraud, who had succeeded General d'Amade in the command of the French force. Some high ground on the west of the Kereves Dere had been won, observation gained, and a better terrain for defence secured.

The great day was approaching. To be or not to be, that was the question. Was the waiting worth the opportunities given to the Turks to improve their defences and pile up reinforcements? Would the improved *moral* show tangible gains? The day opened with a heavy bombardment of the first three lines of trenches by heavy artillery from 9 a.m. until 10.20 at the rate of one round per yard of the first three lines of trenches. The Field Artillery then concentrated for twenty minutes on the wire protecting the first two lines. The French artillery as usual gave freely the most invaluable support under the direction of those distinguished officers, General Deauvé and Colonel Aldebert. At 10.40 the Heavies resumed until 11 a.m., when the barrage lifted, and the infantry dashed forward from the trenches. " In my nine years of war," says General de Lisle, " I have seen many thrilling sights but not one compared to the 28th June. Its success was well-nigh complete, and the troops appeared to move with the assurance of victory. I could see every company and even every man as the tins shone like heliographs in the sun." As the sun would be behind the backs of the attackers each man had been provided with a triangular piece of biscuit-tin tied on to his back. This greatly simplified the work of the artillery, not only from the point of view of safety of our troops, but of expenditure of ammunition, of which there was not a superabundant supply. It must not be forgotten that the cruiser H.M.S. *Talbot*, with the torpedo boats *Scorpion* and *Wolverine* standing close in to shore, gave most effective aid. In addition, machine guns fired indirectly, and in enfilade, from ranges between 1,500 and 2,800 yards, plastered the Turkish front concentrations. The *Talbot's* 12-inch guns, with shrapnel having a cone of dispersion of 200 by 60 yards, must have been terrific, as each bullet weighed one ounce.

On the left the 87th Brigade, with the Borders on the right of Gully ravine and the S.W.B. on the left or west of it (the latter battalion being supported by the K.O.S.B. on the right and the R.I.F. on the left), took the whole of the first system—*i.e.*, three lines of trenches. Through them passed the 86th Brigade to the second line, which was stormed, and the Royal Fusiliers advanced beyond to the high ground above the sea known ever afterwards as Fusilier Bluff. Fusilier Bluff was ours till it was evacuated at 11.45 p.m. on January 8, 1916. The 29th was co-operating on that day with a very sterling force of Scottish Territorials from the 52nd Lowland Division, then just entering on a career of glory, which is recorded in a very full and interesting history by Major Thompson. They were from the Clyde basin, the Lothians, Ayrshire, Dumfries and Galloway, and the Borders—Lowlanders by speech at any rate, although such famous Highland uniforms as the Argyle and Sutherland and the H.L.I. were represented, and many names began with " Mac." If their discipline was unconventional it was effective. To use a slang expression, they were distinctly a " tough crowd." It would be difficult to figure a nicer tone or a friendlier or more soldier-like atmosphere in any unit short of regular veterans, and the 156th Brigade, who were selected by General Hunter-Weston to participate in the operations of the 29th Division on the right of the Krithia nullah, did honour to their country and their comrades. It is sad to think that a portion of that gallant force should have come against one of those extra strong posts that so often escape the attention of the gunners. Nothing is known of special favour shown to the 29th by the French in the support by the Soixante-quinze batteries which gave such puissant aid to the attackers. The historian of the 29th can only record the pride and gratitude felt by the division in the co-operation of the 156th Brigade, and their deep regret at the deaths of Major-General Scott-Moncrieff and the too numerous officers and other ranks. A brilliant exploit was that day performed by Lieutenant James of the 4th Worcesters, who, finding platoons of the

5th Royal Scots without an officer, took command and led them into the first line of the Turkish trenches. For this and a brilliant bombing exploit five days later, in which he was well supported by Regimental Sergeant-Major Felix, he was awarded the tenth V.C. won for the division.

Krithia was still intact, Achi Baba remote. Yet the neat completeness of the day's work had done more than secure a minor tactical success at a cost of about 1,000 casualties. It raised the *moral* of the troops. In gaining five lines of trenches on the left of the ravine, the 29th found themselves unopposed by defences and with only isolated companies of Turks confronting them in the open. Unfortunately our last reserves had been expended. Men felt, and they were not far wrong, that with one fresh division Achi Baba was ours. Anyhow, given a fair chance, they knew they could worst the Turk. But no such chance came again. The troops demonstrated again and again their courage and tenacity, but it was always in defence or against hopeless odds, as at Scimitar Hill.

Naturally enough the enemy made furious counter-attacks—not, as it happened, straight off and by day as heretofore, when successful—but at night and on successive nights. It was fortunate that the 87th Brigade contained a very high average of good shots. Their shooting was a tribute to the valour of the Turks and their own steadiness. On them fell the brunt of the counter-attacks, and no troops could have better discharged the duty of repelling them. While the other brigades had been recuperating they had held the whole divisional front except the portion allotted to the Ghurkas, and were in the front trenches when the Commander-in-Chief visited them on 15th June.

Fusilier Bluff, especially, was the scene of vigorous Turkish attacks, the only result of which was to cover the ground in front of our trenches with six or seven lines of piled corpses. In vain the Turks sought for an armistice in order to remove and bury the dead. The British knew as well as the Turkish Command that the Turks would not advance over that sinister barrier, so there it stayed till the evacuation. On other parts of the front the Turkish bodies were burnt. A captured order by the Turkish High Command made objection on their part an exposable hypocrisy. The orders were to burn our dead while interring their own with rites.

An incident connected with Captain G. R. O'Sullivan of the R.I.F.—winner of the eleventh V.C. for the division—shows in addition to the gallantry of that officer the difficulties of the men at this time. The Turks apparently had unlimited bombs. We, in addition to what could be made up, had only a ration of 100 per division *per diem;* 5,000 would not have been too many. But the step-child among British military enterprises just had to go without, and with dire results. The trenches which were captured with a loss of 1,000 men were only retained with a wastage of 1,500 in a few days of close warfare. But this is a digression.

In the absence of bombs the R.I.F. were obliged to evacuate certain trenches at night and retake them with the bayonet at dawn. On two successive nights, however, Captain O'Sullivan regained trenches with such bravery that he was recommended for the Victoria Cross. With the help of Lance-Corporal Somers—winner of the twelfth V.C.—he bombed the Turks out of trenches which they had won, by lobbing jam-pot bombs, made in the battalion, from the open into the Turkish trench. It was too much for the Turks, and on each occasion they evacuated the trench.

But despite these drawbacks the Turks had given up hope of regaining the lost ground by the 9th July. The 28th June therefore stands out as a successful operation, and Sir Ian Hamilton said so in clear and eloquent terms on 29th June.

SPECIAL ORDER

by

General Sir IAN HAMILTON, G.C.B., D.S.O., A.D.C.,
Commanding Mediterranean Expeditionary Force.

GENERAL HEADQUARTERS,
June 29, 1915.

The General Officer Commanding feels sure that he voices the sentiments of every soldier serving in this army when he congratulates the incomparable 29th Division upon yesterday's splendid attack, carried out as it was in a manner more than upholding the best traditions of the distinguished regiments of which it is composed.

The 29th suffered cruel losses at the first landing. Since then they have never been made up to strength, and they have remained under fire every hour of the day and night for two months on end. Opposing them were fresh troops holding line upon line of entrenchments flanked by redoubts and machine guns; but when yesterday the 29th were called upon to advance, they dashed forward as eagerly as if this were their baptism of fire.   Through the entanglements they swept northwards, clearing our left of the enemy for a full thousand yards.   Heavily counter-attacked at night, they killed or captured every Turk who had penetrated their incomplete defences, and to-day stand possessed of every yard they had so boldly gained.

Therefore it is that Sir Ian Hamilton is confident that he carries with him all ranks of his forces when he congratulates Generals Hunter-Weston and de Lisle, the Staff, and each officer, N.C.O., and man of this division whose sustained efforts have added fresh lustre to British arms all the world over.

(Signed) W. P. BRAITHWAITE, Major-General,
Chief of General Staff, M.E.F.

General Gouraud's wound on the 30th came as a severe blow. It was not that France could not send competent generals to replace him.   General Bailloud, promoted to succeed him from command of the Second Division, gave complete satisfaction to the Commander-in-Chief and his British subordinate commanders.   But Gouraud was Gouraud, and his loss was keenly felt.   On the very day on which he was injured a brilliant operation on the part of the French had gained the fortified network known as the Quadrilateral, east of the head of the Kereves Dere.   Luckily he reappeared in France, to the great benefit of the Allied cause.

The 29th were not again called on for any major operations at Helles until the final evacuation.   July was a quiet month for them, and a certain part of the time was spent at Mudros.   It was a blessed rest after the strain and the stenches of the peninsula.   Castro, a quaint little village on the west coast of Lemnos, and back by hired motor hearse was better fun for officers than the monotonous perambulation of trenches.   But, of course, it was hot, and there was nothing particularly nice to drink or suitable to eat. The 86th and 88th Brigades made a hurried return from Imbros on the night of the 21st and 22nd July, as there was a report that 100,000 Turks were massing and preparations made, immediately to drive us into the sea.   It was said even before this that an observation post had been made on the summit of Achi Baba, that Enver himself might enjoy the sight.   However, nothing serious happened, and outstanding events were the vagaries of a peripatetic naval gun called " Rambling Kate," used for firing at point-blank range at the Turkish trenches, which ended her working days on 13th August by the following trio of shots : the first a clean miss ; the second a use-

ful bull's-eye on a barricade at close range ; and the third and last,
one which made Kate throw a back somersault off her platform and
lie inert at the bottom of the trench ; and the explosion of a mine
known as " Going's Hump " in the S.W.B. sector (called after a
cheery and capable Hibernian, known to all the 87th and most
of the 29th as " John Going." He was at this time a major and
officer commanding S.W.B.), which, being unexpected, created
much stir, not to say consternation.

The 6th of August

The holding battle on the afternoon of 6th August was never
intended to be more than a demonstration in force. But it cost
the 88th dear. As far as the 29th were concerned, they alone were
called upon to advance on the right sub-sector. The 87th Brigade,
by fire from the rear, by exhibition of dummies, by bombing and by
cheering, were to keep the Turks opposite the left sector in a state
of nervous expectancy. The 86th Brigade were in divisional
reserve.

General Cayley has favoured the editor with the following
account of the holding attack carried out by the brigade :—

" As a diversion to distract the enemy's attention from the
movements farther north at Anzac and Suvla, which were timed for
7th August, an attack was ordered towards Krithia on a broad
front. The 88th Brigade was the left of this attack, on their right
being the 42nd Division, and other divisions farther to their right.
Their first objective was the series of H trenches, H12, H13, a front
of over a thousand yards. The brigade was strong at the time,

              4th Worcesters being about 900 strong
              2nd Hants   ,,   700   ,,
              1st Essex   ,,   700   ,,
              5th Royal Scots   ,,   300   ,,

The brigade came from reserve the previous night and relieved the
86th Brigade, the order from right to left being Worcesters, Hants,
Essex, with Royal Scots in reserve.

" The attack was timed for 3.50 p.m., and several hours previous
to this a heavy, steady bombardment on the Turkish trenches to
be attacked was carried out. Shortly before zero (probably half
an hour) this bombardment became intense, and appeared to be
very effectively directed on the Turkish trenches. Again shortly
before zero (probably ten minutes) the navy started a very heavy

and accurate counter-bombardment, not directed so much against the front trenches where battalions were formed up, as against communications and lines for reinforcements. The ground over which the attack had to move was on the left about 100 yards wide (except on the extreme left, where the trenches nearly touched one another) and more or less broken, gradually increasing to about 300 yards on the right centre of very open ground forming a reentrant into the hostile positions, and therefore exposed to enfilade fire as the attack developed.

" Exactly at zero the first waves went most gallantly over the top straight for their objectives, and were followed by the succeeding waves (I think three waves in all for each battalion). To follow the attack from left to right, the 1st Essex apparently at first met with little hostile fire, and gained the front enemy's trench without much difficulty. It was found to be very deep and partly closed in, really the front trench of a regular redoubt. A few men got in, and a bombing fight ensued, but no real entry could be made, and heavy fire was brought to bear on the men outside. A lodgment was made in our extreme left of the trench for a time by men who had advanced from the various bomb saps. But after a time they were counter-attacked out, and the remnants of the regiment fell back to our trenches.

" The 2nd Hants took on from the right of the Essex. Their left had about the same distance to go, but the distance rapidly increased towards their right. They were met with the heaviest fire, and in spite of the greatest determination I never could hear of one of them reaching or entering the Turkish trenches. Their commanding officer for the occasion (*vice* Colonel A. T. Beckwith, who had been wounded on reconnaissance the previous day) was Captain O. H. L. Day. He was killed with many others. The 4th Worcesters on the right had farthest to go. The battalion on their right never seemed to get forward at all, so their flank was exposed from the first. In spite of heavy losses, they, however, managed to get forward, and a good many of them got into the enemy's trenches. What happened there I do not know, but they were probably in small groups, and were counter-attacked and captured in detail. Two officers, Captain Brett and Lieutenant J. M. B. Entwhistle, and about sixty men were reported later as prisoners.

" In that open ground very few of the remainder could get back by daylight. After dark a certain number from each battalion did get in, and parties were sent out to try and bring in wounded, a certain number of whom were collected.

" The Royal Scots in reserve were not employed. The total casualties were over 60 per cent. of the three battalions, the figures from memory being : 1st Essex, 350 ; 2nd Hants, 450 ; 4th Worcesters, 700. Besides being a failure, this was far and away the heaviest day of casualties the brigade had in the whole war.

" That night the 86th Brigade relieved us again, and a very sad and tired remnant retired to the beach. One of the Worcester officers who was captured—Entwhistle—remained a prisoner till the end of the war, and, as I have heard since, did splendid work keeping up the spirits of all by his cheeriness and pluck. I had two or three letters from him during the war. He was finally released at the Armistice, and died at Alexandria from influenza on his way home, one of the saddest incidents I know of in the war. As the attack started we got most encouraging reports from the divisional observation post, which could see over the ground especially on our right, to the effect that our men could be seen entering the Turkish trenches and getting to all objectives. But it was very few who got there, and fewer who got back. The whole thing was really over in less than twenty minutes."

GALLIPOLI

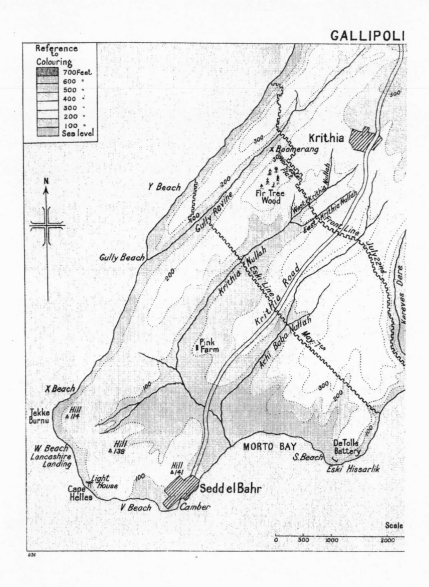

Reference to Colouring
- 700 Feet
- 600 "
- 500 "
- 400 "
- 300 "
- 200 "
- 100 "
- Sea level

Krithia

Y Beach

Boomerang

Fir Tree Wood

Gully Ravine

West Krithia Nullah

East Krithia Nullah

Front Line

Gully Beach

Krithia Nullah

Eski Line

July 22nd

Kereves Dere

Krithia Road

Achi Baba Nullah

May 1st.

Pink Farm

X Beach

Tekke Burnu

Hill 114

Hill 138

MORTO BAY

DeTotts Battery

S. Beach

Eski Hissarlik

W Beach Lancashire Landing

Hill 141

Light House

Sedd el Bahr

Cape Helles

V Beach

Camber

Scale

0   500   1000   2000

936

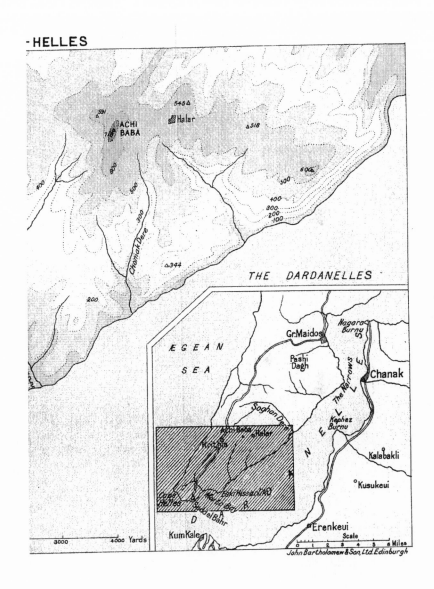

THE DARDANELLES

CHAPTER VI

SCIMITAR HILL

MEANWHILE at Anzac and Suvla the great enterprise had failed. By the 15th August there seemed little hope of a break through. The position had to be made secure if we were even to hold on, and Sir Ian Hamilton felt that a further effort must be made to that end. If the best was to be got out of the young and inexperienced troops, who had lost a good deal of the fire and enthusiasm with which they had started off, they must be toned up by contact with the seasoned brigades of the 29th.

Sir C. E. Callwell in *The Dardanelles* observes : " He resolved upon making a fresh effort to improve the Ṣuvla position and to secure its junction with the Anzac area, hoping at the same time to gain possession of Ismail Oglu Tepe, as capture of this hill would constitute an important step towards securing both Suvla Bay and Anzac Cove from artillery fire. In view of effecting these objects he moved the 29th Division round to Suvla from Helles, and then also disembarked the Mounted Division, that was coming from Egypt, in the northern area. The arrival of the 29th Division, the achievements of which during the campaign had already been common talk in the United Kingdom before the troops operating in the Suvla region had started from home, had, it should be recorded, a most stimulating effect upon the army that was facing the Anafarta hills.

" General de Lisle, previously in command of the 29th Division, had taken over charge, as a temporary measure, of the Suvla force —his place at the head of his division being taken by General Marshall—and on the 21st August a fresh attack on an important scale was undertaken. The engagement took place in presence of Sir Ian Hamilton, although General de Lisle was in executive command."

General W. R. Marshall replaced General de Lisle as G.O.C.

29th. Captain Lucas, who had acted as brigade-major ever since the formation of the 87th Brigade, took over command of the 87th. Shortly before the battle, Colonel Wolley-Dod had been invalided sick, and Colonel Perceval appointed to command the 86th Brigade. Lieutenant-Colonel C. G. Fuller became G.S.O. 1. 29th Division, and his place at the head of Q side was taken by Lieutenant-Colonel L. H. Abbott. Major J. C. Brand of the Coldstream Guards became brigade-major, 87th Brigade.

The 87th were the first of the 29th to land at Suvla Bay. They disembarked early on the 17th August and bivouacked in what seemed, even after Helles, a somewhat exposed situation. The S.W.B. and Borders were sent up that night for a tour of the front trenches held by the 158th Brigade of the 53rd Division. Major Going, officer commanding S.W.B., took over temporary command of that brigade, which had its proper commander in hospital, its brigade-major slightly wounded, and its staff-captain sick. The battalions rejoined their brigade on the night of the 19th–20th in readiness for the attack on the 21st. On the morning of the 18th the Mounted Division under General Peyton landed, and on the 19th the 86th Brigade. The 88th, who were holding the left of the line at Helles, did not leave till the night of the 20th, and were only just in time to march (minus tools and sandbags sent to Mudros by mistake) to the place of assembly west of Chocolate Hill. The G.O.C., along with the commanders of the 86th and 87th Brigades, made a reconnaissance on the 20th, as the result of which the dispositions for the attack on the left half of the IX. Corps were made.

The objective of the 87th was Scimitar Hill, also called Hill 70 ; that of the 86th, Hill 112 lying south of Scimitar Hill. The 87th were to proceed from a point north of Chocolate Hill and march due east ; the 86th to advance by the southern slopes of Chocolate Hill against Hill 112, which lay between Hill 70 and the real objective of the day's attack—namely, Ismail Oglu Tepe, sometimes called Hill 100, and sometimes W Hill.

In the plain south-east by east of Suvla Bay stands Chocolate Hill, a pudding-shaped lump with scrub on it. A thousand yards east of this isolated eminence is the broken ground from Scimitar Hill to W Hill. Between Chocolate Hill and the bay was a dried salt lake, as bare as the palm of a hand. The reverse slope of Chocolate Hill afforded the only cover. It was therefore a place of assembly and a target, and ultimately a shambles. The 87th Brigade had time to dig themselves in at their jumping-off place, and they suffered no casualties during the morning. The 86th Brigade had no choice. It was Chocolate Hill or nowhere for them, and they suffered severely from the counter-bombardment.

The general features of the engagement have been described so authoritatively and so well, that the tale of the 29th's last battle in this theatre needs but a few words. What struck General Cayley, watching from the redoubt on the top of Chocolate Hill, was the poor visibility and the preponderantly naval character of the bombardment, which started at 2.30. The scrub went on fire almost immediately, and added to the haze. The Turks lost no time in laying down a vigorous counter-bombardment. The 86th Brigade, who moved at 3.30 to the assault of Hill 112, found their path barred by burning scrub. They had to turn this obstacle on the right, and as the 11th Division on their right had lost direction and were leaning too much to the left, a certain amount of mixing of units occurred, and in the face of a terrific storm of shrapnel and machine-gun fire the attack petered out. It was a positive inferno : a blazing hot day, a scorching forest fire, and an invisible foe raining death on them.

Meanwhile the attacking battalion of the 87th, the R.I.F., had moved forward at 3.5 some 400 yards to the foot of the slopes of Hill 70. They had few casualties. When the moment for the assault came at 3.30 they were fresh and practically uninjured. The actual attack was pressed with great gallantry by the R.I.F. They stormed the heights ; they even took a Turkish trench on the eastern edge. Possibly they were unwise in venturing so far. They had been warned by the corps commander. But wherever they were they came under cross fire of shrapnel and rifle bullets from both flanks. They were swept off the top, and had to retire to a ledge about 100 feet below the actual crest. A similar gallant attack by the Borders at 4.15 failed to reach the summit. A final effort by the S.W.B. (made just before the superb advance of the yeomanry at 5.50) was directed to the capture of high ground north of Hill 70 which had persistently caused trouble during the previous attempts on the hill. It also failed, and it was the last effort of the 29th, for the 88th Brigade were spared useless slaughter. On the assumption that the gallant yeomen had gained the grand objective, W Hill itself, the 88th were ordered to assist the 87th at Hill 70. But the assumption was ill-founded, and the 88th attack was countermanded. It was just as well. The troops were tired, and about them hung the depression of 6th August, when the brigade was nearly wiped out. Under cover of night the troops were withdrawn to their original positions.

The 29th's last pitched battle on the Gallipoli Peninsula was therefore a failure, and resulted in heavy casualties, which in the case of the 87th Brigade alone amounted to more than 40 officers and 1,100 other ranks. But nothing could exceed the gallantry of the brigades. To mention only a couple of incidents. Captain Wm. Pike was in command of the R.I.F., and under orders to remain with the reserve. But he could bear his inaction no longer when he heard of the difficulties of his beloved regiment. Collecting what men he could, he made a dash for the Turkish trench, into which he disappeared wounded and for ever. In the same battalion Captain O'Sullivan, V.C., " gloriously fell " (in General de Lisle's words) " in upholding the honour of his distinguished regiment. His battalion was swept off the hill by enfilade gun fire. As senior surviving officer he collected the remnants, about fifty, in dead ground below the crest. Then calling for ' one more charge for the honour of the old regiment,' he led them up the hill, from which only one wounded sergeant returned. A very gallant gentleman."

The attack proved clearly that the Turks had been heavily reinforced in this sector. This was confirmed later on, and our Intelligence Branch ascertained that the Turks always maintained troops in the proportion of three to our two, and sufficient in reserve to increase the proportion to five to two in twelve hours.

Trench warfare ensued. It was under less agreeable conditions than those at Helles. There is little to record except the regretted departure of the 5th Royal Scots. This splendid battalion had dwindled down to company strength and had never received drafts. It had earned the praise of Generals Hunter-Weston and de Lisle. The latter in his orders to the 156th Brigade on 27th June had held up the 5th Royal Scots as an example.

The regiment was on its side intensely proud of the honour of having shared in the arduous doings of the division. They had watched, they had imitated, they had gained confidence by being in touch with the superb regular battalions of the 88th Brigade.

The Newfoundlanders took their place, and signalized their arrival in the fighting line by a well-executed minor enterprise. At all times this regiment was manned by the boldest of the British race, and their valour in France and Belgium was one of the glories of the 29th.

On 1st October the 87th Brigade was sent to Helles to join their old friends the 52nd Division, and came under the orders of that great gentleman and soldier, Major-General the Hon. Herbert Lawrence, afterwards Chief of the General Staff in France. It took no part in the minor attacks in November and December which are so interestingly recounted in Major Thompson's *History of the Fifty-second (Lowland) Division.* But nothing could keep " Bomb Kelly " (afterwards Lieutenant-Colonel John Sherwood Kelly, V.C., and then officer commanding K.O.S.B.) out of a scrap, and after the final capture of a trench called G 11 A on 29th December, he and his bombers from the 1st K.O.S.B. did yeoman service in helping the Royal Scots Fusiliers to retain their grip of the hard-won territory. To any one new to the scene of war and with opportunities of associating with the 87th and the three brigades of the 52nd, the contrast was striking. The discipline of the latter was less conspicuous. Orders were given in a sort of friendly question form : " Would you mind bringing me, etc. ? " Of saluting and " sir-ing " there was not much. They seemed to get on quite well without it, and strolled about the Krithia nullah on their various duties, or cooked their dinners, or made their toilet in the trenches with an air of self-confidence and being at home. Their trenches were clean in spite of a lot of individual cooking. A Scotsman just joined the 87th admitted that his spiritual home was among the Jocks. There were links with the 29th. Colonel Casson of S beach, O.C. S.W.B. at the landing, was in command of the 157th Brigade, with the rank of brigadier-general. The 156th was commanded by a brother of Colonel Koe of the 1st K.O.S.B., killed above Y beach.

A good deal of the flavour of the old regulars still hung about the 87th. Orders were given without circumlocution ; there were incessant inspections, constant criticism and fault-finding, insistence on the salute, unending fatigues, and no " bally politeness." Those who have been drumming elementary soldiering into relays of inexperienced reinforcements are entitled to a certain shortness of temper. General Lawrence was appreciative of the work done by the 87th while under his command, and after 31st October twelve officers per week from the Territorial brigades were attached to the 87th Brigade for instruction.

The season began to wear on. If it was still warm enough early in November for enjoyable bathing, there were nights when it was cold, and rain, when it did fall, was heavy. Winter was coming, but its actual arrival was sudden and terrible, though it only lasted a few days. The terrific rainstorm of November 26, 1915,

needs no description in this story. Everybody knows how the
rain turned into snow as the wind veered round to north-north-east.
The sight at Cape Helles, when the snow stopped, was magnificent.
The wine dark sea was still whipped by an icy blast far under
freezing point.   The mountains of the Troad and Samothrace behind
Imbros stood, *nive candidi*, from summit to base, as did Soracte
to the eye of the Roman.   Hostilities ceased entirely.

Of course there was hideous suffering there.   The K.O.S.B.
alone had more than fifty cases of frost-bite.   But it was as nothing
to what the two brigades at Suvla underwent.   The deluge there
was far greater.   It rushed over the Turkish trenches down through
the valley over the top of our trenches.   Barbed wire in No Man's
Land was carried several hundred yards behind our lines.   Ponies,
pigs, and other animals were swept along with débris of timber.
A mule, a donkey, and two Turks were washed over one sap-head.
All were drowned.   Many of our men were drowned.   Bodies were
found in a lake three miles to the rear of where they had been
stationed.   All the trenches except a part of the 88th's sector had
to be evacuated.   They were full of water.   The soaking men had,
perforce, to cower behind the parados on the sopping ground.   Both
sides ceased fire, and sheltered as best they could.   This experience
was bad enough, but worse was to follow.   The north-east blizzard
of the morning of the 27th had a velocity of 80 miles per hour
and a temperature 25 degrees below freezing-point.   Three solid
inches of ice stood in the trenches.   General de Lisle is of opinion
that the suffering of the troops at Suvla and Anzac was more
terrible than anything ever experienced in the war.   Many were
frozen to death at their posts ; still more were frost-bitten, necessi-
tating 400 amputations, and all were at the utmost limit of endurance.   An incident calls for honourable mention.   A labour
company at Divisional Headquarters was composed of unfit or
" C " men of the veteran type.   These men volunteered on their
own initiative to hold certain trenches, and so enable the sufferers
in occupation to fall back to shelter and warmth.   They were
allowed to do so, and spent a week at the front without a grumble.
When the 86th came out, the corps commander, Sir Julian Byng
(now Lord Byng of Vimy), visited all the companies which had been
holding the trenches across the valley.   One company of the Royal
Fusiliers paraded with its captain and three men only.   The
captain, who was R. Gee, afterwards V.C., reported that his trench
strength on 26th November was 137.

The casualties inflicted by " unfeeling nature " were more severe than those of the 21st August. They exceeded 3,000 at Suvla alone.

The storm had one redeeming feature : not a fly survived. The Gallipoli plague rapidly disappeared. The weather became mild and calm. The men worked back into condition for the final phase.

CHAPTER VII

THE EVACUATIONS

Ἀνὴρ ὁ φεύγων καὶ πάλιν μαχήσεται.

On 8th December Sir Charles Monro ordered the evacuation of Suvla and Anzac. This necessitated the construction of successive lines of defence in case the Turks detected the movement of the troops before it was completed and launched an attack. The highest military authorities anticipated heavy casualties. The risks were enormous. No less than three army corps had to be moved. Time was of the essence of the enterprise. The weather was a vital consideration. Preparations must proceed without precipitate haste and yet without rest. The naval and military staffs toiled from morning till night. The men in the platoons earned every night's repose over and over again. The following reminder of the main features of what seemed a miraculous rescue from menaced destruction is borrowed from Colonel John Buchan's *History of the War*.

These were :—

(1) The removal during ten days, under cover of night, of the Heavy Artillery and a considerable body of troops.

(2) The maintenance of secrecy by keeping up artillery and rifle fire, and by accustoming the Turks to quiet nights.

(3) The removal of the Field Artillery and the evacuation of the hospitals, horses, and motor-cars.

(4) The final evacuation by the rearguard of picked troops, after the remaining guns had been put on board. The guns were got off after dark on the evening of Sunday the 18th. The troops left the front at 1.30 a.m. on the following day. The last stragglers were got off by picket boats about 8 a.m.

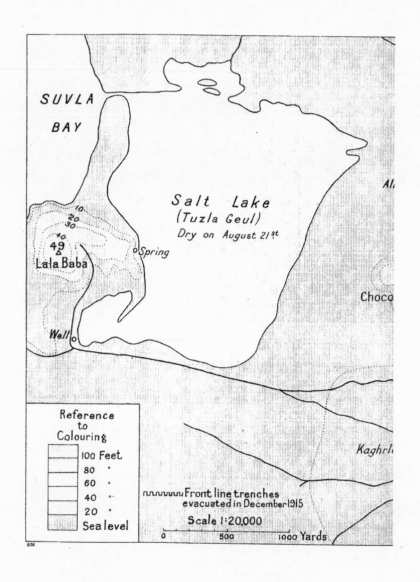

SUVLA
BAY

Salt Lake
(Tuzla Geul)
Dry on August 21st

10
20
30
40
49
△
Lala Baba

°Spring

Well °

Al

Choco

Kaghrl

Reference
to
Colouring

	100 Feet
	80 "
	60 "
	40 "
	20 "
	Sea level

∿∿∿∿∿∿Front line trenches
evacuated in December 1915

Scale 1:20,000

0   500   1000 Yards

9.56

SCIMITAR HILL

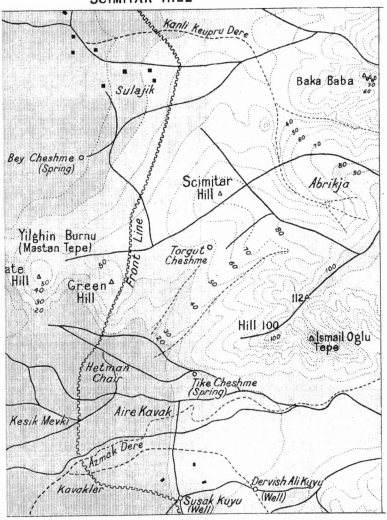

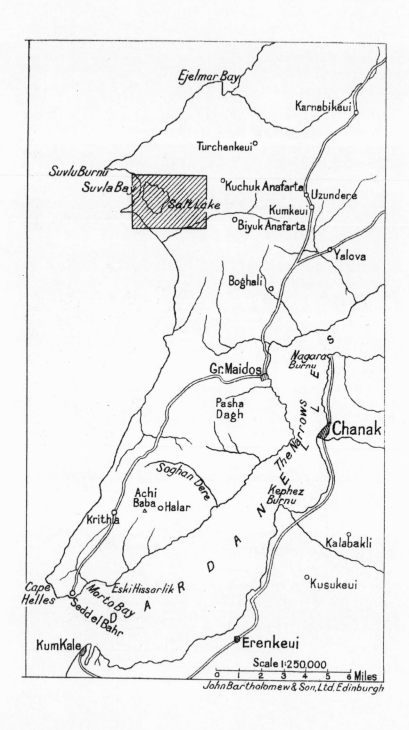

Ejelmar Bay

Karnabikeui

Turchenkeui

Suvlu Burnu
Suvla Bay

Salt Lake

Kuchuk Anafarta

Uzundere

Kumkeui

Biyuk Anafarta

Yalova

Boghali

Gr. Maidos

Nagara
Burnu

S

Pasha
Dagh

Chanak

The Narrows

Soghan Dere

Achi
Baba
o Halar

Kephez
Burnu

Krithia

N

Kalabakli

Cape
Helles

Morto Bay

Eski Hissarlik

R

Kusukeui

A

Sedd el Bahr

D

Kum Kale

Erenkeui

Scale 1:250,000

0   1   2   3   4   5   6 Miles

John Bartholomew & Son, Ltd. Edinburgh

The following vivid account from a contemporary letter has been placed at the editor's disposal by Major-General Cayley, who, as a brigadier-general, commanded the last troops of the 29th to leave the scene :—

" We've managed to get away over 40,000 men without the loss of a single man, horse or mule, gun or cart, and a minimum of ammunition. The only things left were a certain amount of rations, and, of course, odds and ends of stores, water-tanks, corrugated iron, etc. Most of the rations were set on fire as the last parties left, so there won't even be a great quantity of them left to the Turks. The only thing is that in withdrawing we have owned that the job was beyond our powers, and the waste of life had been to some extent valueless. But otherwise I think we were right to go. We were doing no real good except holding a certain number of Turks opposite us. It has been an anxious time, as you can imagine : the constant fear that the Turks had wind of it, and the knowledge that, if they had, the withdrawal would have been an impossibility. It has truly been a most astonishing performance, and luck and weather have been all on our side. In the first place, the Turks appear to have been far worse knocked by the storm than we were, so that they lost all enterprise. Then since the storm the weather has been perfect, allowing our men to recover largely from its effects, and also, a matter of the greatest importance, absolutely calm. It would have been a bad state of affairs if a big gale had sprung up in the middle of the business. Those left might have been in an impossible position, and a great disaster incurred. However, as it all went off without a hitch, it's not much use talking about what might have happened. On the 14th nothing much happened, except that the Turks were deadly quiet and one began to wonder what was up. The brigade that day took over the whole of the 86th Brigade line, so my responsibilities were much increased, as we were holding over 3,000 yards of firing-line with less than 1,500 men, also 2,400 yards of second line with about 600 men. Pretty thin if the Turks meant business—no supports or reserve at all. However, all seemed quite satisfactory, and at night the Turks were only remarkable for the amount of work they were putting in improving their wire entanglements. The 86th Brigade embarked for Mudros that night. Next day, 15th, only normal ordinary amount of shelling and rifle fire. It began to blow a bit and look threatening. Brigade Headquarters moved back behind second line, a better place to command from, while the retirement was going on. We sent all our kit away—rather, all that remained of it—and carried on with a blanket apiece. Luckily it was pretty warm. Of course all supplies, bread, and fresh meat had stopped, so it was bully and biscuit with extras. Unluckily Wilson,* the brigade-major, became very seedy, threatened jaundice, but stuck to his job nobly all through, and a very busy time it was for him, and for Armstrong † too. They were both invaluable to me, and worked absolutely splendidly, as did every one. It was a bit rainy next morning (16th), but not enough to matter, and then cleared up and turned out a grand day. Turks doing nothing, and completely in the dark as to what we were up to. The final orders for the last two days came in, and we then had to make out brigade orders from these—a difficult job, as every man had to be accounted for and the orders made out so that none could possibly be left behind. On the 18th I had all commanding officers up and went into the orders with them fully, and discussed things generally. Then that night, which was the first of the two final nights, all men were withdrawn from the second line and a good many from in front, leaving the firing-line held by about 1,000 men. All those that were withdrawn that night were safely got down to the beach by 9.15 p.m. without a sign from the Turks, and thus half the precious brigade was safely got away. It was the most anxious time of all, as one felt that if this withdrawal could safely be made, there was no reason why the final one should not be equally successful. About 20,000 men were embarked this night from all the beaches ; most of the guns had gone previously, just a few being left to fire from the usual places, so as not to make the Turks suspicious. All this time it was a great relief to know that the Turks were working away at their defences hard, putting up extra wire and generally carrying on as if they were expecting an attack. Also one or two came in to surrender every day, very ragged and half-starved-looking and absolutely ' fed-up.' Later on that night I withdrew another 500 men from the firing-line, to occupy the places behind the line where men would naturally be seen moving about, to light fires, etc., and generally make the place appear as usual. We had been busy getting mines ready and putting them out in front of the firing-line, so as to make the Turks go a bit slow if they did come on. The situation on the last morning (the 19th),

* Captain Percy N. Wilson, D.S.O., the capable and popular brigade-major of the 88th Brigade.

† Captain Pat Armstrong, acting staff-captain, 88th Brigade, of whom more anon.

then, was : 3,000 yards of firing-line held by about 500 men, another
500 or so behind, including Brigade Headquarters, signallers, bearer
companies, and Royal Engineers. The day was absolutely quiet,
not an unusual thing of any kind happening. I took my last walk
round the firing-line in the morning, and saw that every one was in
good heart, as they all were. The arrangement for the night was
as follows : Immediately after dark, all men behind the firing-line
(at least 400 of them) were marched straight to the beach, where
they safely arrived, and were all off and away by 7.15. This left
about 800 men, of whom perhaps 600 men still in front. At 6.45
the commanding officers of each regiment, with about 80 men and
the remains of the machine guns, stole quietly back from the
firing-line. They all got safely away through the second line and
to the beach, where they were all embarked by 8.45. Various
odds and ends made this party up to 400, leaving about 450 still
to go. Of these about 250 were in the firing-line, and 120 with
seven machine guns in a covering position in the second line, which
was about a mile and a half back. At 10.15 every one was withdrawn from the firing-line, except 40 men a battalion—160 all told.
Every one else, except small parties for checking people coming
through on the roads, a few signallers, etc., were withdrawn to the
beach, where they got safely on board by midnight. Meanwhile
I went back to the beach myself about 10.30, leaving Wilson to
regulate the traffic on one road, and my machine-gun officer on the
other with small parties. I went away in style in a motor which
some naval machine gunners had given me the use of. It was
at once put on a lighter after I had done with it. There were now
187 of the brigade still on shore. It must have been a jumpy time
for the 160 men still left in the trenches. But they were all picked
men, and by moving about and keeping up the appearance of
ordinary night-firing they effectually deceived the Turk. They
had to stop out on their own from 10.15 to 1.30 a.m. while the rest
of the carts, mules, etc., were being embarked. All the guns had
gone earlier in the night. All our munitions, except what men were
carrying, was also got away—millions of rounds. A lovely moon-
light night, full moon but slightly hazy, so that it was hard to see
at any distance. Absolute order on the beach. As each party
came down they marched straight on board small steamers which
could come alongside, or on to lighters, to be taken out to bigger
ones anchored close in. An array of men-of-war ready to open fire,
if necessary, lying off. The naval arrangements could not have
been better. Well, we still had telephones out to the trenches,

and all the reports were the same—Turks very quiet, digging and wiring very hard. About 1.30 the last parties came back, were all checked complete at the second line, passed along to the beach (two miles), telephones disconnected, and wires cut. Road parties got together and hurried away. The last man of the brigade got safely down by 3 o'clock. This, I think, was Wilson. The last party of the 39th Brigade, 13th Division, rolled up about the same time, and the brigadier (my brother Walter) and I stepped on to the same lighter, the last of our respective brigades, about 3.30. We went off to a biggish ship which had cabins, and I personally, with Wilson and Armstrong, at once turned in, about 4.30. There were a few of other brigades still ashore, but the last were off before 5 a.m. As a final act, all the remaining stores on the beach were set on fire, but I didn't stay up to see the blaze. So we got away, and came over here peacefully. Not a breath of wind to interfere with the shipping. The whole performance was truly wonderful. At 7 a.m. the Turks discovered we were not in the firing-line, and it being still dusk, opened a very heavy shell fire on the second line and beaches. One would have liked to have seen their faces when they discovered not a soul—40,000 men away without a sound, with all their goods ! ''

Then the weather broke. A day later and an awkward situation would have arisen.

The relief felt by all the ranks in the two brigades at their wonderful escape from a terrible situation did not last long. It took all the philosophy of the veterans and those infected by their spirit to endure the bitter news that they were to be sent to Helles to relieve the 42nd Division and re-absorb the 87th Brigade. Their demeanour was perfect, and in due course they landed ; the 86th on the 15th, headquarters on the 21st, and the 88th on the 22nd. An idea prevailed that the IX. Corps was shortly to relieve the VIII., so to a certain extent the spirits of all the troops in the reunited division were kept up by the thought that their stay would be short, and it was plain to any one that no offensive was in immediate prospect. Nor was there time for brooding. The indefatigable task-master, who controlled their destinies, found the trenches much below his standard of safety, which left nothing to chance. The new arrivals, therefore, were busy with pick and shovel and sandbag. By the 30th December it was at last communicated to the general, brigadier-generals, staffs, and commanding officers that Helles was to be evacuated, and that the

29th were to form part of the rearguard. The prospects were not bright. With luck one may fool a foe by a *ruse de guerre* once. Successfully to repeat the operation with the same *ruse* within a month, in broken weather, in face of the same enemy, now flushed with triumph at the withdrawal of the Infidel dogs from the lines at Anzac and Suvla, and rejoicing in the near advent of siege guns of large calibre, thanks to Bulgaria, seemed beyond possibility—two or three thousand men lost was a conservative estimate.

The gradual percolation of the news through all ranks of the forces produced that state of mind of the rustic in *Paradise Lost*—

"At once with fear and joy his heart rebounds."

Grave danger was about, but it was worth it. It was no fun to be the "bloody sacrifice," but it was evident that the saving of men rather than material was the aim of those in authority, and heart and soul each individual entered on the final stage.

The French infantry, then reduced to 4,000, disappeared on the night of the 1st–2nd January 1916; their guns on Z day.

Any one visiting the middle area between the front and the beach could hardly fail to notice the emptiness of the trenches and the constant inquisitiveness of hostile aeroplanes. They dropped bombs on our camps, while the whine of howitzer shells overhead told of shelling of the vital beaches. Nor were signs lacking in front that the Turks felt that there was a probability of immediate evacuation. Raids occurred every night on the front of the 29th, until the enemy fell a victim to the special *ruse de guerre* which marked the second evacuation. For several nights detailed officers observed the average number of guns, rifles, and flares discharged, and arrangements were made for the same number to be discharged for the last night even after the troops had gone. This, of course, meant a marked reduction in the ordinary noise of a Gallipoli night. At about 10 p.m. for a week in advance of Z day not a shot would be fired for long spells. At first the Turks kept up their fire, but gradually they reduced their counter-fire, and the quiet of the night was only broken by an occasional stray shot. It was this mild fusilade that was imitated by a mechanical device. A rifle or flare pistol was wired in a fixed position. A tin was filled with sand, and hung by a loop of string from the trigger of the rifle or pistol. The sand weighed six pounds. Above this tin was suspended another containing water. An accurate puncture in the water-tin contributed a drip into the sand-tin at the rate of one pound per quarter of an hour. The " pull " being seven pounds, each rifle went off in a quarter of an hour. The rifle could be timed for a longer period by using less sand. Long after the last man of the 29th had left the scene, flares were rising from our lines and the crack of the bullets went on as usual.

Christmas had gone off cheerily. New Year was more sombre. Nothing, however, of moment occurred till Y day, the 7th January, the day before Z day, the close of which was to see the final evacuation of the trenches. It says much for the secrecy maintained that brigade commanders even as late as the 4th had no idea as to when Z day was to be. The Turkish bombardment on Y day was the fiercest felt for some time, but the brunt of it fell outside the sector of the 29th. It was vigorous enough to indicate the likelihood of an assault, and the garrison was all on the alert. Nothing resulted except the flash of bayonets, and a certain amount of movement in the front Turkish trenches. Nobody came over the top on the divisional sector, and it seemed as if the Turks were satisfied with the information thus obtained, that the British were holding in force and were full of fight. To those of us who were present the German staff-officer's account of the heroic sacrifice of Sir Ian's " favourite Staffordshires " makes amusing reading. The rest of us were apparently all massacred ! Can any one touch the naïveté and thoroughness of a German's mendacity when he is out on that tack ? Not that he is by nature a liar ; far from it ! When driven to lie, he lies from a sense of duty—clumsily, doggedly, but in a style to satisfy his audience.

On Z day everything came off according to plan : 17,000 troops left the Peninsula. The staffs of the 86th and 88th might be described as experts ; the 87th's staff proved equally efficient. The brigadier was admirably served by Captain (as he then was) J. C. Brand, the brigade-major, and by Captain M. C. Morgan of the S.W.B., the staff-captain. Any anxieties felt were due to the weather, and the possibility of things going wrong through causes, which no foresight could control. The parties left in relays, and those who had to leave in the dark found the equivalent of Ariadne's thread in the shape of polite policemen posted at intervals to keep them in the right way. Even thus it would be interesting to know if *all* reached the beach according to plan and in perfect formation, or whether Private X. was nearly forgotten at his post. But why trouble, as all were embarked, and only two casualties were caused by tumbles above W beach ? A curious feature of the march down was the leg weariness of the men. The long trench life seemed to have weakened their muscles. Packs were flung away now and again, and the rate of march between 11.45 p.m. and 1.45 a.m. was snail-like. The embarkation has been often described. An odd shell or two, which fell nowhere in particular, the rising wind, the orderly groups, the unceasing queues moving beachwards, the tragic shooting of the 142 faithful horses, which could not be got off, the collecting of odds and ends of units, made an indelible picture on the mind. Those on board the last destroyer will never forget the crash at 4.20 a.m. when the dump went up and lumps of stuff fell on the deck. Utter fatigue kept off nausea when the Ægean ran high. Before daybreak the 29th were away in Imbros, and soon after, in the morning of a fine sunny day, they were boarding the transports in the bay of Mudros. Headquarters had been in peril. The *Prince George* in which they sailed was struck by a torpedo, which did not explode.

Thus ended the ordeal of the 29th on the historic peninsula. It endured for 259 days, save for brief absences on Imbros or Lemnos. The wastage had been appalling. The total casualties numbered 34,011. As the average strength was 7,300, the proportion in a little over eight months meant a renewal four and a half times—*i.e.*, 100 per cent. every two months. The number of those who landed and evacuated was small. Only 14 officers and 1,523 other ranks landed at the start and evacuated at the finish without being invalided during the course of the campaign through wounds or sickness. Only 18 officers and 1,405 other ranks were at the landing and evacuation, who had for varying spells been invalided during the operations. On the other hand, there can be little doubt that out of the huge casualties sustained by the Turks, put by some as high as 500,000, something considerably in excess of 34,011 may be placed at the credit of the 29th. The evacuation brought to the fighting forces no sense of shame. They did as they were told, and lived to fight another day. As far as the 29th were concerned, divisional spirit was as strong as in any similar unit in the British army. All that was required was rest, change of scene, a more generous diet, and the tonic of close-order drill and ceremonial parades. And these were all forthcoming with the excitement of a zig-zag voyage to Alexandria as a prelude.

There remains but one observation—*i.e.*, how it came about that this second evacuation was so successful. The fact is, the Turk was not in a mood for unnecessary attacks. Time was on his side, and the weather was on his side. In a short time he knew he would be able to blow us out to sea. If he had known how matters stood, he might have stormed the front. But his feeler on the penultimate day was a reminder that a good many eggs would be broken before he got his omelette, and the weather on the 8th was most unpropitious. In the circumstances he took his risk, and was probably much relieved to find that his resolute antagonists had outwitted him and vanished, leaving him a considerable amount of material and the territory which was vital to the safety of the Dardanelles.

BOOK II

THE WESTERN FRONT

" To-morrow to fresh woods and pastures new."

PART I—THE INFERNO

CHAPTER I

THE BATTLE OF THE SOMME

" We shall your tawny ground with our red blood
Discolour."

THE voyage from Lemnos was uneventful. A sharp look-out
was kept day and night for U-boats. In due course Alexandria
was reached, and the troops entrained for Suez. A wild hope
had taken hold of many that the 29th might be quartered in the
Cairo area, close to the historically interesting relics of the past.
But the authorities had reserved the pick of the stations for
the Australians, whose gentle dispositions and iron discipline
were calculated to endear them to the civilian population and the
military police. The dullness of Suez prevented the minds of
officers or other ranks from being distracted from the business of
military recuperation. Except for three weeks on guard on the
east side of the Canal the time was spent in close-order drill, rifle
practice at short ranges, route marches, and brigade ceremonial
parades. The climate allowed football, and few who saw it will
forget the thrilling divisional final on 16th February, in the presence
of the corps commander, General Sir Francis Davies, between the
K.O.S.B. and the Lancashire Fusiliers. The representatives of
the 87th Brigade triumphed over those of the 86th, thanks mainly
to the masterly goal-keeping of Second Lieutenant Christison, by
the narrow margin of one goal. Shortly before this the troops of
the 29th had given General Byng, commanding the IX. Corps,
a rousing send-off as he sailed up the Canal *en route* for France
and fame. He and the 29th were to meet once more ; but of that
anon. (See page 147.)

All sorts of rumours were afloat during the two months, which

the division spent in Egypt, as to its next move. It was plain
that the rest of its existence was not to be spent in the land of the
Pharaohs. Some guessed Palestine, others Mesopotamia ; but
the general verdict was France. This turned out to be correct,
and by the middle of March the 29th were once more facing the
very real perils of the Mediterranean.

Strange was the course taken by the transports ; but the
manœuvres were blessed with success, and one by one the vessels
sailed past the Château d'If into the harbour of Marseilles. The
journey northwards was full of interest to the troops, nearly all
of whom must have been visiting France for the first time. The
Rhone valley, the cheering crowds and noble vistas of Lyon, the
rich lands of Burgundy, the loom of Paris, which the troop trains
skirted, the march to billets in the Long area of Picardy in the dusk,
could not fail to stimulate enthusiasm for the fighting necessarily
in store. Here, at least, was a country worth defending, and not
so far away was another land still more precious.

Leave was given generously and speedily, and not a few of
the 29th entered the Solent to the accompaniment of a snowstorm
which was a reminder of the blizzard at the end of November.

The 29th was now only one out of some seventy British divisions
in France and Flanders. Henceforth it would not be the cynosure
of every eye, " the backbone " of any enterprise. Its story would
be domestic. Its actions would be mere fractional episodes in
large-scale operations. It would have to begin as a novice among
old hands at the game of war as played on the Western Front.
As has been pointed out by Colonel John Buchan, by the spring
of 1916 the British army was homogeneous. The old regiments
were manned by new men. The territorials had had more than
a year in which to absorb the spirit and guise of professional soldiers.
The new battalions had received their baptism of fire at Loos. The
utmost to which the 29th could aspire was to be second to none in
the performance of their limited share in combined operations, and
see to it that none in front, on flanks, or behind should be hampered
by any avoidable failure on the part of the 29th. The training of
the Western forces under the supreme command of a born trainer
of troops with vast experience was pretty well stereotyped for all
units. There was bayonet-fighting, bomb-throwing, rapid construction of field fortifications, mastery of the Vickers and Lewis
guns, to say nothing of the German machine gun, co-operation with
aeroplanes, and every sort of tactical exercise. If one division was
to distinguish itself, it could only be by superiority in material,

method, or *esprit de corps*. In regard to material, the 29th was composed of men of the same age, type, and proficiency as those of the average numbered division. Every now and then it might pick up a veteran N.C.O. or regular officer. It had a nucleus of senior officers of outstanding merit. But in the main it drew from the common store, and, if it was to excel, it must be through either or both of the remaining qualities.

The Munsters had left the division, and on 5th May the corps commander inspected the 16th Middlesex, which replaced them. The 16th were the residuum of the erstwhile "Public Schools Battalion," and were always worthy of their origin and their regiment.

The 29th were in the Fourth Army commanded by General Sir Henry Rawlinson (the late lamented Lord Rawlinson of Trent). Along with the 4th and 31st Divisions they made up the VIII. Corps under their old comrade and commander, Lieutenant-General Sir Aylmer Hunter-Weston, K.C.B. It was a happy reunion for both Commander and command, and even those who came to Gallipoli too late to serve under the corps commander, and those who had not been in Gallipoli at all, felt their backs straighten as they looked " eyes left " at him at Marieux on the route march to the French front.

The sector taken over extended south from a little north of the sunk road between Auchonvillers and Beaumont-Hamel (perhaps next to Ypres and Verdun the most famous place-name on the Western Front) to a point about half a mile from the village of Hamel. Hawthorn redoubt and Y salient and ravine were formidable strongholds confronting them. Civilization was represented by the neat little town of Doullens. Divisional headquarters were at Acheux, notable for its chimney, château, and wood. The brigade in reserve occupied Louvencourt. The two in the line had headquarters at Mailly-Maillet and Englebelmer. It had been for long a quiet sector. An attempt to storm Beaumont-Hamel in 1914 had cost the French many lives. Since then the Germans had converted a naturally strong position into what they believed to be, and what seemed to the whole world at one time to be, an impregnable fortress. By a sort of *concordat* the villages on either side were not shelled, and rifle-fire was negligible after Gallipoli standards.

" Mr. Boche ain't a bad feller. You leave 'im alone : 'e'll leave you alone," was a remark dropped by a N.C.O. of the garrison of a front trench from whom a unit of the 29th took over on 4th April. It was not the way of the 29th to leave well alone. Hard work on improving the trenches and wire at once began. Patrols were

out on the first and succeeding nights. Snipers' posts were constructed and used. Whether the enemy noticed the change and
were curious to know who the newcomers were, and what it all
meant, or whether the quiet sector was having its turn of the
periodical raids, is unknown. Suffice it to say that about 9 p.m.
on the night of the 6th April a terrific bombardment of hostile
artillery and trench mortars broke out on the front trenches of the
left sector held by the 87th Brigade. The windows at Acheux
rattled to the vibration, although 15,000 yards from the trenches.
Unlike the Germans with their deep dug-outs and their caves,
our troops had literally no refuge. The intensive bombardment
of the area known as Mary Redan, estimated at not less than
8,000 shells, completely wrecked fifty yards of wire, blocked all
communication trenches by enfilade fire of high explosive, and
destroyed nearly all the garrison. This almost perfect specimen
of a box barrage lasted till 10.30, when it lifted and a party of
Germans rushed into a trench occupied by the S.W.B. and removed
the survivors, about fourteen in number, with a loss of four killed.
It appears that the Germans had by this time a sort of embryo of
the afterwards famous " Stosstruppen " or " Sturmtruppen " in the
shape of a peripatetic raiding party nicknamed by our men " the
Boche Travelling Circus," and that it was this very force, which
somewhat rudely established the presence of the 29th on the Somme
battlefield. The 29th had 6 officers casualties by wounds and about
100 men dead, wounded, or missing. One man was dug out by
our relieving troops uninjured. The chief sufferers were the
S.W.B. They had already lost an officer and a private out patrolling on the night of the 5th, and were eager to demonstrate by a
counter raid the motto " *nemo me impune lacessit.*" Unfortunately,
if the German raid found the division in poor defences, it also
found them without trained junior officers. It was the same in
all battalions. The loss at the Dardanelles of 1,100 officers resulted
in the cadres being filled by officers of no previous war experience.
Many of these were resourceful ; all were brave ; but they knew
so little. Ingenuity is not confined to soldiers, and it is well known
that an officer of the 29th, wounded and captured, succeeded on
one occasion in wording a letter from Germany so as to achieve
three somewhat difficult objectives: (1) pass the German Censor ;
(2) reach the division *via* his own home, to which it was written ;
and (3) convey valuable military information to his divisional
commander in intelligible form. But the direction of a raid
demands experience and luck. Neither element was present,

and the raid failed. But nothing could have exceeded the ardour and zeal shown by the late gallant Captain E. J. W. Byrne and his zealous band in practising for the hazardous enterprise, or their determination on their final departure.

On 4th June what seemed at the time a serious loss to the division occurred. Lieutenant-Colonel Sherwood-Kelly was always spoiling for a fight. On this occasion his brigade, the 88th, were carrying out a raid, in which the battalion which he then commanded—the 1st Essex—was not engaged. Nevertheless, there he was, out in No Man's Land, assisting the raiding party back to their trenches. It was then that he was struck by a shrapnel bullet which pierced his shoulder and penetrated the lung, breaking some ribs *en route*. It was a terrible wound, and little hope was held out for his recovery. However, he made a miraculous recovery, and missing the 1st July, was able to participate in the campaigns in Artois and Flanders, and to render services to the division at the battle of Cambrai, which won him the V.C.

It was, of course, well known that there was going to be a " push " on the Somme. The Divisional Training School was in full swing before the end of May. The defences were improved out of all recognition, although as seen from the air they presented a poor appearance as compared with the elaborate rectilinear completeness and depth of the lines of the Germans, who moreover in Y ravine possessed a steep-sided, well-hidden sanctuary. Current rumours had it that the German garrison preferred to hold the sector permanently, rather than be relieved with the risk of being transferred subsequently to a more dangerous sector. Even in April the general plan had been discussed in conferences at Army, Corps, and Divisional Headquarters. As the 29th's attack totally failed, it is unnecessary to consider the objectives in detail. Generally, it was to pierce the German front system between and including Beaumont Hamel and the Ancre. Everything turned on the artillery preparation during the week preceding the day of assault, the 1st July. In the 29th's sector, which presented great difficulties to the attackers, the volume and accuracy of the gun fire was not impressive. Something overwhelming was required in the way of destruction to enable troops to cross 350 yards of No Man's Land at a slow walk laden with heavy equipment, in the face of trenches arranged, thanks to the way the ground rose to the east, ridge upon ridge, so that tiers of fire could be brought to bear on them, those behind firing over the heads of those in front. It was hoped that the explosion of " The Great Mine " under the Hawthorn redoubt (see Map) would help the assault. After much consideration it was decided to fire it ten minutes before zero. The Germans took the broad hint that something was going to happen, and there was no element of surprise. It must also be remembered that the whole way from Gommecourt to the Ancre the enemy had excellent direct observation of the British lines. Here he had massed the bulk and flower of his defensive troops. The 29th had come up against a stone wall. The story of the 1st July for the 29th is confined to that day alone and to a comparatively short period of it. The attack took place over a frontage of 2,000 yards. The 87th had the right half. The 86th had the left half, including the village of Beaumont Hamel, as part of its objective. The 87th had the R.I.F. on the right, the S.W.B. on the left, and in reserve the K.O.S.B. and the Borders. The 86th had the Royal Fusiliers and the Lancashire Fusiliers in the front line, with the Dublins and the 16th Middlesex in reserve. The reserve battalions of both brigades marched up on the evening of the 30th June, the 87th in front.

The reserve brigade left their billets at Louvencourt and followed the rear reserve battalion of the 86th. Their place in the line was behind the 87th Brigade. The whole of the brigade and divisional reserve reached their places of assembly in the trenches without a casualty. Even among the troops holding the line there were few casualties. The villages of Auchonvillers, Mailly-Maillet and Englebelmer, and Mailly Wood did not receive attention from the hostile guns. Moreover, the deep dug-outs constructed during three months of strenuous toil afforded safe refuge in times of retaliatory cannonading.

The 1st of July

For many the attack at 7.30 a.m. on 1st July was the first experience of going over the top. For too many it was the last. The main advance was preceded by the explosion of the mine under the Hawthorn redoubt. Two platoons of the Royal Fusiliers with four Vickers machine guns and four Stokes mortars rushed forward to hold the crater. Unfortunately, the enemy forestalled them on the farther top of the crater and prevented farther advance. There then ensued one unbroken rattle of hostile machine-gun fire for one hour. The same fate was in store for the troops, who advanced under cover of the fire of Stokes mortars in the sunk road on the extreme left of the sector.

The 87th had no better permanent success. The R.I.F. did succeed in penetrating the first line. Their steadiness in crossing No Man's Land was that of troops on parade. But though on the right the trenches were crossed by portable bridges, in the main the wire proved a complete obstacle. The same applies to the S.W.B. The effort of the first line of assault was in vain. The reserves meanwhile suffered from the enemy's gun fire *sans coup férir*, and it was a damaged mass of troops who at 7.35 clambered over the trenches of the K.O.S.B. and Borders. With the exception of a few of the leading sections of the latter, the second wave did not reach the first. The 87th Brigade was practically knocked out.

The 86th Brigade had been held up through cross machine-gun fire in the case of the 2nd Royal Fusiliers on the Hawthorn ridge, and by machine-gun fire from every direction in the case of the Lancashire Fusiliers.

The barrage on the left sector was so intense that it was not until 7.55 that the supporting waves left their trenches. The Dublins on the right failed to reach the wire ; the 16th Middlesex reached the crater with heavy loss. All attempt to advance was abandoned after the death of their adjutant. The attack had failed. What would the fate of the 88th be ? If they went forward they went to certain death. But when the military machine gets in motion it is hard to divert or stop. Those in command had imperfect and rather encouraging reports. If our men were really fighting in the Station Road on the right—*i.e.*, well behind the enemy's front line—they must be supported, and a determined effort made to prevent them from being cut off and undone through the very brilliance of their success. Accordingly the G.O.C. ordered a fresh attack to be carried out by the Essex and Newfoundlanders. The latter were ready first, and launched a determined attack at 9.15 a.m. Many eye-witnesses have testified to the superb steadiness of that astonishing infantry. Undaunted by a hail of machine-gun fire, they went forward till out of 700 men a mere handful remained.

These men from a far land spent their blood like water for their distant kindred, their love of justice, and the *Pax Britannica*. The site of their glory is a little bit of extra-territorial Newfoundland dedicated for ever as a consecrated memorial to valour. No one should neglect to read the chapter on Newfoundland's contribution to the war in the *Times' History of the War*.

And then it was the turn of the Essex. They were badly

mauled by shell fire. It was impossible for any men to get through the barrage, and thus ended the attack by the 29th. The 4th Worcesters were ordered for a combined attack with troops of the 4th Division but, mercifully, the arrangements broke down and the attack was cancelled. The Hampshires took no part in this disastrous but glorious day.

The casualties were severe. They numbered 5,000. The loss of officers, in spite of the fact that they were dressed like privates, was disproportionately heavy. Certain units suffered as compared with others. The 87th Brigade had the heaviest loss—over 60 per cent. of its available strength. The 86th ran it close, and had even heavier casualties among officers—viz., 74 as against 72. The Newfoundlanders lost more than 90 per cent. of those in the actual assault and 84 per cent. of their available strength. The Middlesex were close behind them.

The want of success undoubtedly depressed the troops, who had done all that was humanly possible. They wondered whose fault it was. They were somewhat cheered by a sympathetic message from General Joffre, who said that the success farther south could not have been achieved but for the gallant attacks on the north. It has been put like this :—" The happenings of the 1st July should not be looked on as a disaster. To the Higher Command and (*a fortiori*) to the historian the doings of individual units—*e.g.*, divisions or corps—must be regarded in their proper proportion. The attack of the right corps of Allenby's army and of the two and a half left corps of the Fourth Army, though locally unsuccessful, made possible the success of the right corps of the Fourth Army and of the French. The gallant and strenuous attacks on the left were essential to the success gained on the right, and all have their due share of the general success." But the feeling that the " flowers o' the forest were a' wede awa' " was a very real one at the time. The 29th was unaccustomed to failure, without inflicting more than they got. It set itself dourly to work to prepare a new line from which others might attack later on, but rest and such change as the Western Front could give was needed to restore tone to the sorely tried battalions, and time was needed to enable drafts to be absorbed and trained.

The following description of Beaumont Hamel, as it was on May 9, 1917, noted by a most competent military observer, gives an idea of the strength of the German fortress, and the fierceness of the final bombardment to which it succumbed :—

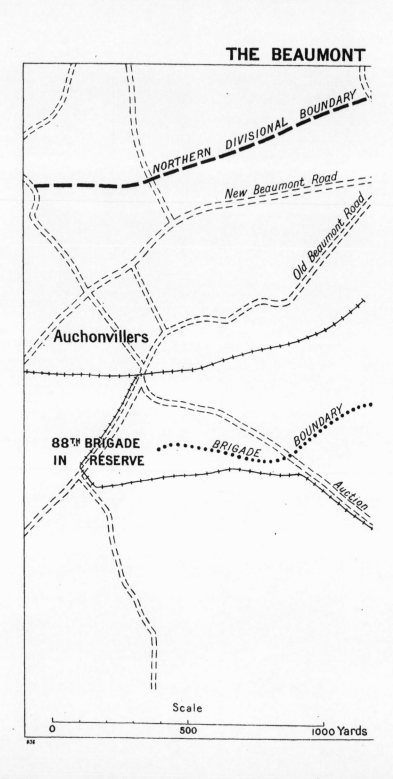

THE BEAUMONT

NORTHERN DIVISIONAL BOUNDARY

New Beaumont Road

Old Beaumont Road

Auchonvillers

88TH BRIGADE IN RESERVE

BRIGADE   BOUNDARY

Auction

Scale

0   500   1000 Yards

036

HAMEL FRONT 1·7·16

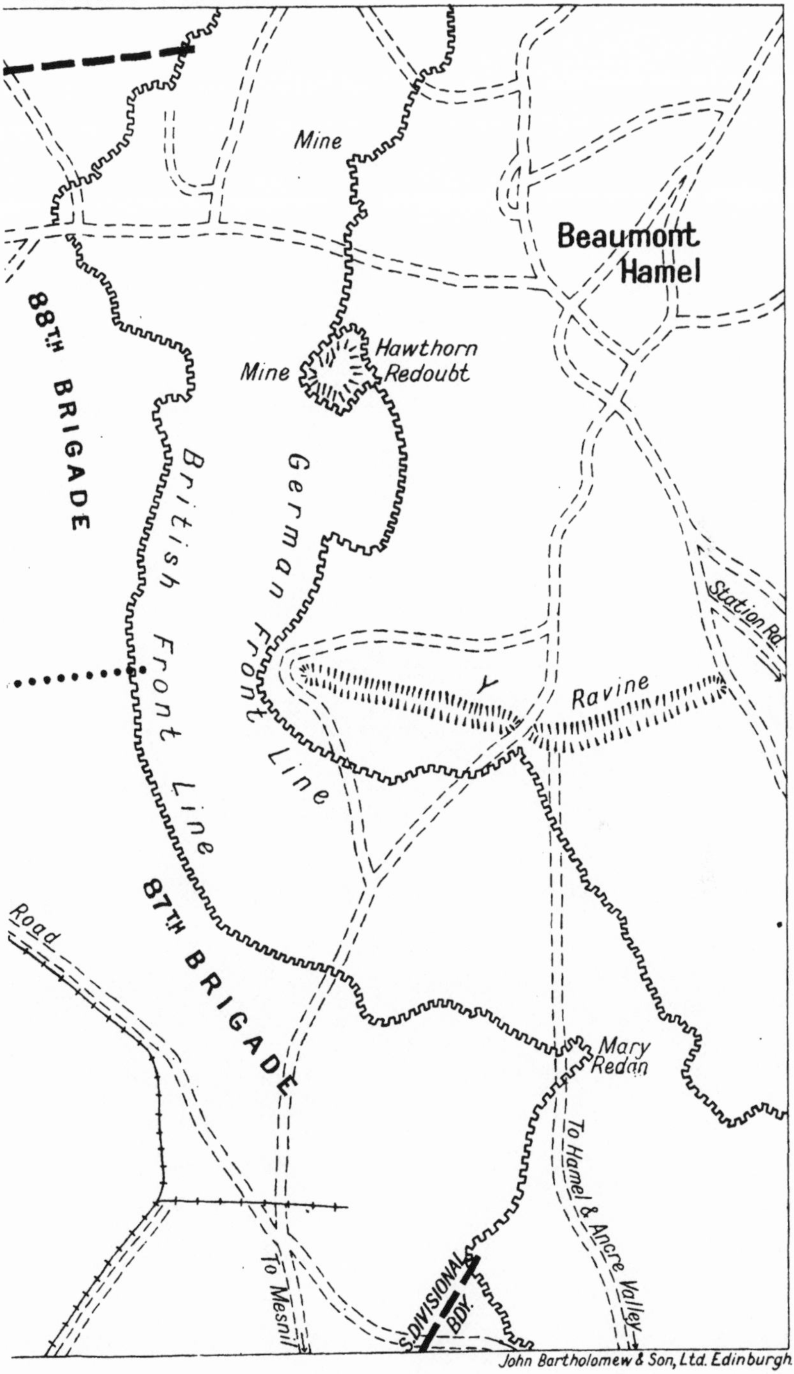

Mine

Beaumont
Hamel

88TH BRIGADE

Mine
Hawthorn
Redoubt

British Front Line

German Front Line

Station Rd

Ravine

Road

87TH BRIGADE

Mary
Redan

To Hamel & Ancre Valley

To Mesnil

DIVISIONAL BDY.

John Bartholomew & Son, Ltd. Edinburgh.

" It is a wonderful sight. There is nothing to be seen of Beaumont Hamel or Beaucourt. The whole ground is overlapping craters. All along the road between the villages wagons have been blown off the road. Every tree in the area is shattered. Our mine on 1st July is enormous, 100 yards by 50, and 30 to 40 feet deep.

" It was short of but just caught the German front line. The dug-outs within 80 yards of it had all their entrances filled with débris and the occupants probably buried. But the timber is intact and the shafts have not been blown in. They have since been opened again, possibly by the Germans to dig out their own men. There are shafts running from each of the two forks of Y ravine which appear to lead into the deep dug-outs in the firing-line about 50 yards away. We discovered graves of several men in this brigade close to the German lines. Auchonvillers had been levelled flat, except the last farm our side, and the house at the railway crossing. In Mailly the rear half was fairly intact. The people are beginning to cultivate in the neighbourhood of No Man's Land. A very few roads have been kept up. The remainder are quite impassable for a car."

The Ypres Salient (an Interlude)

The 29th were relieved by the 25th Division on 24th–25th July and said good-bye to the Ancre for ever, save for a railway journey in the dark in the following year. Their next appearance in the battle of the Somme was at a sufficient distance, and under sufficiently changed conditions, not to awake painful memories. Meanwhile even a journey by march and train to Proven was not without its revivifying effect. Ypres was for once a sleepy hollow. The sector between the Menin road and Langemarck was in a state of disrepair, in places quite useless for protection against small-arm fire. In many places water and mud were over ankle deep. The division were soon hard at work mending the trenches and wiring. The latter was the more clamant duty. The 86th Brigade on the right did a fine piece of work in wiring the difficult Railway Wood subsector in one night. It was a highly dangerous enterprise, and the men were much fortified by the gallantry shown by the brigade-major, Captain W. M. Armstrong, in walking up and down in front of the working parties. " Pat " Armstrong was one of the assets of the 29th. He had gone to Gallipoli as General de Lisle's A.D.C., and after being G.S.O. III. had been recently made brigade-major to Brigadier-General Williams of the 86th Brigade. Nobody could resist his charm of manner. No one was ever more warmly welcomed than he, wherever he turned up. He had a personality of a most engaging kind, besides being a valorous and cheerful soul.

But to return to the Ypres Salient, the work of the 29th earned the praise of the army commander, General Sir Herbert Plumer (now Field-Marshal Lord Plumer) for the improvement in the defences effected by the division. It was a compliment after the heart of the G.O.C. The difficulties were enormous. The ground was water-logged, and a trench, dug at night, filled with water to within two feet of the surface in six hours. The only solution was to use frames shaped like a capital A placed in the trench upside down, and to make breastworks for protection above the ground-level. The water could then drain away under the duck-boards. The army commander showed that he had meant what he said. Otherwise he would not have seen his way to arrange for the visit of the King of the Belgians to the front line. His Majesty, not content with visiting Ypres and Brigade Headquarters, went round the front, inspecting troops and getting round dry shod. At one point he was within 50 yards of the German line. His Majesty was evidently favourably impressed, for on September 28, 1916, the corps commander was able to issue a Special Order, which ran thus :—

> The King of the Belgians and Prince Alexander of Teck were each impressed by the smartness and fine appearance of the officers and men of the 29th Division, and Sir Aylmer Hunter-Weston desires to congratulate all ranks on the good impression that the division has made on the Sovereign of our gallant Allies.

A Special Order for the army commander followed on 2nd October :—

> The army commander has received excellent reports of the work done by the 29th Division both on their defences and in their area generally, and he wishes, before the division leaves, to convey his appreciation to the divisional commander, brigadiers, and commanding officers.

The 29th were in this sector for exactly two months. The outstanding events were a phosgene gas attack on the night of

the 8th–9th August which cost us something like 300 casualties.
It was curiously local in its effects, and the R.I.F. in the Potijze
area bore the brunt of it. The transport horses of the R.I.F. got
back to their usual station behind Ypres, but all died next morning
towards midday.

What might have caused a panic among transport units travers-
ing Ypres was stopped by a driver of the divisional train. The gas
was thick near the Cloth Hall, and some of the transport were moving
at a speed which might easily infect others with panic. It was then
that the driver, knowing what was the matter and how best to deal
with the situation, dismounted, turned his wagon so as effectually
to block the roadway, put on his gas mask, and *filled his nosebags
with hay and put water into them*, and remained where he was. A
sergeant-major soon appeared, and gave instructions to the less
instructed. An awkward incident passed by and the driver received
the M.M. Otherwise, wastage in men and animals was at a minimum
during the tenure of this sector.

The second event was a gracious visit on August 14, 1916, of
His Majesty King George V., accompanied by the Prince of Wales.
His Majesty had tea with General de Lisle at Divisional Headquarters at Nine Elms Camp, Poperinghe. He showed the keenest
interest in the welfare of the 29th and in every detail of camp
life.

The third event was a simultaneous raid resulting in the capture
of several prisoners and identifications. The late Lieutenant
W. de H. Robinson of the Borders won the M.C. for his admirable
handling of his party, which secured eight prisoners. The 29th
had once more got going. A little while longer and its *annus
mirabilis* would commence—the year of the Kaiser's birthday, of
Arras, Ypres, and Cambrai.

It only remains to put on record the splendid support given to
the 29th while in the Wieltje sector by the 20th Divisional Artillery
under Brigadier-General John Hotham. The efficiency, the promp-
titude, and the accuracy of the shooting won the admiration of
all ranks. For the gunners secured a quiet life for the toilers in
the trenches. If hostile fire commenced, it was returned sixfold.
The Germans finally gave up promiscuous firing. To some of us
the presence of the 20th Divisional Artillery meant the renewal of
old friendships. The regret at parting was mutual on the side of
infantry and artillery alike.

BACK TO THE SOMME

On 5th October the division handed over the line to the 55th Division and entrained for the Somme. Divisional Headquarters were at Corbie, and for the remainder of the Somme battle the 29th were in the right half of the salient won by the bloody battle which had raged from the 1st of July to the end of September. Roughly speaking, the scene of their activities was between the road, which runs from Flers to Ligny Thilloy on the left, and Sailly-Saillisel on the right. Their communications missed Albert and crossed the Ancre west of Méaulte. Montauban was the battle headquarters of the division. The deplorable weather of the end of September and beginning of October had slowed down operations. In the bleak, east-windy downpours of chill October the roads proved inadequate to the vast amount of heavy traffic to which they were subjected. They were impassable to an ordinary bicycle. They taxed the skill of the most intrepid motor cyclists imaginable, the runners of the British army. In places they collapsed, and the imprisoned vehicle had to be extricated by caterpillars, the passage of which did not improve the surface of the roads or the stability of their bottom, such as it was. The congestion equalled that of London at high pressure, and it never seemed to cease. The A.P.M., Captain J. S. Mellor, who combined tact and good-nature with a will of iron, had his hands full in regulating it. Motor vehicles of every kind, guns, troops, and a certain number of equestrians poured along in unending streams. The detritus had to be flung to the side, where it formed quite an imposing but treacherous bank. Roads acquired the character of lanes. Here and there the country could be crossed on foot, but as a rule it was covered with water-logged shell-holes, and to stick to the road was the wiser policy. A couple of instances will suffice to indicate how operations were retarded. On 13th October a divisional staff car took an hour and a half to return from Longueval and two days later it took two hours from High Wood to Ribemont. The distance in either case was under twelve miles. In the later stages of the Battle of le Transloy a soldier stuck so deeply in the mud close to the firing line that the only way by which he could be rescued before dawn —then at hand—was by undoing his braces and pulling him out of his trousers, and his boots, which, mercifully, were " gum " boots. Such was the world in which the 29th found itself for the first time : a modern stricken field of battle, where underground dens were the choicest dwellings, where a normal trench was a luxury, and where the outposts shivered in isolated pockets not knowing whether the wet and the wind were worse or better than the cruel frosts of winter.

It will be remembered that the 88th Brigade had suffered less than the others on the 1st of July. Consequently, when the 29th were called on to assist the 12th Division under General Scott, it was the 88th which hurried on in advance and were the first to be sent into battle. The 12th Division belonged to the XV. Corps of the Fourth Army. General Cayley has furnished the editor with an account of two most creditable attacks made by his brigade from Gueudecourt, which had been originally wrested from the enemy by the 21st Division on the 29th of September.

In the first engagement the dash of the Newfoundlanders was matter of comment by captured German officers, who declared it could not have been surpassed. It was high praise from the Sixth Brandenburg Division, known as the " Iron " division. In the second an important trench, appropriately named Grease Trench, was captured and held by the Hants and Worcesters in spite of pouring rain and a start at 3.40 a.m.

GUEUDECOURT

" Early in October 1916 the 88th Brigade was detached from the division, and sent ahead from the salient to the Somme, where they were attached to the 12th Division.

" On 12th October the brigade took part in an attack in a very difficult sector. We attacked from Gueudecourt, the objective being two lines of enemy trenches, an advance of about 500 yards in all. The 1st Essex on left under Lieutenant-Colonel A. C. Halahan and the N.F.L.D. on right under Colonel A. L. Hadow were the battalions who carried out the operation, which was entirely successful in the end. Zero hour was at dawn. The troops on the right and left of the brigade failed to get their objectives, which made the flanks rather insecure.

" The left of the Essex attack was quite successful, a good many prisoners being taken, but their right failed to get on. However, the Newfoundlanders took their trenches in style, and finding the trench on their left, which should have been taken by the Essex, still full of Germans, they started bombing down it, and after a most strenuous fight cleared and captured it. They did *not* make any prisoners, but slew many Germans. Captain Butler was one of the many heroes of the occasion, and claimed to have personally bayoneted fifteen Germans. Knowing him as I did, I do not doubt it for an instant. Major March was in command of the advanced part of the Newfoundlanders and did splendidly, organizing the bombing attack and personally leading most of it.

"An Essex subaltern had a startling experience (I do not remember now what his name was). A good large party of Germans surrendered to the Essex, when suddenly the German officer went for the Essex subaltern, and they had a rough-and-tumble fight, which ended in the death of the German officer, and, as I understand, of all the party who had surrendered. The total bag of prisoners was about 130, and undoubtedly many more were killed in the close hand-to-hand fighting. All trenches captured were held. It was an extraordinarily satisfactory day for the brigade, as they were, as far as I know, the only troops successful in reaching and retaining their objectives on a battle front of many miles.

"On the 18th October the brigade was again taken for an attack from their captured trenches in front of Gueudecourt.

"The other two battalions of the brigade were, this time, engaged, 2nd Hampshire on the right (under Colonel Middleton) and 4th Worcesters on left (under Colonel E. T. J. Kerans). The attack was equally successful, all objectives being gained and held, in spite, again, of the failure of troops on the flanks. Zero hour was 3.40 a.m., and the rain was pouring down, making the ground nearly impassable.

"Part of the Hampshires' furthest objective was found to be a trench which was only partially completed and very shallow, and not yet occupied. However, they surprised a working party of the enemy, and accounted for them by death and capture.

"The troops on their right failing to come on, the Hants took an extra 300 yards of trench for them and consolidated and held it. The Worcestershires had some lively hand-to-hand scrapping, and took pretty heavy toll of the enemy. Their left flank being in the air owing to the failure of the other troops, they had to make a defensive flank back to our required starting-point, which they successfully held and beat off various local counter-attacks.

"A yarn, which I believe to be true, as it was told me the day after the battle, illustrates the German character well, and also the coolness of our men.

"A private of the Worcestershires (name unfortunately unknown to me) was told off to take back on his own eight German prisoners. He went off gaily, but when he got about half-way back he met a strongish party of Germans who had not been mopped up. He wasn't put out at all, and started to fire on them, and got his prisoners to load spare rifles for him, of which there were several lying about, so that he could keep up rapid fire ! The prisoners carried out his orders like lambs, one of them also being instructed to roll a cigarette for the firer, which was also done. The German party was finally routed, and the soldier brought in his eight prisoners in safety.

"The brigade machine-gun company under Major Morris did splendid work, getting guns forward with the leading waves, so making the holding of them against counter-attacks materially easier. Also before zero hour, they got a gun or two out into shell holes well in advance of the starting-line, and from thence splendidly helped the advance by their covering fire. The bag of prisoners in the second attack was about 150 and many more slain."

On 19th October the 87th relieved the 88th. It would be more accurate to say the relief began, for it was not completed even by 10.30 a.m. on the 20th. The cross-country tracks were impassable, and the extra traffic blocked the roads. The result was that the two battalions detailed to relieve those of the 88th in the line did not start on their final lap of about five miles till 8 p.m. The experience of the S.W.B. is characteristic of Somme fighting. They did not finish the relief of the Hampshires till 11 p.m. on the 20th, after twenty-seven hours, during which period they had six officer casualties. They had no greatcoats, and by a caprice of the weather the thermometer dropped to about 10 degrees below freezing-point.

The 86th relieved a brigade of the Twelfth Division on the night of the 20th–21st October.

There was an attack planned for the 25th. It was postponed, and eventually the division were relieved on 30th October by the First Australian Division. The tour in the line had opened the eyes of all ranks to the prospect of the amenities of a winter campaign in the Somme area. There had been more kicks than ha'pence going, but a few prisoners had dribbled singly over, having either had enough of it or lost their way. All had been heavily shelled at intervals. The 88th alone had " got a bit back." Nothing of special moment happened to the 29th during what was left of 1916. It was transferred from the XV. to the XIV. (Lord Cavan's) Corps, and from 18th November (when it relieved the 8th Division) until 12th December, when it was relieved by the 20th Division, occupied the Lesbœufs-le Transloy sector shortly to be described. The most noteworthy happening was the temporary loss to the division of Brigadier-General Lucas, who handed over to Lieutenant-

Colonel R. Bray of the 2nd West Riding Regiment on 7th December. He had well earned a rest, if rest it could be called, training a brigade at home. He was an " original member," so to speak, and had from the start won the confidence of those over and under him. We have followed his career in Gallipoli, but he had seen hard service from the very start of the war both in the staff and in his regiment. Colonel (afterwards Brigadier-General) Bray, who had been commandant of the European Volunteers at Shanghai, succeeded him at 87th Headquarters.

The remainder of 1916 was passed in the Cavillon area. Divisional Headquarters was at Cavillon and the 86th were at Picquigny, the 87th at Soucs and the 88th at Molliens Vidame. Thus ended an inconspicuous, somewhat disillusioning, but very educative year for the 29th. On the 16th January of the year of Arras, Ypres, and Cambrai, the 29th were still engaged in the last stages of the battle of the Somme. They had that day taken over from the 17th Division the le Transloy sector within a mile of that village in a south-westerly direction. The Fourth Army was not engaged at this time in any major operations. The Fifth or Reserve Army had ever since November shouldered the chief burden of the campaign. The capture of Beaumont Hamel by the 51st Division and the exploits of the 63rd in front of Beaucourt-sur-Ancre on the 13th and 14th November had roused the whole nation to enthusiasm. That action was not without its anxious moments, and it is a special pride to the 29th to feel that one of its future brigade commanders, Lieutenant-Colonel Freyberg, then commanding a battalion of the 63rd (Naval) Division, by the greatest gallantry and military genius contributed greatly thereto. The following is from the pen of a distinguished soldier : " At nightfall on the 13th, after the most bloody casualties it was realized that the attack had again failed, but Lieutenant-Colonel Freyberg, though wounded, collected every man who had got through the left of the German defences. This party of about 350 he led during the night up the spur to attack Beaucourt redoubt. He took the redoubt and the remainder of the ridge, and next morning 5,000 Germans between this ridge and the Beaumont-Hamel defences surrendered. By his initiative, fine leading, and bravery Lieutenant-Colonel Freyberg won the battle of the Ancre. Probably this was the most distinguished personal act in the war." In addition to the immediate award of the V.C. he was marked out for promotion, and in February 1918 he was at the youthful age of twenty-seven appointed to command the 88th Brigade.

It was the pressure of the Fifth Army on the southern flank of his awkward salient that no doubt ultimately caused and accelerated the date of the enemy's retirement in March 1917. None the less the activity of other parts of the line helped to undermine his *moral*. The 29th started the 1917 campaign by two brilliant minor exploits by which it re-established its reputation as a first-class fighting division. The 87th, then commanded by Brigadier-General R. N. Bray, D.S.O., and 86th under Brigadier-General Williams, showed that they could follow the good example set by the 88th at Gueudecourt.

The training which the 87th had received at Cavillon had been directed with a view to the capture by a surprise attack of the second line of trenches on a front of a thousand yards, bisected by the road running due south from le Transloy to Combles. For some reason this large-scale raid has failed to be vouchsafed an official name. "The Affair at le Transloy," or "The Kaiser's Birthday Raid" might answer the purpose; for the day chosen was the 27th January.

The attack was carefully prepared. The XIV. Corps had had the habits of the enemy under close scrutiny for weeks, and it was established that "Stand-to" occurred at 5.30 a.m. This was accordingly selected as zero hour for the start of an intense barrage by the 15th Brigade R.H.A. and the 147th Brigade R.F.A. of the 29th Division, as well as by the 76th Brigade R.F.A. of the Guards Division and the 17th Brigade R.F.A. of the 17th Division. Artillery of the 20th and 5th Australian Divisions operated on the flanks, while the 28th Heavy Artillery group fired on selected targets in the back area. The infantry selected for the enterprise were the R.I.F. and Borders, who had practised in a facsimile of the hostile trenches with flags to represent the barrage. The R.I.F., under Lieutenant-Colonel R. R. Willis, V.C., of the Lancashire Fusiliers, one of the heroes of the landing on W beach, were on the right, and the Borders under Lieutenant-Colonel F. G. Morris on the left, and both moved forward from the assembly trench close behind the barrage. The left-half sector of the brigade was held by the N.F.L.D., and, as will be seen, it could not have been in better hands. The S.W.B. were to "mop up" and support if necessary. But in that capacity neither they nor the reserve were required. The front and support trenches were captured with ease, except where a strong point on the extreme left of our attack held out for a quarter of an hour, during which all the officers of the Borders became casualties. However, with bravery and resource,

Corporal Robins, in charge of a Lewis gun, worked round the strong point until, by enfilade fire, he compelled its surrender with three machine guns and the whole garrison. Two reserve points known as Ersatz A and Ersatz B gave less trouble, as the barrage had passed over them. The task accomplished, the captured territory was put into a position of defence.

It was a creditable performance, executed with great dash, and the G.O.C. was well pleased with the fruits of the training and the outcome of elaborate preparations, in which long-range machine-guns, smoke shells, and elaborate reconnaissance had played a part. The greatest care had been taken to keep the machine-guns warm. It was noted by a competent observer that the German machine-gun fire was less brisk than usual. He put it down to frozen barrel casings. The losses had been comparatively light. The casualties amounted to 132. The enemy captured totalled 394, of whom 9 were officers. As usual, the element of surprise had brought easy success. The captured troops were Würtembergers of a famous division and some odds and ends from other units. The *Times* of January 30, 1917, called them "the Kaiser's picked men." Their *moral* was good, and they frankly admitted that they were completely taken by surprise and that our lads had had a " walk over."

Many individual acts of gallantry were performed. The following two are typical.

Sergeant Mott, Borders, found his platoon held up by a machine-gun in a small strong point. He was already wounded in the face, but he worked round the flank and single-handed charged the gun himself, throwing himself on the firer and holding him until his men came to his aid. For this act Sergeant Mott won the thirteenth V.C. for the 29th.

A bloodless victory was gained by a sergeant-major of the N.F.L.D., who, as already explained, were on the left flank of the attack. He happened to detect signs of willingness on the part of some Germans to surrender. Without a moment's hesitation he dashed across No Man's Land, and returned in triumph with no less than 70 prisoners.

The consolidation of the captured ground by the 2nd Monmouthshire Pioneers under Lieutenant-Colonel Bowen's personal supervision was a remarkable feat. The ground was frozen to a depth of eighteen inches, and, of course, as hard as iron. Yet the line was dug in twenty minutes in the face of hostile fire at close range.

The success of this little affair or minor operation brought congratulations from the Commander-in-Chief, as well as from the

Commander of the Fourth Army. Sir Henry Rawlinson's message of 4th February ran thus : " This operation was skilfully planned and exceedingly well carried out by the two battalions concerned. The artillery brigades who did the barrage work deserve high praise for the accuracy and efficiency of their fire, as shown not only by the reports of the infantry but by the evidence of the air photos. The whole enterprise is one which indicates that the 29th Division has reached a high standard of efficiency very creditable to all concerned and to the divisional commander in particular."

Sir Douglas Haig sent the following : " Congratulate the 29th Division warmly, and in particular the 1st Border Regiment and the 1st Royal Inniskilling Fusiliers, on the success of their operations carried out this morning." A special article, as above noted, appeared in the *Times*, and it had an excellent effect on the public at home and the troops at the front, including the 29th.

The 86th Brigade was able to show its mettle before the 29th came out of the Somme. The division were relieved by the 20th Division on 9th February and rested in the Méaulte-Heilly-Bussy-Rainneville area until 21st February, when it once more relieved the 17th Division in the Saillisel sector. More ground had been taken over from the French, and the 29th, although the centre division of the XIV. Corps, held ground farther to the right of the Somme front than ever previously, and faced east with a very slight tilt northwards. The 20th were on its right and the Guards on the left.

Attention has already been drawn to the effect of the pressure of the British Fifth Army on the garrison still clinging to what was left of the Ancre salient. The fall of Pys and Miraumont on 17th and 18th February naturally suggested Bapaume and Irles as the next points to be evacuated. It was considered advisable that a reconnaissance in force should be made, to feel the weight of German resistance in the area south of Bapaume. There was secondly a tactical advantage to be gained by a slight thrust forward, so as to capture and consolidate a trench called Potsdam, which commanded a view of the valleys to the east and north-east, and a trench called Pfalz, which, besides possibilities in the way of observation, was essential in part, if not in whole, for protection of Potsdam, if and when won. Thirdly, the success of the operation would improve the defences. In particular it would wipe out a re-entrant in our front line, the tip of which was 250 yards from Pfalz. If the Germans held in force and were in fighting mood, it promised to be a stern struggle. There could be no surprise. The wire in front of Pfalz was on the reverse slope, and it was vital that it should be cleared. This task was entrusted to trench mortars. Meanwhile, so far as visibility allowed, the Heavy Artillery had bombarded strong points and trench junctions. The attack was to be made at 5.25 a.m., an hour before dawn, and the men who were to take part were trained to march by the guidance of tape and compass bearing. They were also carefully trained in the use of German bombs, both stick and egg-bombs. Some 2,000 of these were expended by the 86th Brigade in practice.

That brigade was under command of Brigadier-General W. de L. Williams, C.M.G., who had allotted the 2nd Royal Fusiliers, under Lieutenant-Colonel G. A. Stevens, and the Dublins along with a company of the Lancashire Fusiliers, all under Major N. P. Clarke, for the enterprise. The Royal Fusiliers were on the right, the Dublins and Lancashire Fusiliers on the left, or northern sector opposite Potsdam. The front of attack was about 1,100 yards in width.

The weather conditions were poor. The long iron frost of January and most of February had broken. The shelled ground reverted to its former condition of a muddy morass or quagmire. Going was slow, only ten yards a minute, but so accurate was the creeping barrage that it was possible to keep within twelve yards of it. A wounded officer was met, when returning, by the G.O.C., who asked him what the barrage was like. He replied, " General, it was like a wall. I walked across No Man's Land, my hands in my pockets and my pipe in my mouth. On reaching the German trench we just leant up against the barrage and, as it lifted, we fell into the trench."

The attacking troops were formed up on the parapet in good time. At scheduled time down crashed the barrage. They were off. No Man's Land was crossed, and the objectives gained except in the sector opposite the flanking company of Lancashire Fusiliers and the leftmost of the Dublins. Those of the Dublins who had reached the trench on the right bombed northwards to help their comrades held up by uncut wire. There was long bitter fighting at close quarters and some slaughter done round the dug-outs. Lieutenant McFeely of the Dublins did brilliant execution with his revolver. The result of a desperate struggle was that the Dublins and Lancashire Fusiliers gained and held their objectives. Meanwhile the 2nd Royal Fusiliers had met with stubborn resistance in their attempts to exploit their success southwards and eastwards by bombing. Liberal as had been the supply of bombs carried up and indefatigable the work of the carriers in keeping up the supply by crossing and recrossing No Man's Land, supplies proved insufficient in the face of the gallant bombing attacks of the enemy. Indeed, had it not been for the capture of a good store of German bombs and the ability to use them, it would have gone harder than it did with the Royal Fusiliers. As it was, they had to give way, but enough was gained materially to improve the position on the divisional front. For conspicuous gallantry in repelling these attacks Lieutenant J. F. Dearden earned the D.S.O. The enemy's attacks were not renewed after 6.30 p.m. The work of the Monmouths in consolidating the ground captured was beyond praise. Thanks to their labours and to the gallantry of the N.F.L.D., who had been attached to the 86th as reserve battalion, two attacks on the 1st March and two more on the 2nd against the northern and southern barricades were frustrated. The southern barricade was actually advanced and the British firmly seated until the general advance.

It is sad to record the death of Lieutenant-Colonel A. J. H. Bowen, the gallant commander of the Monmouthshire Pioneers, who had just earned a bar to his D.S.O., a few days after the 28th, while supervising the work of consolidation. He was not a regular soldier, but so completely a soldier by temperament and self-culture that he was indistinguishable from the very finest type the British army can produce. The G.O.C. was not exaggerating when he said that Bowen's death was a loss to the whole army. Lord Cavan sent a message that his loss was deplored by the whole corps.

This sanguinary and desperate conflict resulted in the capture of 2 officers and 71 other ranks. Many of the enemy were killed and wounded. The three objects of the raid had been attained, but the cost had been considerable. Our casualties amounted to 19 officers and 363 other ranks. One of the wounded was the acting brigade-major, Major J. M. Meiklejohn of the Borders, afterwards O.C. Div. M.-G. Batt., who was twice forward and the source of much valuable information.

The battle was a microcosm of the macrocosm of the Somme— the wearing-out battle. Laborious planning, arduous training, determination and tenacity were applied to get to grips with and to fight the enemy until he had had enough. The effect of the fight, which won the whole of Saillisel, was to stimulate the 86th and indeed the whole of the 29th with fresh military ardour. The four actions between October and March had established its reputation as a first-class fighting unit. Lord Cavan, the Commander of the XIV. Corps, sent his hearty congratulations and thanks for "grit and tenacity during a trying day. The capture of Potsdam trench was quite up to Gallipoli form. It is of utmost importance, and I know the 86th Brigade will hold on and keep it. Artillery support and barrage quite admirable."

General Sir Henry Rawlinson, commanding the Fourth Army, sent the following :—

"Please convey to 29th Division and especially to 86th Brigade my congratulations on their successful attack yesterday. The tenacity in holding on to Potsdam trench and the efficient support of the artillery are deserving of high praise. The plan was well conceived by the division commander and staff and very gallantly executed by the Dublin and Royal Fusiliers."

The Commander-in-Chief added his congratulations on the success of a minor operation.

The compliments to the divisional artillery were well deserved. It had played a notable part in the action, and the infantry felt a special debt of gratitude to Lieutenant Hallinan, R.F.A., who, seeing the dearth of officers owing to casualties, organized and led bodies of the infantry most gallantly. For this he won the M.C.

On the 4th March the 29th were relieved by the Guards Division and to a minor extent by the 20th. On 20th and 21st March the 29th said farewell to the Somme and the Ancre, and moved to rest quarters at and round about Cavillon.

THE SOMME - WINTER FIGHTING 1916-17

Scale
0   500   1000   2000 Yards

Grévillers

Frémicourt

Bapaume

Bancourt

Thilloy

Riencourt les
Bapaume

le Barque

Ligny-Thilloy

Villers
au-Flos

Beaulencourt

Gueudecourt

le Transloy

Rocquigny

Flers

Lesbœufs

Moulin de Morval

Bois
Delville

Morval

Sailly-Saillisel

Longueval

Waterlot F^{me}

Ginchy

Bois des
Bouleaux

Saillisel

Bois des
Trônes

Guillemont

Combles

Frégicourt

Bois
St Pierre Vaast

John Bartholomew & Son Ltd Edinburgh.

CHAPTER II

MONCHY-LE-PREUX

" A City set on an Hill."

" The most violent counter-attacks were directed against Monchy-le-Preux. The struggle for this important position held by the 29th Division (Major-General de Lisle) was exceedingly fierce. The enemy's attacks were supported by the full weight of his available artillery, and at one time parties of his infantry reached the eastern defences of the village. To the south and the north, however, our posts held their ground, and in the end the enemy was completely repulsed with great loss."—Lord Haig's Dispatches, page 95.

(On 23rd April.) " British battalions (29th Division) gained the western slopes of the rising ground known as Infantry Hill." . . . (On 24th April.) " Very appreciable progress had also been made east of Monchy-le-Preux." . . . In " the course of these operations of 23rd and 24th April we captured a further 3,000 prisoners and a few guns."—*Ibid.*, pages 97, 98.

" There was also very heavy fighting around Monchy, where the famous 3rd Bavarians were in action against the not less famous 29th Division."—*History of the War*, by Colonel John Buchan.

THE brief mentions of the 29th in the official dispatches and a representative history of the war cited above indicate plainly to the reader that he is not to expect the sensational in the ensuing chapter. The ragged ends of a battle with limited objectives do not appeal to the imagination in the same way as do the dramatic bounds forward at the opening. The 29th were not called upon to take part in the earlier phases of that tremendous British effort, which between the 9th and the 13th April had hurled the Germans out of their trenches north and south of the Scarpe to an average depth of four miles, secured the Vimy ridge through the valour of the Canadians and taken 13,000 prisoners. Their task was to defend the territory gained, to push forward as much as possible in the direction of certain tactical points east of Monchy and, by incessant pressure on the enemy, keep his forces in Artois, when he would like to have them on the Aisne. Eager hearts were expecting great things to happen at the Chemin-des-dames. For at least a month rumours had been flying round the British front concerning the irresistible vastity of an impending French attack on a scale to which we could never aspire, and directed by brains which are not vouchsafed to British generals by a discriminating Creator. The battle of Arras was merely the Prologue. The Play was to begin on the 16th April elsewhere.

Five miles south-east by east of the railway station of Arras stands the village of Monchy-le-Preux. It had been a thorn in the flesh of the troops attacking from Arras south of the Scarpe. It stood on the summit of a conical hill, more than 350 feet above sea-level and more than 200 feet above the Scarpe, sufficiently isolated to command to north, west, and south extensive views of the surrounding country. To the east the ground dipped a little but retained the character of a plateau. About a mile east of Monchy the ground rose at the eastern edge of the plateau to a conspicuous knoll known as Infantry Hill. A place of such tactical importance as Monchy was naturally well fortified and strongly held, and it took the efforts of four divisions before the Germans were driven out of it by the combined efforts of the 37th (Infantry) and 3rd (Cavalry) Divisions on the bitterly cold and snowy 11th April. There was little doubt that the enemy would make strenuous efforts to recover this vital observation point, and it was of cardinal importance that the British should not lose their grip of it, but should, if only to improve their defensive position, press the Germans still farther back by the capture of Infantry Hill. Monchy was the key to the position of the VI. Corps, commanded by General J. A. L. Haldane, and its loss would have serious consequences for the whole of the Third Army of Sir Edmund Allenby. Ever since its capture the Germans had massed quite an abnormal concentration of heavy artillery, which henceforth day and night throughout April and May poured a steady flow of shells into Monchy. Only after sundown was there a lull. Fortunately the village contained excellent deep dug-outs made by the Germans and some good cellars. The enemy had also paid the VI. Corps the compliment of sending troops of the finest quality to contest possession of this important battlefield. There were all the materials for a struggle of the grimmest nature fought out under conditions of weather and ground enough to depress the human soul to the depths of misery and dejection. Trench construction was hampered by a phenomenon very characteristic of Artois—the region which has given us the world-wide name of artesian wells—namely, the discovery of water at levels hardly below the surface. The trenches in the north-eastern outskirts of Monchy were always water-logged, and 400 yards east of the village a likely site for trenches had on one occasion to be abandoned on account of the persistent oozing up of water in the most unlikely of places, due presumably to underground fissures.

The 29th's share in the later stages of the First Battle of the Scarpe in April and in the earlier stages of the Second Battle of the Scarpe (to use official terminology) consisted of a tour in the trenches of about a fortnight in April. There are no tactical successes of importance to record. In spite of the efforts to be recounted Infantry Hill was never won. It was not until June 14, 1917, that it was stormed by the 3rd Division as the result of an admirably planned surprise without a barrage until a minute and a half after zero and in broad daylight (see *Sir D. Haig's Command*, vol. i., page 350). The guns of the 29th Division Artillery assisted materially in this success and in repelling a counter-attack the same evening. The story of the infantry of that division is one of an inconspicuous round of duty done in spite of cold, wet, dirt, and danger. The battle casualties in April amounted to 4,340. Those of May swelled the grand total for the Scarpe fighting to more than 7,000. These appalling figures for a month's fighting tell their own tale.

The 29th spent the time, after handing over to the Guards on March 4, 1917, in resting and training and absorbing reinforcements in the Méaulte-Bussy-Ville district of the Ancre. On 20th and 21st March the brigades found their way to the Cavillon area, a delightful bit of unspoilt country on the lower Somme, where training was continued until a gradual move was made in the direction of Arras by easy marches beginning on the 29th.

At this point of time when the 29th has once more found itself, and is making ready for the ordeal of battle, a word in regard to training may not be out of plaee. The low standard of training of junior officers prevailing in the Somme battle has already been pointed out. Much had been done in the three months in Flanders to effect an improvement, and good results were seen in the later

fighting on the Somme.   But the wintry conditions and the development of the barrage, to say nothing of the greater use of
machine guns, Lewis guns, trench mortars, Stokes mortars, and the
return to rifle fire made a special effort necessary in the early spring
of 1917.   The old system, by which in regular units the commanding
officer is responsible for the training of his men, was no longer
adequate.   The necessity for an even, uniform, and all-pervading
standard was paramount.   There was a shortage of commanding
officers with sufficient experience.   Hence the growth of Army,
Corps, and Divisional Schools.   Coming to the 29th, the G.O.C.,
on ascertaining that the wastage in France was likely to average
something like 100 per cent. every six months, immediately set on
foot the following system, with a view to the rapid imparting of
practical instruction in minor tactics.   No one, who has experienced
the bewildering feeling of helplessness, when detailed to instruct
men in tactical exercises without guidance, will underrate the
importance of the help given to officers through the personal efforts
of the G.O.C.   On every occasion that the division went into
reserve, he personally lectured company and platoon commanders
with the aid of the blackboard and many ingenious *memoria technica*.
The principles enunciated were then put into practice under his
own supervision.   Nothing was left to chance.   Before every operation situations similar to those likely to occur were described in
detail, and then a manœuvre was executed as like that of the
impending operation as he and his staff could devise.   After this
manœuvre had been carried out satisfactorily, the officers of each
unit were summoned to a conference and personally catechized by
their general.

But even more important than these special and careful
preparations was the general instruction, which showed the inter-
relation between discipline and mobility and pugnacity, the importance of drill and smartness, of a drill-like practice of tactical
exercises, as tending to promote precision in manœuvres, and of
inspiring in subordinates faith in the ability and bravery of their
leader.   In turning over the pages of a little brochure, in which
the quintessence of the lectures is contained, one is struck by the
business-like and practical character of the instruction, and the
arresting language in which it is couched.

" A creeping barrage doesn't creep ; it jumps."

" When you are held up by a strong post, and are uncertain
which flank is the best to turn, put your hand in your pocket and
pull out a coin.   If it shows heads, go to the right ; if tails, to the

left. It is better to go to the wrong flank without hesitation than keep your men under fire at close range."

" Turning a flank is not being able to fire through the side windows, but into the back door." (The wonderful fruit borne of this aphorism will be recounted in a subsequent chapter.)

" The pickets on the line of observation are like the eyes, and the force in support is like the mouth of a human face. Make a ring round a diagram of a company on outposts and look. As we observe with the eyes, and the mouth supports the body, the relative position of the platoons can never be forgotten."

" Zero is only an approximation. Watch the barrage."

" A barrage is not a line, but a belt."—" The best troops do not need to shout."—" Regard a thick barrage as a luxury."—" Ground won must never be given up."—" The counter-attack, which takes place two hours after capture of the objective, is the most dangerous. Therefore see your front is properly patrolled."

" When you think of attack formation, think of the ace of diamonds."

" Target practice is for duffers and snipers. Field firing competitions are the real battle practice."

The use of flags and tape, the uselessness of whistles, the necessity for a simple prearranged code of signals, so that orders may be given and carried out during the fight without a sound, tests for correct marching, how to acquire skill with the rifle, the arrival at perfection through the study and elimination of " characteristic faults," all find a place in the curriculum. My first introduction to the G.O.C. in Egypt was when he asked me, " What is the characteristic fault in the slope ? " Of course, I did not know. " Moving the head," said the general, with a kindly smile. If I live to be a hundred, I shall never forget that piece of instruction.

General de Lisle was always enthusiastically supported by the brigadiers and officers commanding battalions, and hardly a day passed that units could not be seen exemplifying one or other of the four cardinal principles of instruction—explanation, demonstration, execution, and repetition. In particular much attention was paid to advances or retirements made under the covering fire of units on either side, usually by alternate sections. Constant reference will be made in the coming battles to this manœuvre under the name of Fire and Movement. Subsequent events will show the tactical results attained and the superb uplift to *moral* effected by the intensive training through which every new-comer, and most old hands were put in the 29th.

Meanwhile the diversion of the troops while resting and in reserve was not neglected. It was felt that something more elaborate than the usual concert or sing-song was required, and this meant the dedication of certain men possessed of musical or theatrical talent to an intensive study of singing, acting, scene-shifting, lighting, making-up and dressing, and to rehearsal after rehearsal. They were excused the trenches with the completest approval of their comrades. Unless the troupe was to endure, the time in training it would be thrown away. Much talent had been lost to the division in the Somme. To give one instance, a private in the Borders, at a concert given at Acheux late in June 1916, played accompaniments for all and sundry with mastery and exquisite taste. A few days later he fell on the 1st July, and the division was minus a real musician.

The K.O.S.B. had produced an excellent clown when occasion required ; the 87th Brigade had sported a team of pierrots ; but the idea of a divisional troupe, no doubt, was due to the numerous divisional troupes of fame, notably the " Bow Bells " of the 56th (London) Division.

Anyhow, it is interesting to know that two days after a " very good " show, given by the " Bow Bells " in Arras, on May 24, 1917, after voice trials, Major J. G. Gillam, D.S.O., and Captain L. C. Shadwell, both of the divisional train, selected the following fifteen to start the new troupe on its career. There is nothing like a good name, and as the half-diamond was the badge of the 29th, chosen by the G.O.C. because the diamond formation is normally the best in an advance, it was called " The Diamond Troupe." The names are : Private Giordano and Private Threlfall, 87th Field Ambulance ; Corporal Pollard, Inniskilling Fusiliers, and Corporal Stannard, Royal Fusiliers ; Private McKinlay, K.O.S.B. ; Corporal Dean, Hants Regiment ; Private A. Hill, Middlesex Regiment ; Corporal Sykes, Border Regiment ; Private Morris, Border Regiment ; Private Nicol, S.W.B. ; Private Palmer, Middlesex Regiment ; Private Holmes, S.W.B. ; Private Price, Royal Fusiliers ; Private Wilson, K.O.S.B. ; Privates Hangle, Labour Corps, Stannard, Palmer, and Holmes formed the orchestra. After about a month of rehearsal the troupe commenced to give performances in a marquee, in which a stage had been set, complete with curtains and a small amount of scenery. The costumes and makes-up were at this time rather crude ; but seeing the difficulties which they had to contend with, the actual performances were of a good standard. The singing was very good, and all the turns both amusing and diverting.

The first theatre in which the troupe played was at Proven, where a fine canvas theatre had been erected with a very good stage. The troupe had its own electric lighting plant, which it carried about with it. This was under the supervision of Private Price, who was a really clever electrician, though at this time very few, if any, effects at lighting were attempted. These were to come later. The first part of the performance was a pierrot show, and the second part consisted of variety turns. Considerable strides were made whilst the troupe were at Proven, during which time the conversion of Private Threlfall from a smart R.A.M.C. orderly to a dainty and bewitching lady was commenced. And no member of the Diamond Troupe was put through half the work that " Queenie " had to do before she became the very perfect and clever artist who captivated London during January 1918. Diet for the complexion, and dentistry for the smile marked the first stage of her career. In addition to this, " Queenie " was made to make up her face every morning until she became perfect in the art. This did not take long, but the result was most marked. Her hair was then considered, and with new wigs her appearance was greatly improved. Last of all, new dresses were designed and made for her, and eventually her trousseau, both dresses and underclothing, were worthy of a real lady. Every conceivable thing was done to turn this boy into a girl, and the details to be thought of were considerable. Lace handkerchiefs, silk stockings, scent, brooches, rings, bracelets, flowers, ribbons, and chocolates, necklaces, long kid gloves and satin shoes all played their part, and the amusement obtained and created during a shopping expedition to Dunkerque was considerable. Let it be said here that neither in the " Queenie " pieces nor in any other turn was there anything of coarseness, vulgarity, or broad jest. Dickens's " young person " would have been as safe as with a volume of *Punch*.

I find from an unerring source that it was towards the end of September that the troupe suddenly found itself. In one month it had made immense strides. When I find the G.O.C. speaking of the able management (or rather co-operation with the manager) of Lieutenant-Colonel E. T. Wright, D.S.O., who rejoined the 29th as officer commanding train in August 1917, I draw the conclusion that his arrival and interest had something to do with an improvement, which was not only *post hoc* but *propter hoc*. But a business head, authority, a critical faculty, and organization must have talents to play with. Major Gillam was an admirable producer, especially of operatic scenes, and all the early triumphs

of the troupe were won under his management.   The orchestra of
three—violin, 'cello, and piano—was excellent, and the mainstay
of every performance.   In Captain Shadwell the 29th possessed a
lyrical bard, who not only could supply the light, topical, frivolous
comic matter, so dear to the average Briton, but rise to the stirring " Song of the Twenty-ninth," which forms the final appendix
to this story.   Wedded to the music of Arthur Saunderson, this
song, sung by Private Hill early in October 1917, took the division
by storm, and it is impossible to picture a divisional gathering of a
festal nature in which it would not be sung.   One of the favourite
productions of Shadwell's lighter muse was a song, " In these Hard
Times," sung by Private McKinlay, a verse of which runs
thus :—

" To-day my rations I went to draw, but I never had such a shock
        before.
The 'Quarter,' smiling blandly, gave me a jam tin grandly.
I looked inside, and when I spied the plum and apple, he softly
        sighed,
As he winked his eye at me, ' It's like this, don't you see ?
        In these hard times you've got to put up with anything ;
        In these hard times you mustn't pick or choose.
        You might have got more, you might have got less,
        But it's all you'll get to-day, I guess,
        For the strawberry jam's for the sergeants' mess
                In these hard times.' "

A useful recruit was Private McArthur, whose droll singing of
Shadwell's " 365 days " convulsed his audiences, also a parody
of that almost too popular song, " They wouldn't believe me."

The custom at this time was for each artist to choose and
rehearse his own turns, and submit them to the manager for his
final approval ; but concerted numbers were always drilled and
rehearsed by the management, in order that lighting, costumes,
music, and action should all combine properly.

Probably the most difficult and trying of all the turns produced
by the troupe was a duet entitled " Some Sort of Somebody,"
sung by Hill and " Queenie."   But at the same time both the
members of the troupe learnt more of acting than in any other
piece.   To show the work put into so small a turn, which was
taken off after a very short run, the rehearsals continued daily
for a solid month, during which time " Queenie " learnt to walk
and run as a lady, how to use her hands and feet, her handkerchief,
how to arrange her frock and pat her hair into shape—such small

and insignificant details that the audience would never dream that each separate action had had to be shown and practised diligently and continuously.

The first part of the programme—the pierrot show—lasted about forty-five minutes, and the second half—the variety show—about the same length of time. Two popular turns of the second half were Nicol's bicycle act, during which he rode both a very small and a very high single wheel with extraordinary dexterity, and the sketch at the end of the show, entitled "The School," which every one who ever saw it will easily remember.

During the time that the division was preparing for the Cambrai battle the troupe was performing in a very fine wooden theatre in the camp, and there a scene from *Faust* was most ably produced by Major Gillam. Hill and Corporal Sykes, who had a very good tenor voice, took the parts of "Faust" and "Mephistopheles" respectively, and "Queenie" was the vision. And a beautiful vision she was.

When the division went into the battle of Cambrai the Diamond Troupe went to a Casualty Clearing Station and performed there each night to the patients, and later they moved into a good theatre at Péronne. It was at this time that Colonel Wright took over the management from Major Gillam, who had left the division. Up to now the performances had been arranged anyhow, the turns sometimes being decided only a few minutes before the curtain went up, with the result that the performance as a whole was often ragged, and delays occurred between the turns owing to the artists not having time in which to change properly. The programmes were now most carefully thought out with the purpose of giving variety between each turn, at the same time allowing each player the proper time in which to dress. Four grand performances were given at Péronne to crowded houses, which gave a great fillip to the troupe, who were quick to see that, with improved organization, they could very easily give a vastly superior and better finished performance than they had been doing in the past.

One of the smartest bits of work which they did was on their return to France after an invasion of London. Arrangements had been made by Colonel Wright for them to play for two nights at the headquarters of the XXII. Corps at Abèle on their way up to the division from Boulogne. They arrived at Abèle at 3 a.m. on the morning they were to give their first performance—worn out with their journey. By 8 p.m. they had their scenery mounted, the lighting battens and footlights fixed and were ready for the show, which was an unqualified success.

Steps were now taken greatly to improve the lighting system. New battens were made, new limelights were purchased, and eventually the stage could be lighted with any one or all of five different coloured lights. Hours were spent after each evening performance trying the effects of various lightings, each combination being noted and scheduled for future use. It is only fair to give the greatest credit to the electrician, Private Price, and Privates McKinnon and Scott, who worked the limelights. For hours they patiently practised the various changes, which occurred during the performances, and never once did they fail to carry out the printed instructions, or " lighting plots." There is little doubt that the lighting of the performances of the Diamond Troupe was far in advance of anything done by other troupes in the field.

After their visit to Abèle the troupe went into a wretched theatre in Poperinghe, where they continued their rehearsals—the Harlequin and Columbine Scena, written by Captain Shadwell, with music by Corporal Stannard, being commenced there at the beginning of February. This scena was probably the most finished production of the troupe, the parts of Harlequin and Columbine being taken by Hill and " Queenie " respectively.

The troupe next played in a canvas theatre near Vlamertinghe, the entrance to which was extraordinarily muddy. The theatre was a very good one, and performances were given right up to the time when the division was hurriedly drafted to the Merville area to hold up the advance of the enemy. The troupe was left at Vlamertinghe at the theatre, but soon had to clear out as the theatre was destroyed by shell fire. They then went down to Boulogne under Captain Shadwell, who had been left in charge of them. There they played for about six weeks at the various hospitals, where they were greatly appreciated and most hospitably cared for. After the advance of the enemy had been stopped, the division went to Wallen Cappel, and the troupe then took the riding-school theatre in St. Omer, where it played for several weeks. Two or three gala performances were given—one by command of Lieutenant-General Sir Beauvoir de Lisle, who had by this time taken over the XV. Corps. At one gala performance about 120 nurses were entertained at the invitation of the G.O.C. Early in June 1918 the troupe moved to a theatre, or rather a barn which was being used by the 87th Field Ambulance for a theatre. The stage was greatly improved, and some members of the 87th Field Ambulance Concert Party joined the Diamond Troupe. After this the troupe played for various periods at a home-made theatre near Hazebrouck, in the centre of the division's rest area ; later at Roubaix Theatre, after which they were more or less lost to the division, which had commenced to take part in the general advance. The troupe rejoined the division when it was in Germany, and gave performances at Würmelskirchen until they were granted leave about Christmas 1918. Unhappily, during the time they were on leave the War Office issued an order that any men in England on leave from France might obtain their discharge on application, and all but three or four took advantage of this.

The Diamond Troupe thus stole silently away just when it might have been of the greatest value to the rest of the division during the weary days, when men were waiting for their discharge. All the costumes, etc., were sold to other troupes, many of whom were started by units, who, however, found the direction of a concert party considerably more difficult than they had imagined, with the unhappy result that several of them had to close down after only a few performances.

Though the life of the members of the Diamond Troupe was comparatively easy in comparison with the other men in the division, yet their work was very exacting and trying, the air of nervous excitement before and during the performances being considerable.

Allusion has been made to a trip to London. This was undertaken by order of the G.O.C. in aid of the benevolent fund of the division. The Royal Court Theatre was hired for the week January 21–26, 1918. Of the difficulties and thrills of anxiety experienced by Colonel Wright (now O.C. entertainments) and his troupe one might make a long story. But space forbids. The properties and costumes went astray for a time on the railway. Advertising was costly and inevitably delayed pending the settlement of house and date. Bookings were small at first. The first dress rehearsal on Sunday, 20th January, took six hours. Stage instructions had to be framed, and this took three hours more. Next morning the costumes were completed, and wigs, etc., adjusted by 11 a.m. The first performance, attended by the Lord Mayor and Lord Derby, the Minister of War, began at 2 p.m., and although the house contained a number of free sitters it was a complete success. Two performances a day were given during the week— on the last three days crowded with " good money."

Her Majesty Queen Alexandra graciously honoured the troupe and the division by attending the matinee on Saturday, 26th January. With time for the advertisements to have their effect the financial results would have been even better than they were. A clear profit of £750 was, however, most satisfactory, and the troupe won such kudos that the Minister of Munitions wished it to tour the chief munition centres on tempting terms. But the duty of the troupe was to amuse the fighting-men, and the offer had to be declined. The value of the Diamond Troupe to the *moral* of the troops surpassed the best expectations of its promoters. It took as if by magic the minds of the weary soldiers off their woes. Nothing could improve on what Sir Philip Gibbs wrote in the *Daily Chronicle*, September 20, 1917, after a visit to the 29th in Flanders :—

" A week ago the Germans began to bombard a section of our trenches pretty heavily with 5.9's, which are big things, making a horrible noise and a worse mess. In that part of the line there happened to be a battalion of the Royal Fusiliers, who are mostly London men, and it must have surprised the enemy a good deal to hear, through the din of their shell-fire, the sound of singing. It was a popular song called " In these Hard Times," and it was roared out in a great chorus by men who knew they might be blown to pieces between one verse and another.

" Last night I heard some of the same men singing the same song. It was in a big hall of sticks and canvas which holds 500 men, and is so designed that it can be removed and put up elsewhere in a couple of days. Five hundred men were there, packed tight, and all with their eyes fixed with fascination upon a little lighted stage where there was a world of comedy and song which witched these men's souls away from the war zone.

" The war was not far away as gun range goes. When I came out of this soldier's theatre and walked along some duck boards to an officer's mess, the night was filled with the flashing of shells and with the white glare of Véry lights going up along the line. The men came out, too, into the darkness back to their billets and camps, and they were whistling and humming the songs they had heard, and laughing still at the thought of the trick cyclist who rode his bike any old way with marvellous skill and fearful grimaces.

" ' A topping show,' said an officer, ' it brightens up the men no end.' There was a discussion as to the new frock of the young fellow who played the girl's part, falsetto voice, and a golden wig.

' She looked a peach,' said a senior officer, ' but I think the frock was three inches too short.'

" A tenor and a baritone had done the dual scene out of one of Verdi's operas as well as one could hear it on a London stage. The men whistled with shrill syren blasts in their appreciation of high-class stuff ; and the orchestra of three—with a violin, a 'cello, and a piano—had played their part splendidly and kept everything together in a wonderful way. But, of course, it was laughter the men liked most, and when a mimic Charlie Chaplin twisted his ridiculous hat, and when a ' Zummerzet ' yokel described his love affairs, or when a tall droll-faced Jock played the simpleton sub-limely, they had their fill of it.

" ' It takes a lot of organization,' said the O.C. entertain-ment, ' but it's worth it a hundred times. We might have lost the war if it had not been for laughter. Imagine what it is for men just out of the trenches to see a show like this. It is fairyland to them. They just drink in the light and the music. Besides, it keeps up the *esprit de corps*. Did you notice how they were stirred by that divisional song ? '

" There had been a hush when that song was sung, for it brought back to some of the men who heard it the days of battle in the Dardanelles and in the fields of the Somme or in the quagmire of Flanders where the ghosts of brave comrades were."

From the Cavillon area the division passed through the Vignan-court, Beauval, and Lucheux areas. In the last-named village Brigadier-General Lucas rejoined on 3rd April and took over com-mand of his old brigade, the 87th. General Bray, who went to command a brigade of the 57th Division, left with the heartiest wishes of all who had come in contact with him. He had carried out the difficult task of filling a gap with equal tact and military skill. It was his brigade that scored (*si parva licet componere magnis*) the most complete success of any operation on the Somme. The brigade were sorry to part with him, but they were very glad to get their old friend back. The arrival of a " burial and casualty " officer on the 4th was a reminder of the perils ahead. The march continued by Le Cauroy and Couturelle to Bavincourt. By this time the 29th were in the XVIII. (General Sir Ivor Maxse's) Corps. On the 9th the roar of the guns told of the great battle begun, and as the news of territory and prisoners captured came trickling in, the spirits of the troops rose. On the 13th the 29th joined the VI. Corps and took over the line close east of Monchy from the River

Cojeul on the south to a point north of Monchy from which the Scarpe was visible. Divisional Headquarters were in the Petite Place Château in Arras. Already the troops had been moving into Arras and out again on the battle side on the 12th, and the 88th under General Cayley were in position by the morning of the 13th, having taken over from the 12th Division during the previous night. To the right of them were the 87th Brigade, whose front extended southwards towards the Cojeul by the morning of the 14th. The 86th Brigade were in reserve in Arras.

Infantry Hill concealed a large amount of ground, and its reverse slopes were a likely point of assembly for an attack on Monchy. The corps commander naturally wished that the hill should be captured as soon as possible and a defensive flank formed to connect the sharp salient thus created with the northern defences of Monchy, and the 88th received orders to attack at first at 5.30 a.m. and then (after cancellation) at two p.m. on the 13th. In the opinion of all concerned in the 29th this was too sudden an undertaking for freshly arrived troops. The G.O.C.'s request for delay was acceded to, and the attack was timed for 5.30 a.m. on the 14th. It was the turn of the 88th to undertake the task. The Essex and the N.F.L.D. were the battalions selected for this local attack on a two battalion front. In reserve for the actual defence of Monchy were a company of Hants in Monchy, and the remainder on Orange Hill about a mile and a half behind, and in support on the flank towards the 87th were the Worcesters, whose right rested on the great road from Arras to Cambrai. Monchy was ours and no more. There was no proper assembly trench on the east of the village, and one had to be dug by the Hants after dark on the 13th about 100 yards east of the village and facing the objective. In the foreground, in a trench called by us " Shrapnel " trench, were the nearest German garrison, about 300 yards away.

When the first troops of the 29th entered Monchy, it had been knocked about and burnt here and there, but was practically undamaged. It had something of the character of a residential suburb, and the well-built brick houses contrasted favourably with the mud hovels of Picardy. Unfortunately, dead horses of the cavalry blocked the streets, and these, with the bodies of dead men, combined to send out the most appalling stench conceivable. When the Germans began to shell in earnest the place fell down like a pack of cards. It was unrecognizable after the intense bombardment of the 14th April. In ten days it had ceased to exist. The last thing to fall was an enormous crucifix which stood near a pretty little villa known as " The Red House." Those who cowered in cellars and dug-outs beneath the muck and rubbish found Monchy for two months a hell on earth. The wounded suffered indescribably, and the courage and devotion of the Rev. J. W. Hunkin, M.C. (and bar), chaplain to the divisional artillery, in carrying water and the little treats soldiers love, and his words of cheer and consolation, will never be forgotten by the survivors of those to whom he ministered, or those who knew of it. One wonders how many of those, who flocked in hundreds to hear him preach in Arras, are still above ground.

No account of the 29th's doings in and around Monchy can dispense with the setting of frightfulness and filth. But before proceeding to the events of the 14th April it is worth pointing out that the British quality of being able to take punishment and make fun of dangers and discomforts was strongly in evidence. One short anecdote will suffice as an illustration. The Rev. Kenelm Swallow, M.C., chaplain to the S.W.B., was stationed in a disused gun-pit covered with a sheet of corrugated iron in among a battery of artillery. There were piles of ammunition on one side, and numbers of wounded and dying on stretchers. The battery was spotted, and everybody felt apprehensive that their end might come any moment, as the German shells began to fall near. " In the middle of all this a man with a cinema camera arrived and calmly started to photograph the bombardment of Monchy village, whereat a weary and witty Cockney, standing by, remarked, ' I suppose the British public 'll soon be paying a bob to have a look at this. Well, we're better off. We get *paid* a bob a day for looking at it ! ' "

The sporting proclivities of the race are exemplified in the following tale. During an otherwise quiet night on the Arras front in 1917, heavy fire was opened by a Lewis gun in the front line. The company commander went to find out the cause. The Lewis gunner said he had been firing on a German patrol which he thought was in a shell hole close in front. While he was talking to the Lewis gunner, a few pithy and unmistakably English remarks were heard in front, and on being told to come in, a man of the company appeared, much shaken, and carrying a partridge. During the day he had sniped two over the parapet and had crept out after dark to get them. He was duly told off by the company commander, who had an excellent partridge for dinner the next night.

Punctually at zero the barrage dropped and crept forward by lifts of 100 yards every four minutes. The guns were firing at extreme range, and there was plenty support for the Essex on the left, though hardly a full ration for the N.F.L.D. on the right, who suffered casualties from machine-gun fire. However, the attack appeared to be proceeding satisfactorily, and the garrison of " Shrapnel " at once beat a hasty retreat. Reports sent in showed that the objectives had been reached and the work of consolidation in full swing. Very soon afterwards a change came over the scene. A terrific bombardment fell on Monchy and on the batteries behind Orange Hill, where the Hampshires were, and masses of the enemy were seen emerging through the mist from the direction of the Bois du Sart, north-east of Infantry Hill. A strange thing had happened : attacks had been planned by both sides for the same morning, and we had only forestalled the Germans by an hour. It was a terrible situation for the two battalions in the air, 1,000 yards from any support, outnumbered and attacked on three sides by the 3rd Bavarians. Nothing is known of the fight on Infantry Hill, but one thing is certain, that a stiff and gallant fight was put up. Most of the Essex (and presumably the N.F.L.D.) prisoners were taken wounded. Otherwise in the absence of resistance the enemy would have swarmed into Monchy instead of dribbling up, as they did, in parties. Their attack formations must have been broken up by the resistance of the N.F.L.D. and the Essex, very few of whom ever came back.

The situation was serious in the extreme. The Headquarters personnel and battalion reserves of the Essex manned street barricades and kept small parties of Germans, advancing from the north-east, from gaining any foothold in the village. To the south-east, 2,000 Germans were developing, with the support of a barrage, a strong attack on the line, none too strongly held by the Worcesters. But what was worse, the enemy had swarmed over " Shrapnel " trench, and was already in some strength in our original trench of assembly. The slightest indecision, and Monchy was lost. It would be two hours before the reserves could come up, if they could get through the barrage.

Lieutenant-Colonel Forbes-Robertson, then officer commanding N.F.L.D., at once summoned the entire Headquarters personnel of the N.F.L.D. and some stragglers of the Essex. The whole party were some 20 strong. The little party, with a machine-gun, made a dash across the open of 100 yards to a hedge on a bank between the south-east outskirts of Monchy, where Headquarters were, and the trench of assembly. Vigorous fire was immediately opened on the Germans. Forty were shot dead at short range.

The colonel was a marksman, and with the rifle he alone accounted for over 30. By good luck one of the German machine-guns was knocked out from the north by a good shot from one of the brigade machine-gun company, and the gallant little party were able to hang on in spite of losing two killed almost at once and others, that finally reduced the number to 7. By their vigilance and coolness under the leadership of their commanding officer the N.F.L.D. remnant smothered every effort made by the enemy to leave the cover of either the assembly or " Shrapnel " trenches. They held their ground till relieved in the afternoon by the 2nd Hants, who had come through the barrage unscathed. Lieutenant-Colonel A. T. Beckwith, D.S.O., officer commanding Hants, had noticed that the heavy German barrage between his men and Monchy was, fortunately, not in a continuous line, the southern half being 100 yards behind that to the north. Taking advantage of this, he passed his companies through, adopting a course like the letter S, and reached Monchy with but few casualties. Colonel Beckwith then re-established the defences of Monchy, and reorganized all the troops in the village.

Meanwhile the Worcesters had shown their usual steadiness and intrepidity. It was essentially their deadly rifle fire that broke up the German attack. All seemed to be well, until in the afternoon hostile shelling broke out again, and a fresh attack was launched from the Bois du Sart. This time it was dispersed by artillery, and for the rest of the day the 29th were not called upon to meet infantry attacks.

Colonel Forbes-Robertson won the D.S.O. for his action in saving Monchy. Lieutenant Keegan, signalling officer, N.F.L.D., won the M.C. Where all have done well it is superfluous to pick out names, but the names of Captain Tocher, the medical officer, Sergeant Gobby, and Corporal Parsons call for record.

The division suffered casualties amounting to 45 officers and 1,227 other ranks. As can readily be imagined, the losses fell heaviest on the Essex and the N.F.L.D. The former had 17 officers casualties (1 killed, 9 missing), and 585 other ranks, 475 of whom were missing. The latter lost 17 officers (10 missing) and 469 other ranks, of whom 318 were missing. In reflecting somewhat sadly on the chances of life, which again so cruelly went against these two battalions, there is the consolation that, unlike those who fell on the 1st July, they were not the mere recipients of wounds and death. They gave as good as they got. The attack on Monchy was a much bigger affair than the local thrust of the 29th eastward. Monchy was not in a state of defence. It had been so constantly shelled that it was a shambles of animals and combatants. Nothing could have been more opportune than the upset to a set plan of the enemy by the two battalions. Much sympathy was felt for them, and appreciation of the results of their self-sacrifice was voiced by the corps commander and by Sir Edmund Allenby himself, who called in person to tell General de Lisle how pleased he was with the result of the day.

That evening the 86th relieved the 88th in and around Monchy, and that intimacy grew up between the Lancashire Fusiliers and the battered village which earned for their energetic and able commander, Lieutenant-Colonel M. Magniac, D.S.O., the affectionate soubriquet of the " Mayor of Monchy." Meanwhile the 87th stayed in the line, but Headquarters were moved on the 16th from the cross-roads at Feuchy Chapel three miles east of the railway on the Arras–Cambrai road to a point three-quarters of a mile south, called Airy Corner. Lieutenant-Colonel J. Sherwood-Kelly, officer commanding R.I.F., was gassed by a shell on the day before, when in the very act of descending the steps of Brigade Headquarters dug-out. *Mirabile dictu*, he was back from hospital on the 18th recovered. Truly a man of iron! As the Germans proceeded to pour 8-inch shells into the cross-roads, the change was a wise one, and yielded an excellent view of the stiff fighting in which the 50th Division was engaged, and by which Wancourt was captured on the 18th. On the 19th–20th April the 87th were relieved by the 15th Division, and retired to Arras, where, for once, the sun shone. After two days there the brigade returned to the line, this time to the trenches east of Monchy, the K.O.S.B. on the right facing Infantry Hill, and the S.W.B. on the left facing the Bois du Sart, with the R.I.F. in support behind the K.O.S.B., and the Borders behind the S.W.B. An attack was impending.

The 23rd and 24th April 1917

The French attack of 16th April in the Aisne had failed in its main object, which was strategic. To the most optimistic eye the end of the war was as far off as ever. This is no place for discussion of the difficulties in which the British Higher Command were placed. Suffice it to say that the decision come to was that the First and Third Armies should attack on both sides of the Scarpe on a front about nine miles wide. The objectives were limited and not unduly remote, the first objective of the 87th at the nose of the Monchy

salient being less than half a mile off.   In the sector of the 88th
between Monchy and La Bergère on the Arras–Cambrai road, the
distance would be about twice as great.   If things had gone well,
Infantry Hill and the Bois du Sart and Bois du Vert were to have
been attacked in the afternoon.   These two natural forts would
have to be captured, if the position of the VI. Corps was materially
to be improved.   They dominated the hillsides north and south
of the spurs of Infantry Hill.   For example, on the south divisional
front, including a little copse about to be mentioned, the ground
sloped eastwards like a glacis, destitute of cover and in full view
of the Bois du Vert.   Similarly, the northern flanks suffered from
the Bois du Sart and from Pelves and the banks of the river Scarpe,
both of which gave excellent positions for machine-guns, which our
aeroplanes could not locate.   The enemy could therefore afford
to be a little less sensitive about being pushed back on the top of
the ridge.   It was the flanks of the 29th which suffered worse than
the centre, and the flanking divisions fared worse still.   The fact
that they could not keep pace with the 29th in the attack on the
23rd is evidence not so much of superhuman merit on the part of
the 29th as of the stubborn resistance met with by its neighbours.
As is well known, the Second Battle of the Scarpe was fought with
varied success.   It was preceded by a terrific bombardment and
counter-bombardment.   Monchy was plastered with high-explosive
shells.   It required alertness and foresight to get the attacking
troops to the assembly trench, giving Monchy a clear berth.
There was much desperate fighting on all parts of the battlefield, and heavy slaughter of the Germans as they advanced
to counter-attacks over ground swept by our guns.   Over 3,400
prisoners were taken by the 25th April, when the battle began to
die down and Guémappe was at last taken by VI. Corps troops.
But our own losses were heavy, as will be seen when the doings of
the 29th are recounted.

As already stated, the 87th were to advance east along the
plateau from Monchy itself.   The Worcesters (under Lieutenant-
Colonel E. T. J. Kerans), supported by the 2nd Hants (under
Lieutenant-Colonel T. V. P. McCammon, who was wounded in
the course of the fighting), the two comparatively untouched
battalions of the 88th, were to march straight for the Bois
du Vert and form a line with the K.O.S.B. on their left, the
divisional objective being roughly a north and south line through
a point 200 yards west of Infantry Hill.   As the right flank was
refused at the start of the day, it is evident the battalions of the

88th had farther to go than those of the 87th. In reserve, under command of Brigadier-General Williams, who was fighting his last engagement in the 29th before being promoted on 30th April to command the 30th Division, was the 86th Brigade, beside which lay the remnant of the N.F.L.D. Along with the 1st Lancashire Fusiliers and the 16th Middlesex, they occupied the reserve trenches north of the Arras–Cambrai road, while the Royal Fusiliers and Dublins were in Arras. At 4.45 a.m. on Monday 23rd April the barrage dropped. Cheered by a tot of rum—taken during that most cruel period for the best of nerves—the last five minutes before zero (the 29th believed in moderation, not in pussy-foot), the troops once more went over the top. The barrage was on the lines of that employed on the 14th, and so effective was it that the K.O.S.B. reached their objective with few casualties, some of which were due to impetuosity, and proceeded to dig in. The enemy guns fired over their heads and over those of the R.I.F., who moved steadily forward in support and dug in behind the K.O.S.B. in readiness for a further advance. Farther to the north the S.W.B. captured two copses and extended the line of the first objective northwards until it was found that a further extension would leave their flank in the air. A defensive flank had to be formed. The Borders dug in close behind the S.W.B. as soon as they found contact with the enemy.

Meanwhile the 88th, commanded, in the regrettable absence of General Cayley, who had been badly gassed on the 22nd, by Lieutenant-Colonel A. T. Beckwith, D.S.O., were progressing steadily. The Worcesters, under Lieutenant-Colonel E. T. J. Kerans, reached their objective and began to dig in, but not without heavy casualties. For instance, in X Company only one officer, Captain H. Croome-Johnson, was not hit. There was in consequence a good deal of chaos, and it is to be regretted that the name of a bold and capable lance-corporal, who did much to extricate that company from confusion, has been lost. Their supporting battalion, the Hants, were unfortunately caught by the German barrage which started four minutes after zero, and had many casualties. Once through the barrage they did excellent work mopping up parties of Germans on their right flank to the number of 52 in prisoners alone. On this flank also there was difficulty, possibly owing to the uncomfortable angle at which the great road slanted, which made it draw troops like a magnet. The division on the right diverged to the right, and in order to fill the gap thus formed the N.F.L.D. were sent forward to occupy the original

jumping-off trench of that division immediately south of La Bergère. The result of the thrust forward of the 29th and the difficulties of the units on either side was that the 29th held a salient
of freshly dug trenches 1,200 yards (at the end of the day) in front
of the formations on either side. At 11 a.m. orders came to consolidate and to abandon the idea of further advance. The situation was precarious and called for moral and physical strength
in the forward troops. Counter-attacks were directed as early as
10 a.m. from Pelves on the Scarpe against the S.W.B., which were
beaten off by machine-gun and infantry fire. Another menacing
attack recovered Guémappe for the enemy and came within 20
yards of the 88th. Fortunately the Middlesex had been sent forward as a support and the right flank held. The infantry attacks
now ceased, and from noon till 4 p.m. an intense barrage of 5.9
shells rained in and around Monchy. Very heavy casualties
were inflicted on the Worcesters and Hants on the right, and a
fierce hand-to-hand fight raged at the small copse mentioned on
p. 115, near the divisional boundary, which terminated in a local
withdrawal of our troops to the trench already described, called
"Shrapnel." The rest of the line to the north held, and machine-
gun fire made it very difficult for the Germans to advance beyond
the bit of shallow trench gained. At night the 88th were withdrawn to Arras, and the remainder of the division worked hard to
consolidate the gains of the day and protect the flanks.

It had been intended that the attack should be resumed on
the following day at 4 p.m., but the attack was cancelled when
it was represented that the 29th were far ahead of the divisions
on either side. The only operation was the recovery of the bit of
trench lost by the 88th, by the 2nd Royal Fusiliers in co-operation
with the division on their right. The advance from " Shrapnel "
was carried out with steadiness and few casualties. The position
proved, however, to be untenable. It was ranged to a nicety, and
such a hail of shrapnel and machine-gun bullets poured into it
that, after reinforcements had been thinned out by casualties, an
experience like that suffered by the original garrison, it was seen
that the situation was never likely to improve, and a return was
made to " Shrapnel." The cancellation of the general attack, in
spite of anxious precaution, never reached the Dublins, and they
incurred regrettable, because avoidable, losses in consequence.
That night the division was relieved by the 3rd Division, save a
company of the 1st Lancashire Fusiliers, which joined the remainder
the following night.

The casualties were heavy and fell with disproportionate severity on the 88th and brought their losses for the 14th and 23rd and 24th up to 2,000, and particularly on the Worcesters, who lost 14 officers and 414 other ranks, or about 88 per cent. of their battle strength. The Hampshires had 16 officers and 275 other ranks casualties. The little remnant of N.F.L.D. lost 2 officers and 60 other ranks. The brigade had more actual casualties than either of the much stronger brigades. The total casualties for the two days were 91 officers and 1,905 other ranks.

The effort was by no means fruitless. Quite apart from the capture of some 50 prisoners, the advance had enabled the divisional artillery to advance by a superbly executed manœuvre at full gallop to the valley immediately west of Monchy, and from their new position to inflict heavy losses on the enemy as he massed for counter-attacks or was caught on the move. Eye-witnesses have testified to the splendour of the spectacle, and the incredible speed with which the guns were once more in action.

Great care had been taken to make the fullest use of machine-guns. Long range barrages to protect the flanks and harass the enemy in such places as the Bois du Vert and Bois du Sart were laid down, the range amounting to 2,500 yards. Two sections, eight guns in all, fired about 10,000 rounds from a point south of Monchy. The gallantry and ingenuity of the teams were beyond praise. Guns would be buried, barrels would be perforated, men would be stunned, yet in a little while the men would shake themselves and carry on, the gun barrels would be plugged somehow, and the tap-tap-tap would resume. Only five machine-guns were damaged beyond repair. Undoubtedly they killed and wounded many Germans. The casualties of all three companies were very high. Second Lieutenant R. Street was a serious loss to the 86th Brigade Machine-Gun Company, for he had had much experience of the Western Front and was a first-class officer.

On the 25th April Lieutenant-Colonel M. Magniac, D.S.O., was killed, a very serious loss to the Lancashire Fusiliers and the division. He had deserved well for the improvement effected in the defences of Monchy, and during his period of command that fine fighting battalion was most efficiently organized and led. Major Ellis, acting O.C. Borders, was paralysed by a direct hit upon his headquarters, but made a wonderful recovery, and was able to participate in the May fighting. A promising young officer fell in the person of Second Lieutenant G. D. L. Nicholson of the Worcesters, son of Major-General Sir Lothian Nicholson, under whom the 88th Brigade subsequently fought in 1918. Every one in the 29th had done his duty, and done it well. It would have been more than human nature can compass, if the 88th had left the line elated. They had suffered too heavily for that. The 87th, on the other hand, who were less severely tried, came out with their ardour stimulated and in capital spirits. On all sides could be heard rumours of satisfaction in high places with the performance of the division. And indeed of that there was no doubt. On the 26th the corps commander, General Sir Aylmer Haldane, wrote a personal letter to General de Lisle in which the following passage occurs :—

" I shall be glad if you will convey to the famous 29th Division my high appreciation of their gallantry and valuable work in and around Monchy during the past fortnight. The position there is the key to the front of the corps, and to a considerable extent that of the corps on our flank. Thanks to the bravery and staunchness of your officers, non-commissioned officers and men, that position has been maintained and consolidated, and important ground to the east secured. I am very sorry indeed to lose so splendid a body of troops, whose deeds while with my corps show that the great reputation they gained a year ago and since is safe in the keeping of those who now form its battalions, batteries, field companies, and administrative services. I am afraid your losses have been heavy, but I cannot feel they have done other than contribute materially to the complete success which is daily proving nearer for the British army. Many thanks to you personally for your assistance and loyal co-operation."

A fortnight was spent in the Couin area west of Arras resting and training. Reinforcements arrived, but not in time to absorb much instruction while in reserve. The division was able to return to the line up to strength, but it was *minus* Brigadier W. de L. Williams, who had never ceased to live up to the reputation he won on April 26, 1915. His place was taken by Brigadier-General Jelf.

The 29th were to have taken part in the Third Battle of the Scarpe, fought indecisively on 3rd and 4th May. On the 2nd the 87th were actually as far east as Observation Hill, two miles from Arras. The main road towards Cambrai was being shelled by a long-range gun, and the troops moved along a rough track 300 yards north of and parallel to the big road. If the supremacy of German aeroplanes had been a feature of the battle of the 23rd April and a matter of comment by the G.O.C. 29th, it was certainly not a feature of the 3rd May. Ours were omnipresent and those of the enemy absent. The brigade was withdrawn on the 4th, when the attack did not succeed, and the whole division returned to billets until the 14th, when it paid its last visit to the Monchy sector. The story of the 19th May admits of very brief treatment.

On the night of the 18th a man was missing from the front line. It was considered probable that he was a deserter. The incident was reported, but cancellation is a big business to undertake on mere suspicion, and the attack went forward as planned. The bulk of the attackers were met by an almost instantaneous burst of shrapnel and machine-gun fire as they went over the top. A company of R.I.F., which reached its objective, was cut off, and only a few survivors returned to tell the tale. The German S.O.S. signals went up within five seconds of zero, and the barrage fell in forty more seconds. Nobody in the 29th, who was there, attributes the bulk of the 75 per cent. of rapidly inflicted casualties to anything else than the murderous treachery of the deserter. There is also little doubt that the enemy had by now stabilized his defences and did not intend to let us get any farther.

The attack was a local affair, to be carried out by the R.I.F. and Borders and a company of S.W.B., the objectives being a line on Infantry Hill some few yards in advance of that held, and was intended to include a copse at the north end called Bois des Aubepines. It is doubtful if it ever would have been made, had it not been necessary, by hook or by crook, to aid the French and keep the enemy from recovering the offensive. The hour selected was 9 p.m. and the supporting barrage consisted of five groups of artillery, advancing at twice the speed of previous engagements in this area. The work of consolidation would have the advantage of the cloak of darkness.

It was a well-planned enterprise. It was attempted with gallantry and determination, but it was inevitably a complete failure. Machine-gun fire was most destructive, and the wind was wrong for sending a whiff of gas into the Bois du Vert—a regular nest of machine guns. Many individual acts of bravery were performed. Sergeant Albert White of the S.W.B. gained the fourteenth V.C. for heroically charging a German machine gun and losing his life while thus trying to help his comrades. On 20th May the battered brigade was relieved by the 86th and returned to Arras.

On the 23rd May the 29th sustained a serious loss by the death of the brigade-major of the 86th Brigade, Captain " Pat " (i.e.,

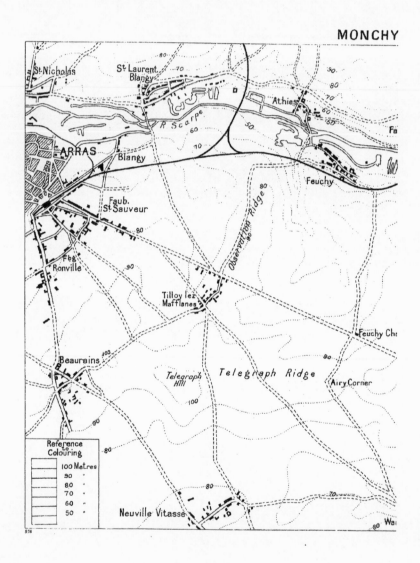

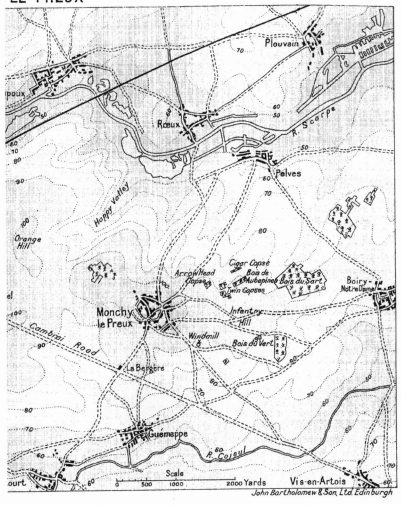

Plouvain

70

60
50

poux

50

Rœux

50

R. Scarpe

50

Pelves

60

Happy Valley

70

90

80

Orange
Hill

100

Cigar Copse
Bois de
Aubepines   Bois du Sart

Arrow Head
Copse

Twin Copses

Boiry-
Notre Dame

el

Infantry
Hill

Monchy
le Preux

100

Windmill
Bois du Vert

80

Cambrai   Road

90

80

La Bergère

80

80

70

70

60

80

Guémappe

70

R. Coisul

60

ourt

60

60

70

70
60

Scale

Vis-en-Artois

0   500   1000   2000 Yards

John Bartholomew & Son, Ltd. Edinburgh

W. M.) Armstrong of the 10th Hussars. He had been on the divisional staff since the early days of the Gallipoli campaign, and had
made his mark on many occasions. His friend Lieutenant Layard
of the Borders was missing as the result of the abortive attack,
and Pat had been searching No Man's Land for several nights
and taking grave risks, until a sniper laid him low. He was uni-
versally mourned by every one who knew him, from the general
commanding downwards. He had an attractive appearance, was
handsome and well-built, and had a breezy way with him. A
corporal hit off one secret of the hold he had over others by the
remark : " Pat was the bonniest officer of them all."

Strange to relate, when the 29th were dedicated to another
attack on the 29th May, again a man was missing. Again the
German barrage fell at zero, but this time on empty trenches. The
coveted trenches were reached on the 30th, but they were found to
hold water. Indeed, the brigade sector east of Monchy was cut in
two by water in our own front line. Moreover, they were found
to be exposed to enfilade fire from a machine-gun concealed in a
wooded knoll 500 yards to the south-east. It was therefore *re
infecta* in a sense that the division after relief by the 3rd Division
said farewell to the Monchy battle-ground and proceeded to the
Bernaville area for training. There was a shade of disappointment
at the meagre results which they had to show for the terrific casualties
mentioned at the outset. The meagreness was more apparent than
real. The class of fighting necessary to settle up accounts and
liquidate a battle by stabilising a new line is always costly. But
there were to be no more hurried improvisations in the 29th's
career. To the unusual richness of its military experience were to
be added the elaborate attacks of the autumn, the co-operation
with tanks in the miracle of the advance on 20th November over
the Hindenburg Line, the defensive tactics of the battles of Cambrai
and Lys, and the offensive which finally proved that the long lane
of the war had a turning.

CHAPTER III

THE BATTLE OF YPRES, 1917

" The abomination of desolation."

By universal consent the Third Battle of Ypres represents the utmost
that war has so far achieved in the way of horrors.   What the future
holds it is idle to imagine.   But the cramped theatre with its slimy
canals, beeks, sloughs, bogs, and inundations ; its shelled duck-board
tracks, its isolated outposts, its incessant shelling and incessant rain,
its mists and fogs, its corpses and its pestilential, miasmic odours,
outdid anything that even the Somme or Arras could boast, and it
dragged on from the 31st July till the 10th November, 1917.   The
craters were more numerous and the mud was deeper.   There was
also the added horror of mustard gas, which could cling about a dug-
out for days in spite of fires.   It was lethal, but was still more
effective as an incapacitator.   It was first felt on July 12, 1917,
and in ten days had inflicted 3,500 casualties.   Among the early
victims were 40 men of the divisional artillery.   The Divisional
Artillery History mentions that on the night of 23rd-24th, in consequence of a steady rain of gas shells, gas masks had to be worn
at the batteries for six hours.   The back areas were regularly
bombed from the air.   In short, to be in the line was the severest
possible test of the manhood and discipline of officers and men, and
to be in reserve meant little tonic for the nerves, apart from ceremonial parades, band competitions and the priceless diversion of
the " shows " put up by the various divisional troupes, which by this
time had become indispensable to the British army on the Western
Front.

The reasons for the Flanders campaign, its objectives and execution are outside the scope of this narrative.   They will be found in
the official dispatches and general histories of the war.   As General
de Lisle has remarked, every one hoped that the great battle would
end the war.

If the mighty effort, by which between the end of July and the middle of November the Ypres Salient was flattened out by advances on the north and south flanks, and the enemy was slowly pushed back, until all but a minute portion of the Passchendaele Ridge had been won from him, produced results disappointing alike to soldier and civilian on our side, we learn that it was a source of anxiety to Ludendorff and his subordinate commanders on the Western Front. To the Germans as well as to the British the whole area was an inferno, and in many units a weakening of the *moral* set in. As the authoritative dispatches and text-books show, the plan of attack was a series of methodically planned, limited advances under cover of heavy artillery fire. There was even, to take an instance, at the divisional headquarters of the Guards Division a model of the German trenches opposite their sector. It was a class of warfare which demanded precision in minor tactics and an eye for a fight. The 29th Division, given time to absorb its 8,000 reinforcements, to replace the havoc wrought by the combats at Monchy, gave fair promise of utility. It was welcomed back into the XIV. Corps, still commanded by Lord Cavan, and for the first time into the Fifth Army, commanded by General Sir Hubert Gough, as a unit likely to give a good account of itself. It was known to be commanded by a general who was a tactician from his youth upwards, had the uncanny gift of noticing, known as the " Adjutant's eye," and a positive genius for making instructions " fool-proof." Unlike Mr. Squeers, who sent out the boys to " clean winders " without accompanying them, the G.O.C. was known to have given a demonstration at Arras of " how to dig." He had not commanded the 29th for two years without influencing his subordinates, and all the commanding officers in the three brigades inculcated the spirit of hard work in training into their commands. The 29th were also fortunate in possessing N.C.O.s who not only led those under them, but helped the young officers over them to learn their part. The sequel will show several typical acts of valour and enterprise performed by N.C.O.s that are a tribute to the fighting spirit become second nature through years of service in crack regular battalions. The fights, in which the 29th took part in Flanders in 1917, are (1) the Battle of Langemarck, which involved the crossing of the Steenbeek on 16th August by all except a few posts already on the east of that rain-swollen Styx ; (2) the Battle of Broodseinde on 4th October in its most northerly sector ; and (3) the thrust from Langemarck over the Broembeck to the edge of Houthulst Forest on the 9th October, known as the Battle of Poelcapelle. The objectives were invariably reached and tenaciously held. No calamities occurred such as that of 14th April. The casualties were the result of the steady drain upon the strength of all units through shells, machine-gun bullets, gas, and sickness, due to the terrific physical strain imposed on the troops, who had to toil through liquid mud to fight and then consolidate, as well as possible, in the dripping rain. Compared with Flanders, the Monchy plateau was dryness itself, and the wintry gloom of the Somme was forgotten.

We left the division making for the Bernaville area not so very far from the scene of its original invasion of France. It was a nicely wooded countryside, attractively " accidenté," with good billets, training ground, and not too remote from the amenities of Doullens and Abbeville. What officers and men required was rest and a little mild diversion, exercise, sport, and a moderate amount of training. Those who were not on leave drank in in good weather the pleasant air of a Picardy summer, and went fresh to the combat in the north. The principal event was the Divisional Horse Show organized by General Lucas, and held in a sequestered little valley near Gorges on the 16th. The weather was splendid, the show a success, and the local population delighted. The school children were given a good " blow out." The 29th had the place to themselves, the only other troops being some units of the R.A.F. Other items of entertainment were the combined sports of the Monmouths and the Field Ambulance on the 14th, and the sports of the K.O.S.B. held on the 23rd in the presence of and after inspection by Lieutenant-General Sir Charles L. Woolcombe, their Colonel-in-Chief. Those harbingers of troops about to move, the advance parties, had already vanished north in motors, and soon the impending move made itself felt. On the 26th it actually began. The troops entrained at Doullens and detrained at "Hopoutie."* They marched to the Proven area to various camps. The first to take over the line were the 87th Brigade, who on the 28th in torrents of rain relieved a brigade of the 38th Division, who were to rest and train for the fresh attack just on the right of the Guards. The point of junction was the Ypres Canal, where the allied front shifted from the west to the east bank about three miles north of Ypres. The Guards held the Boesinghe sector—*i.e.*, those trenches which lay immediately west of the canal. The left extremity of those taken over by the 87th rested on the east bank, but slanted almost immediately away from the canal towards the extremity of the

* This railhead was close to Proven. At first sight the name seems to be good Vlaamsch, but on closer scrutiny turns out to be still better English.

salient at Wieltje.   Once arrived in the line the troops of the 29th found that they were responsible for the work of maintaining the trenches hitherto performed by two companies of Royal Engineers and a pioneer battalion.   The existing trenches were wet and had to be repaired.   Two miles of new trenches had to be dug.   All kinds of stores had to be carried into position in vast quantities. Every night of the three weeks' tour of the front saw a carrying party, 600 strong, toiling under heavy burdens.   It has been calculated that during this tour the 29th carried something like 3,040 tons of stores.   It was a severe strain on the endurance of the troops, who, be it kept in view, were constantly shelled.   The Germans appear to have enjoyed a complete ascendency in the air at this period.   On the 28th June an observation balloon was brought down, the occupants escaping in parachutes.   On the 29th June at one time twenty-one hostile planes were over our lines and not a British plane in sight.   No doubt the reports of the airmen caused the unpleasantly good shooting with armour-piercing 11-inch shells on the 3rd July and conveyed details regarding the expected attack.   The K.O.S.B. found the enemy on the alert, when they visited the opposing trenches on the night of the 6th-7th, and contented themselves with throwing bombs and retiring.   The 88th relieved the 87th, and on the 11th the Germans attempted a raid on the Worcesters, who repelled the attack in hand-to-hand combat. Several dead were left on the parapet, and one wounded prisoner was taken.   The same brigade carried out two successful raids on the 18th, but captured only one prisoner.   The following night, just before handing over, three simultaneous and successful raids were made.   Thus the troops had other things to do besides mere labour, and as the result of the heavy shelling the division suffered over 900 casualties.

The three weeks in reserve, which followed, were welcomed by the troops, and indeed were essential for the units if they were to achieve any results in the coming battle.   Several new unit commanders had arrived, and no less than 8,000 fresh troops, to replace the losses at Monchy, had to be instructed in the best methods for attack.   In addition to practice manœuvres, lectures were addressed by the G.O.C. to the company officers and platoon sergeants of each brigade.   There were also brigade exercises without troops for senior officers.   As to the company commanders, they were interviewed by the G.O.C. himself, and catechised as to what action they would take in all sorts of hypothetical situations capable of arising in the course of the battle.

At 3.50 a.m. on July 31, 1917, the Second and Fifth Armies attacked, with results that fell far short of what had been hoped. No doubt the heavy rain was partly responsible for the comparatively small haul of 6,000 prisoners, of which about 3,400 were taken by the XIV. Corps, and the shallowness of the breach in the hostile defences. But rumour added that want of training was the cause. As a result the 29th worked harder than ever at the training ground at Herzeele, west of Poperinghe.

The first troops of the 29th to engage in the vast battle were the artillery. They left the Arras battlefield on the 21st and 22nd June, and after a short rest at Montenescourt and Gouves, two villages between Arras and St. Pol, proceeded northwards on the 1st July by road. It took them eight days to reach Houtkerque in Flanders. Nine days later both brigades were in position, and in action by the 17th July, forming part of the right group of the left artillery of the XIV. Corps, and under the immediate orders of the C.R.A. Guards Division. The trench mortars had covered the distance from Artois to Flanders in one day by motor lorries, and were already in action by the 12th. From the 15th to the 27th they plastered the enemy wire and strong places with over 2,000 rounds, while the guns co-operated in that colossal bombardment which proclaimed in no uncertain tones the approach of a battle. Brigadier-General Ashmore left on the 28th for London to take charge of the anti-aircraft defences there, and Brigadier-General G. H. A. White succeeded him as C.R.A. It was a wonderful sight to see the tanks under General Hugh Elles on the nights of the 28th-29th and 29th-30th cross the canal. The barrage put down on the 31st by the two brigades gave complete satisfaction to the Guards.

The Guards were the most successful of any British troops engaged that day. They and the French on the extreme left between the Guards and the inundations made considerable progress north-east towards Wijdendrift. This occasioned an attempt on the part of the 15th R.H.A. to advance on the 1st August across the canal to new forward positions. The mud, the congestion of traffic, and the shelling made this impossible for all but four guns of L Battery under Second Lieutenant (temporary Captain) A. E. G. Leadbetter. But this battery found the mud on the other side impassable, and it was not till the 4th that they were able to go into action. Their leader—one of the bright and ardent spirits, who were characteristic of the 29th—fell, to every one's deep regret, on the same day. He was quite young; indeed, he was killed within a few days of his twenty-first birthday, and was not even of age, but had an old head on his young shoulders, and he had discharged responsibilities as adjutant of the 17th Brigade R.F.A. and as staff officer to a large group of nine to ten batteries in a manner entirely satisfactory to his superiors. He had only been recently promoted to command L Battery, a remarkable distinction for a mere boy. By the 6th all the divisional artillery were over the canal and settled down to the work of preparing for the advance of their own comrades of the 29th, who relieved the Guards on the 8th. It may be mentioned here that the system upon which heavy artillery was employed in the XIV. Corps was very satisfactory from a divisional point of view. A general scheme was prepared by the general and artillery staffs in conference, and sent to divisions for remarks and suggestions, which were sympathetically received. The G.O.C. suggested attention to a group of block-houses, which he knew to be a source of anxiety to the men in the line. On the morning of the 15th the howitzers, with less than half a dozen rounds, silenced the garrisons for ever, to the delight of the infantry, whose confidence was greatly strengthened.

In the Wijdendrift-Langemarck sector the battle was over on the day it opened, and the 29th started very much from the line won by the Guards on the 31st July. The 38th Division, under Major-General C. G. Blackader, had been almost equally successful and had taken the important point of Pilckem, and the XIV. Corps front was pressed close up to the Steenbeek. The sector taken over was known as the Boesinghe sector from the village just west of the Ypres Canal. Divisional Headquarters was at St. Sixte Camp. The front line, if line it could be called, consisting of isolated trench lengths full of water and shell craters in the same state, ran along the top of the Pilckem ridge from the ruined hamlet of that name north-westwards to the junction with the French. Even on the top of the ridge the clay soil held the heavy rainfall, and the ground was a marsh. In the lower stretches it was more like a lake. The Steenbeek itself with its overflow was a serious military obstacle. Life in its immediate neighbourhood must be made intolerable for the enemy, so that posts could be made on the right bank as bridge-heads to cover the crossings. Time would show whether the successful crossing of the Ypres Canal by the Guards could be paralleled by an equally successful crossing of the Steenbeek. It came true. Troops of the 86th, which was the reserve brigade in the operations, successfully carried out this minor operation on the 10th-11th August. With the exception of a group of ruined buildings known as Passerelle Farm, all objectives were occupied with insignificant losses and 20 prisoners were captured. The following night the important strong point of Passerelle Farm fell to the 16th Middlesex. Thanks to this operation a line of posts was established, and a bridge-head secured on the far side of a swollen stream with few crossings, greatly facilitating the start on the morning of the attack. On the night of the 12th-13th twelve double wooden bridges were carried up by troops of the 87th assisted by Royal Engineers and placed in position over the Steenbeek. During the night the first two waves of the leading battalions crossed the stream and formed up on tapes ready for the fray. All night long on the 15th-16th our heavy artillery poured gas shells on and around the German gun emplacements, a treatment which seemed to have a sedative effect. On the 16th the volume of hostile shelling was at no time excessive, although hostile aeroplanes were active all day.

The 16th August

At 4.35 a.m. the enemy seemed to realize that something was afoot, for he put up a mild firework display that changed into a magnificent spectacle when our barrage crashed down at zero.

At 4.45 a.m., under the protection of a terrific and exact barrage, the remainder of the infantry crossed the Steenbeek and the whole force moved forward over the quaking morass. The divisional front was a little less than a mile wide. The final objective was a little less than a mile off. The 87th and 88th Brigades advanced side by side. On the right were the 88th, next the 20th Division, the Hampshires under Major T. C. Spring being on the right, and the N.F.L.D. under Lieutenant-Colonel A. L. Hadow, C.M.G. (Norfolk Regiment), on the left. Next the N.F.L.D. came the S.W.B. under Major H. G. Garnett, and beyond them, in what may be termed the post of honour—*i.e.*, that next the French—were the K.O.S.B. under Lieutenant-Colonel A. J. Welch and (subsequently) Major C. A. G. O. Murray. Careful preparation for liaison with the French troops on our left had been made by General Lucas and Colonel Welch, and was rewarded with excellent results. The going was deplorable, and perhaps the N.F.L.D. suffered in this respect more than any other unit, noticeably between the first and second objectives. Both of the wing battalions were ahead of the units adjoining them. The Hampshires, who had some of the hardest fighting of the whole day, despite heavy casualties were able by enfilade and reverse fire to help the 61st Brigade of the 20th Division to capture Langemarck. The K.O.S.B. met with stubborn resistance. The French did not start at the appointed time, but when they did, their advance was facilitated by the enfilade fire of our men, and the Franco-Scottish combination reached their second objectives. Perhaps our allies were able to say something, by no means for the first time, about " *les écossais toujours fidèles.*" At any rate the Scotsmen were delighted with their neighbours. Two instances will suffice to show the kind of obstruction and the way it was overcome. Sergeant W. H. Grimbaldeston, K.O.S.B. (of Blackburn, Lancs.), found that his company was being held up by machine-gun fire from a block-house. He made up his mind that that block-house must be turned and silenced. He arranged for covering fire, and under its protection stole round the flank of the building. The back door was the Achilles heel of the pill-box system of defence. A few bombs might kill the whole garrison. The gallant sergeant reached the back, threatened the garrison with grenades, and captured the fort single-handed along with its six machine guns and its entire garrison of 36. For this splendid act of courage and skill the division for the fifteenth time could boast of a V.C. award. One would think it improbable that this daring act could be rivalled on the same day and by a man of the same unit. Yet it happened. Company Sergeant-Major John Skinner of Pollokshields won the sixteenth V.C. for the 29th while assaulting the second objective. His and another company " rested " for twenty minutes behind the shelter of the barrage while the remaining companies consolidated the captured ground. To quote Captain Currie, his company commander, when the second zero arrived and the troops advanced, "We met with strong opposition during our attack, three block-houses especially giving a great deal of trouble, and holding us up on the left flank. The French having failed to move, my company's left flank was ' in the air.' At this time I had only one officer besides myself (one officer, Second Lieutenant Murray, and most of the N.C.O.s having been either killed or wounded). The three blockhouses were spitting out a terrific fire, and we were obliged to take cover and move gradually forward by squads in quick rushes. At this period Company Sergeant-Major Skinner and I crawled as near to the blockhouses as possible, and succeeded in disabling two of their guns by rifle fire. Company Sergeant-Major Skinner, after we had got within about 70 yards of the blockhouses, crawled forward on his own initiative, while I covered his advance with my rifle. After ten minutes he succeeded in reaching that on the extreme left, and going round the back of it bombed the team of gunners with Mills bombs and compelled the garrison to surrender. The second blockhouse he put out of action by inserting bombs in the loopholes where the guns were mounted. By this time I had passed orders for the company to advance, and we succeeded in reaching the third blockhouse, though only after suffering heavy casualties. Company Sergeant-Major Skinner's haul was six machine guns, about 60 prisoners, and a few trench mortars. This feat he performed practically single-handed, and it was at his own special request that I allowed him to attempt what appeared to be a hopeless task." What follows about Skinner is *verbatim* of his admiring and appreciative G.O.C., except the last rites, which is from the pen of the Rev. Kenelm Swallow, chaplain to the S.W.B.

In those days it was the custom for those who had gained the V.C. to be given fourteen days' leave to attend the investiture by His Majesty. On the occasion when Sergeant-Major Skinner received his cross, His Majesty held the investiture in the quadrangle at Buckingham Palace, and Skinner marched up proudly bearing the D.C.M. with a bar and the Military Medal. His left fore-arm was a band of gold, for he wore eight wound stripes.

After the ceremony he made many friends, and at the end of his leave, when he reached Folkestone, he was sent to hospital. We heard in France with regret that this remarkable man was being sent to the Reserve Battalion at Edinburgh, but two days later, when his brigade was carrying out some practice manœuvres, the division commander saw him with his company, and expressed pleasure that the rumour of his going to Edinburgh was unfounded. On asking particulars, Sergeant-Major Skinner looked confused, but finally explained that he was certainly unfit to travel when he reached Folkestone, but was quite himself again after a couple of days. He was then told he would have to go to Edinburgh. " Me for Edinburgh, sir! That was a bit too thick," he added. " They gave me a warrant for Edinburgh, but did not know I had my return leave warrant in my pocket, so I ' chanced my arm,' and here I am, sir. Besides, sir, I have a bit of a bet on with Quartermaster-Sergeant Ross, who has also been wounded eight times, as to who might get the ninth wound." It was just at this time that an agitation was being made that any one more than twice wounded should not return to the front, yet this gallant warrant officer, who had won every possible decoration and had been eight times wounded, preferred to risk a court-martial and rejoin his battalion rather than remain at home. Skinner won the bet. He received the ninth wound straight between the eyes, in the Passchendaele salient, early in 1918. A wounded man missing from patrol the night before was crying out in No Man's Land, and Skinner went over the top to bring him in. Of all the most gallant men in the 29th, Skinner was among the bravest of the brave.

The Rev. Kenelm Swallow writes, " I happened to be up at his company headquarters a few hours before the dawn when he was killed, and subsequently officiated at his most remarkable funeral at Vlamertinghe in the pouring rain, when his body was brought to the grave on a gun carriage drawn by a magnificent team of horses, and thence carried and laid in the grave by six brother V.C.s, all of the 29th Division."

The character of the fighting was the same in other units. Bogs had to be crossed. Pill-boxes had to be surrounded or turned. The barrage had to be watched. The task set the 29th admits of very brief statement. To the four attacking battalions was assigned the capture of the first two objectives, each about 500 yards from the starting-point. Thereafter an advance was to be made from right to left as follows. The Essex, under Lieutenant-Colonel Sir George Stirling, D.S.O., of Glorat, were to pass through the Hampshires and take the main German trenches about 750 yards off. As at the beginning, so at the end, the right of the 88th rested on the almost invisible ruins of the Ypres–Staden railway track, and it was here that the farthest advance had to be made, as the German trenches slanted westwards to a point which, on the left of the divisional boundary, was only a few yards ahead of the second objective. Next to the Essex came the Worcesters, under Lieutenant-Colonel C. S. Linton. They were to pass through the N.F.L.D. and take the third objective after a shorter journey than the Essex. One battalion, the Borders, under Lieutenant-Colonel A. J. Ellis, D.S.O., was enough for the still shorter advance assigned to the 87th.

It only remains to be recorded that a very satisfactory liaison was throughout maintained with the 61st Brigade of the 20th Division. In the recently published history of the Light Division it is stated at page 163 that the co-operation of the 29th Division on the left of the 61st Brigade could not have been better.

The shape of the captured ground was not unlike the profile of the top part of a case for containing an upright piano. The area won was only three-quarters of a square mile of a " desolate shell-ploughed landscape, half liquid in substance, brown as a fresh-turned field, with no movement upon its hideous expanse, although every crevice was swarming with life, and the constant snap of the sniper's bullet told of watchful unseen eyes." It might be asked what this was worth on a day when the 29th, alone of all units engaged, took the full allotted objectives (doing it according to the time-table and at a heavy cost). One shell accounted for Colonel A. J. Welch, the adjutant Captain Lewis, and Regimental Sergeant-Major Douglas—in short, the headquarters personnel of the K.O.S.B. The S.W.B. lost, among others, Captain W. Ross and Captain G. A. T. Robertson. Both were sorely missed, for they were officers of experience and tried ability, and both in command of companies. Lieutenant-Colonel F. G. G. Morris of the Borders, then in command of the 16th Middlesex, a unit not taking part in the battle, was killed in the small hours of the 17th by a shell. His death was a serious loss to the division. It was the same tale elsewhere. From the 15th to the 18th (both inclusive) 88 officers and 2,024 other ranks became casualties. The answer is that it must have been and was worth it. The affair of the 16th August was over by noon. General Lucas and Captain Brodie Mair (whose death since the close of the war has grieved his many friends and closed a military career full of promise), his brigade-major, were able to combine between them a comprehensive visit to the forward troops of the 87th. The men were everywhere proud and elated. It was the biggest and most successful show of the war as far as the 29th was concerned since the prodigy of April 25, 1915. Anxiety was removed by the crowning mercy of an alert artillery, who in the evening scattered a gathering German counter-attack from the direction of Ney Wood to the four winds. Luden-dorff had regarded the 31st July as a serious reverse. The 16th August was another nasty knock (" *ein neuer grosser Schlag* "). The German system of defence was once more in the melting-pot, and the massive Teutonic heads of the directing spirits of the German General Headquarters and the Fourth Army, commanded by von Below, were in close conclave in search of a solution. Alas, that the weather so assisted the efforts of Staff-Colonel von Lossberg, upon whom Ludendorff greatly relied. But this encouraging news had not reached our troops. Their happiness lay in duty done. While the Hampshires smiled over the discovery that the oddments of crumbled bricks really *was* Martin Mill, and recalled the conquest of Langemarck's western outskirt, the N.F.L.D. could think of Denain Farm and of brotherly hands stretched, like those of Help, to extri-

THE BATTLE OF LANGEMARCK 16TH AUGUST 1917

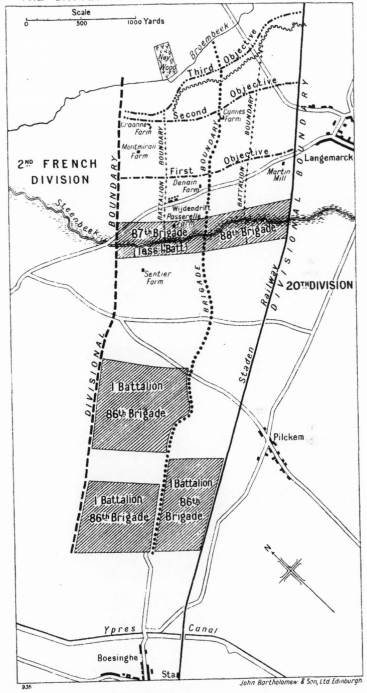

Scale

0   500   1000 Yards

Ney Wood

Broembeek

Third Objective

Second Objective

Craonne Farm

Cannes Farm

Montmirail Farm

First Objective

Denain Farm

Martin Mill

Langemarck

2ND FRENCH DIVISION

Steenbeek

Wijdendrift

Passerelle Farm

87TH Brigade (less 1 Batt.)

88TH Brigade

BOUNDARY

BATTALION BOUNDARY

BOUNDARY

BATTALION BOUNDARY

DIVISIONAL BOUNDARY

Sentier Farm

BRIGADE

20TH DIVISION

Railway

Staden

1 Battalion 86th Brigade

DIVISIONAL BOUNDARY

Pilckem

1 Battalion 86th Brigade

1 Battalion 86th Brigade

Ypres Canal

N

Boesinghe

Sta

936

John Bartholomew & Son, Ltd. Edinburgh.

cate stuck comrades from the slough of despond, that came between
their first and second halt.   They were profoundly conscious that
on that day they were better men than the enemy.   The S.W.B.,
as well as the N.F.L.D., could think of Cannes Farm, and the
K.O.S.B. of Craonne Farm.   The men of the second wave were
conscious that their work earned, as it afterwards obtained, a long
list of awards.   Tired but pleased, the two brigades handed over
the line to the safe keeping of the 86th, now under temporary
command of Brigadier-General H. Nelson, of the Borders, *vice*
Brigadier-General Jelf, evacuated sick, and retired to the reserve
stations near Woesten, west of the canal.   But the battalions of
the last assault had not been content to sit on the final objective.
They had pushed forward down to and across the Broembeek, so
that before the 19th the 86th were able to establish nine posts on
the far side of the stream.   It so happened that Sir Hubert Gough,
the Army Commander, visited Divisional Headquarters in order
to congratulate the division on its success and subsequent exploitation.   On learning the full extent, he issued an Army Order calling
on all divisions to do likewise.

About this period senior American officers came to be attached
to divisions to acquire experience.   The first of these to arrive at
29th Divisional Headquarters was Colonel Drum, a very remarkable man, who impressed every one by his ability and capacity
for work.   Later General O'Ryan, commanding the 27th New
York Division, and Colonel Bandholtz, his chief staff-officer, came
to Divisional Headquarters for a week.   These visits did a lot
of good both to the American officers and also to ourselves.   The
questions were so searching that all felt the necessity of being able
to express clearly the views and ideas, which had not perhaps been
hitherto properly crystallized.

On 28th August the brigadier appointed permanently to succeed
Brigadier-General Jelf arrived to command the 86th, and took over
from Colonel Nelson.   He retained his command till the 29th were
safely ensconced in the bridgehead east of the Rhine.   This was
Brigadier-General G. R. H. (Ronnie) Cheape, M.C., of the 1st Dragoon
Guards, still a young man, a Fife laird, and an adept at the wild
sports of the Highlands.   He was strong and sinewy, clear-eyed and
hawk-nosed, and incapable of fatigue.   Of a famous sporting family,
he had played polo and hunted hard.   Most important of all, he was
a fighting man, and although he was only now introduced into the
29th, he knew that it was a hard-hitting, resolute unit.   If General
Williams' ripe knowledge and skill were lost, the brigade secured

as their commander, whose tenure was almost as long, one of the ablest of the younger school. Cheape could never have been a conventional soldier, and a predominantly English and entirely non-Scottish unit had frequent opportunities of listening to the strains of Duncan Lamont of Mull's bagpipes. The general was a fine judge and performer himself, and that he had an eye for the picturesque use of the pipes will be found by any one with the patience to follow the tale of the 29th. In a word, he was just the man for the 86th, and they were just the men for him.

September was a quiet month for the 29th, after relief by the Guards on 28th August. On the 12th, General Hunter-Weston paid them a visit. Sports were held, and the G.O.C. VIII. Corps gave away the prizes. A Gallipoli race was run, and there were many hearty greetings. There were brigade sports, and covetous eyes involuntarily turned to the elegant cups made by a tinsmith in the 87th Brigade Field Company Royal Engineers out of biscuit-tins. When they were awarded to the athletic prize-winners, unquenchable laughter arose among the warriors around. There was a dog show, and another award that roused even more mirth. The K.O.S.B. had entered a fine pantomime dog composed of two of the lords of creation. This unique animal was given, and we assume made short work of—a bone. There was boxing, and there was a fancy dress mule race. Everything went with a swing. With men like these recuperation is a certainty. If the sound of the drum is a source of martial inspiration, the 29th were well off. On 14th September, after a ceremonial parade, which not only won the most charming compliments from M. le général La Capelle (not to be confounded with the Teutonic von Kapelle, of whom presently) but actually satisfied the G.O.C. 29th, there came the great drum competition open to the whole corps. It was won by the Essex, the R.I.F. being second, the K.O.S.B. third, and the Irish Guards fourth.

On the 29th September a most regrettable blow was sustained by the 88th. The whole of Headquarters (except Captain T. H. Toose, the staff-captain at rear Headquarters), including Brigadier-General Cayley, Captain P. N. Wilson, the brigade-major, and the assistant staff-captain, and the signal officer, were gassed. The same fate befell the Essex. Major F. C. Dinan actually died, and Major Mair had to be sent from 87th Brigade Headquarters to command the battalion pending arrival of a new commanding officer. In the latter case one shell did the mischief by a direct hit on the pill-box occupied as Headquarters.

The 4th October

The battle of 4th October was one of magnitude from the point of view of the British army. Five thousand German prisoners were taken. Many more were slain, and Ludendorff, while claiming successfully to have withstood the weight of an exceptionally heavy bombardment and a heavy infantry attack, admitted the wastage of enormous force as the price he had to pay (" *doch wiederum nur mit Einbusse ungeheurer Kraft* "). From the point of view of the 29th, it was a minor operation. It really belongs to the story of those two fine battalions, the 1st K.O.S.B. in a minor degree, but principally to the " Old Dubs," *alias* the 1st Royal Dublin Fusiliers, who on this occasion, under the command of the gallant Major A. Moore, D.S.O., put up a great fight for the honour of the division. The reason for the small call on the 29th was that they, who were astride the Ypres-Staden railway, were on the extreme left of the front of battle, and had merely to round off the new battle line to the point of junction with the old, where the Borders were alert but stationary. The rôle of the K.O.S.B. was to capture and consolidate three isolated strong points, one actually on the railway, and the others to the north-west of it. This entailed an advance of from 250 to 400 yards. Two platoons were allotted to this operation and were successful. The Dublins had to advance on the right of a two-company front 1,000 yards to the point where contact was expected with the 10th Brigade of the 4th Division. In their path lay quite close a formidable blockhouse known as Chinese House. Farther away and more to the left was a fort on the objective line known as 't Goed ter Vesten Farm. As the line extended left, the advance was echeloned back so as to face to the flank of the line of the general British advance.

The Dublins were under orders in two days to join the 16th (Irish) Division owing to difficulties regarding recruiting in Ireland, and it was at their special request that they were nominated for this important enterprise in the sector held by the 87th Brigade and placed under the orders of Brigadier-General Lucas, who drew up the plan of attack in consultation with Brigadier-General Cheape. They asked to be allowed to take part in one more fight for the 29th. They were in extraordinarily fine form, and it boded ill for those Germans who confronted the brilliant fighters and far from gentle foes, that Irish troops can show themselves on their day. Undeterred by the usual, inevitable, dripping downpour, under

command of Major A. Moore, D.S.O., they marched up to the
line by companies singing Irish Republican songs, the band in camp
speeding them off to the strains of " When Ireland is a Nation."
Only the day before, when practising for the attack, they received
a visit from the G.O.C. He chatted a while with the groups of
extended men. When he came to the last platoon he asked, " Now,
who is going to win a V.C. to-morrow ? " Like a shot a sergeant
jumped up and replied, " I am, sir, or I will leave my skin in dirty
old Belgium."

The troops reached the forward positions with very few casualties.
As may well be supposed, the divisional and corps artillery had not
been behind the standard of the rest of the battle. Particular
attention had been paid to 't Goed ter Vesten and Chinese House
by the heavies, and a 6-inch trench mortar of the 20th Division
had given special and effective attention to the former. An elaborate series of barrages, " creeping," " standing," " back," and
" distant," and " machine gun " had been arranged. At 6 a.m.,
summer time, the troops advanced. The K.O.S.B. took and consolidated their objective. They seem to have met with little
opposition and sent back twelve prisoners. But sometimes, when
the troops of assault and those standing-to in the original line are
spared, the links behind suffer. No one who was not there, tells
that intrepid veteran Major William Simpson, D.S.O., M.C., of the
K.O.S.B., can realize the intensity of the shelling experienced by
the transport on the night before the battle. It cost the K.O.S.B.
Q.M.S. William Crombie—an indispensable if ever there was one—
and it was a mystery how the supplies got forward. The Dublins
attacked with what General Cheape calls " extraordinary vigour."
The divisional commander is of opinion that nothing could have
stopped the Dublins that day. It was no scrambling, aimless rush,
but an ordered progress. Then, as always, the difficulty lay in keeping in touch with the unit on the flank. To provide for possibilities
General de Lisle's standing orders were that two platoons, one
behind the other, should follow the attacking line, and behind the
rear platoon should follow two machine guns, in order to guard
the flank. On the 4th October, writes Brigadier-General Cheape,
" this plan proved invaluable. There was a counter-attack on
the right flank and the 4th Division were being driven back. Our
flanking party then opened direct enfilade fire on the advancing
Germans. These in turn fell back, and the 4th Division took up
their ground again." The objectives were taken in scheduled
time, and the eager Irishmen pressed on to the brink of the swollen

THE BATTLE OF BROODSEINDE 4TH OCTOBER 1917.

String Houses"

Conde House

Olga Houses

Kortebeek Farm

Poelcapelle

To Ypres

Final Objective

1st Objective

Ferdan Ho.

CORPS BOUNDARY

DIVISIONAL BOUNDARY

Starting Line

Koekuit

Broembeek

Kwafterwester Farm

Chinese Ho.

Final Objective

L.T.M. Section

I Coy.

Flanking Det.

I Coy.

I Coy.

I Coy.

I Coy.

4TH DIVISION

1st Royal Dublin Fuslrs
Batt. H.Q.

I Coy.

I Coy.

BATTALION BOUNDARY

BATTALION BOUNDARY

I Coy.

Langemarck

Martin Mill

Steenbeek Railway

1st Border Regiment

Batt. H.Q.

I Coy.

I Coy.

1st K.O.S.B.
Batt. H.Q.

Steenbeek

Scale

0   500   1000 Yards

John Bartholomew & Son, Ltd., Edinburgh.

936

and impassable Broembeek. And now for the seventeenth V.C. and Sergeant Ockenden! It was won in full view of the whole battalion. Ockenden was acting company sergeant-major. He saw a platoon officer near him knocked out, and, having identified the machine gun which was holding up the advance, he rushed it. He managed to kill all the crew but one man, and him he chased and slew in the open amid the cheers of his comrades—he and they, be it noted, being under fire all the time. Later in the day the same warrior attacked a farm, killed 4 Germans, and took 16 prisoners.

It was a great day. It looked as if the " Dubs " had determined to leave a name for valour behind them. At the time of the counter-attack alluded to they never lost a foot but stuck firmly on. That night they were relieved by the 2nd Royal Fusiliers of their own brigade. They had made a *beau geste* for what looked like, but was not, the finish, for, as we shall see, the " Dubs " came back. Despite the heavy going, the headlong tumbles, the clogged breeches of the rifles, on which their lives depended, and the difficulty of avoiding a " mix-up " with the units on the right, they had accomplished their task at a cost of casualties to 15 officers and 325 other ranks. The small number of prisoners passed through the cage is hardly commensurate with the number of those who surrendered. There were some casualties through shelling on the way back. A large number of Germans were killed at close quarters in hand-to-hand fighting.

About an hour after the Dublins had taken their objective the G.O.C., with Captain Nickalls, his A.D.C., arrived at battalion headquarters to convey his congratulations to this battalion in person. The shelling had been nothing out of the way that day, but there was enough to make a registered duckboard track the least desirable of localities. A 5.9-inch shell burst so close to the general and his A.D.C. that it blew them into the mud clean off the track. They were seen to clamber out, pick themselves up, and proceed on the even tenor of their way as if nothing had happened, without haste, without rest. Three men who happened to see the incident took off their tin hats and cheered their divisional commander. And small wonder! added the eye-witness. In these days a not-infrequent visitor to the forward areas of the 29th was H.R.H. the Prince of Wales, then on Lord Cavan's staff. A few days after the day of the " Dubs " he happened to drop in at a certain headquarters in the course of his tour of duty. His *incognito* was preserved in the case of one officer, who, not having a notion who he was, treated him with an easy familiarity which the illustrious visitor seemed to enjoy.

The 9th October

THE BATTLE OF POELCAPPELLE

The 9th October was the last fight of the Third Battle of Ypres in which the 29th took part. If the fight was on a smaller scale than that of the 4th, though on a three army front, the 29th were more deeply involved than on the 4th. Out of a total of just over 2,000 prisoners captured by the Franco-British forces that day, the 29th secured 7 officers and 494 other ranks, 30 machine guns, and 2 trench mortars at a cost of 51 officers and 1,110 other ranks. The three remaining battalions of the 86th and three battalions of the 88th took part in a very creditable operation by which, in co-operation with the Guards Division on the left, and the 4th Division once more on the right, one portion of the line was advanced 2,500 yards towards Houthulst Forest. This time the brigade of the 4th Division in the line happened to be the 12th. The left battalion of that brigade was the 2nd Battalion Lancashire Fusiliers. The right battalion of the 86th Brigade was the 1st Battalion of the same famous regiment. Thus the two regular battalions fought side by side. At no time did the Lancashire Fusiliers require extraneous aids to the combative spirit. Their steadiness was proverbial throughout the division. But their blood must have coursed the warmer that day for the meetings and the greetings with their brethren across the invisible line of the divisional boundary. As usual the weather conditions were deplorable. All night before the attack began the rain poured down in torrents. The myriads of shell holes were brimful of water. It was only with the greatest difficulty and only because of the reconnaissance of regimental officers, the system of traffic controls, the energy of brigade staffs and battalion commanders, and the discipline of the troops that the tapes were laid in the dark and the troops reached their positions in the line in time.

The following incident is not without its point. On the 88th Brigade front the advanced posts had been withdrawn, so that the heavy artillery could shell a suspicious-looking wood near our line. At dusk in the torrents of rain the posts did not return to their correct positions, and heavily engaged the taping-out party, whom they took for a German patrol. After the difficult task of taping out had been performed and our posts had been advanced to cover the tapes, an officer from brigade headquarters who had supervised the work made his way to a dug-out close at hand where the commanding officers of the attacking battalions were to collect. " Colonel ——, I think your men might have a bit more musketry practice when we get back to rest." " What," said the colonel indignantly, " how do you know ? You've only just joined the brigade." " Well, sir, three of your posts fired at us at about fifty yards and failed to hit us," was the reply, amid the plaudits and nudges of the other commanding officers.

During the assembly one of the battalions of a division was found marching parallel to our front line about 700 yards in rear of it, and the officer commanding refused to believe that he had mistaken his route. During the argument that ensued, a German Véry light disclosed the remains of a tall building in Langemarck village, and our neighbour was persuaded that he was standing on a double-line railway track which had been completely obliterated by previous shell fire. The trespassers were put on their right road just in time to prevent blocking the assembly of one of the 29th's units.

The fact that the N.F.L.D., on the extreme left next the Guards, took four and a half hours to go the six miles to the jumping-off place indicates how slow progress necessarily was. It would have been quite impossible to have adopted the ordinary course of sending the first line of assaulting troops up to the line the night before. The Lancashire Fusiliers and the Worcesters had taken over the defence of the line on the night of the 7th–8th, and even with the advantage of proximity to the place where the tapes were laid, they were only just in time for zero at 5.20 a.m. The 2nd Royal Fusiliers were in support of their comrades of the 86th, and they also had a weary march over duckboard tracks until formation on a line of crater holes.

It was the first occasion on which Brigadier-General Cheape had commanded the 86th in any important operation. He was able to say of them that they never missed their objective from then onwards to the end of the war. Brigadier-General Nelson was in command of the 88th, and it was his first important engagement in that position. The reputation he gained that day he enhanced at Cambrai, but this is anticipating. The 1st Lancashire Fusiliers were commanded by Lieutenant A. H. S. Hart-Synnot, D.S.O., East Surrey Regiment. The 2nd Royal Fusiliers were under Lieutenant-Colonel G. A. Stevens, D.S.O. The battalion in reserve for counter-attack purposes, if needed, the 16th Middlesex, was under Lieutenant-Colonel J. Forbes-Robertson, D.S.O., who had commanded the N.F.L.D. with so much distinction at Monchy. The battalion in reserve of the 88th was the 2nd Hampshires, under

Lieutenant-Colonel T. C. Spring. It will be remembered that the operations of the 4th had pushed the right front of the divisional sector considerably in front of the left. As the Guards and the French were moving farther to the north-west, it is evident that the 29th's new front would be a segment of a mild arc more or less at right angles to the general line of advance. The Worcesters and N.F.L.D. had therefore to advance 2,500 yards astride of and parallel to the railway to be level with the Guards, while the two fusilier battalions had only some 1,650 yards to go. If the objectives were reached the 29th would have a front of about 1,110 yards. The chief difficulties, once the initial effort of getting into position had had successful results, were as follows. An enemy strong point called Bear Copse had been spared by the misty days of early October from the drastic treatment intended to be meted out to it by the heavy artillery. The Broembeek was rightly estimated as a serious but not insurmountable obstacle. Previous active reconnaissance and patrolling had ascertained its passability. It was therefore decided not to repeat the operation of the 16th August and cross before zero, but to trust largely to surprise in order to get across at zero. There were various blockhouses, chiefly along the railway line, and the right brigade, being in advance of the left, might expect enfilade fire from Koekuit, a ruinous " clachan," once a hamlet on the road from Langemarck to the Forest of Houthulst.

Except possibly for July 1, 1916, there was more elaborate staff work done in connection with the 9th of October than with any other engagement in which the 29th took part. The first objective was to be taken by two companies of each battalion engaged, the second by the remainder. The barrage was to pause for an hour between these two movements, and again for another hour after the second. During this period the work of consolidation was to proceed under cover of a smoke screen. Then was to come the final act in the day's drama. The support battalions were to pass through the leaders and capture the third and last objective, about 700 yards beyond the second, in one wave.

Bad as the weather was, and wet and chilly as the early part of the night was, especially for those in front, it must be conceded that soon after midnight the rain stopped and a drying wind blew.

Punctually at zero down fell the barrage, and on Bear Copse, that dreaded nest, there rained fifty Stokes bombs, with the gratifying result that the machine guns were silenced and the large garrison surrendered themselves and the copse, leaving in our hands two

Minenwerfer and a large dump of ammunition. The infantry on the left crossed the Broembeek and advanced. On the right the Lancashire Fusiliers met with stubborn opposition at first from a strong point, Olga Farm, which held them up for nearly a quarter of an hour. Their losses were severe, but they gained and consolidated the first objective. But in consequence of the line running thin, the 2nd Royal Fusiliers reinforced them with a couple of companies, and the combined fusilier force advanced to Condé House by rushes from shell hole to shell hole. There they captured 200 prisoners, but were unable to advance farther through the fire of two forts to the east. It was just then that the Germans, unfortunately for themselves, happened to counter-attack. They did so strongly in eight lines from the direction of the two forts. They were met by rifle and machine-gun fire, that of the liaison party (described in connection with the Dublins) on the right being most effective. But what was worse, the barrage for the third objective fell at 8.55 and finished off the counter-offensive. The composite force and some odds and ends of Worcesters, N.F.L.D., and even Guardsmen, prepared for the final advance. It was 10 o'clock, however, before anything could be done. The 12th Brigade of the 4th Division had been held, and it was necessary for Second Lieutenant Le Mesurier of the 1st Lancashire Fusiliers to form a flank party. At 10 a.m. the resistance suddenly collapsed ; the limit of advance was reached and consolidation begun. It was a desperate day's work. The two fusilier battalions had shown themselves supreme in attack and defence, and their valour is epitomized in the feats which won for each battalion a V.C. The eighteenth V.C. for the 29th was won by Sergeant Molyneux of the 2nd Royal Fusiliers, who led his section with conspicuous bravery in hand-to-hand fighting, accounting for many killed and capturing a machine gun and 20 prisoners. The nineteenth was won by Sergeant Lister of the 1st Lancashire Fusiliers. He rushed a machine gun alone, and after a fight with the crew he captured it. He then called on the garrison of a fort known as Olga House to surrender, and 100 men laid down their arms. Before leaving the 86th we must revert to the subaltern and his defensive flank. He had to stay there until, last of all the original attacking force, he was relieved by the Middlesex. His men, originally 30 in number, had dwindled down to four. But when at last the five survivors reached camp, their comrades of the battalion turned out as one man and cheered them to the echo. " Whatever honour," says General de Lisle, " Lieutenant Le Mesurier may gain in life, none can equal the spontaneous approbation of their comrades in the ranks so freely offered to himself and his four men."

The Broembeek crossing played a more important part in the adventures of the 88th. Indeed, the most important hindrances in the path of the 86th, "Kortebeek Farm," "Olga House," "Condé House," and "Tranquille Farm," were all on the left bank—*i.e.*, that from which the troops started. But the left brigade and the Guards on their left had almost immediately to cross that swollen stream and its adjacent marshes. Plan things as one may, in execution confusion is apt to arise where nature drives people to form queues to cross bridges. The N.F.L.D. in support got mixed up with the Worcesters in advance. Stray guardsmen found their way into 29th territory, and it is quite possible that the Guards sector was similarly invaded. However, the advance proceeded in spite of opposition from men firing from dug-outs in the railway embankments, and the first objective was reached up to time.

The twentieth V.C., won by Private Dancox of the Worcesters, has the special interest attaching to a feat of gallantry by a soldier not usually fighting in the ranks. His imagination had been stimulated by talk round about him on the all-absorbing topic of pill-boxes and machine guns and how to outwit their wily occupants by slipping round the corner and getting in by the back door. As he was sanitary orderly to the headquarters of the battalion, no doubt the discussions, he heard, were on the highest level. Anyhow, on the 9th he asked permission to rejoin his company for the fight. This request was granted, and he was posted to a mopping-up party, who, during the halt on the captured first objective, were detailed to search the ground in front and on this side of the protective barrage. Sure enough a machine gun was located, but it was behind the barrage. Boldly risking his life Dancox passed through the barrage and applied his knowledge of "how to get in by the back door" with such practical effect that when the barrage lifted he was seen returning with a machine gun under his arm, a broad smile on his face, and 40 prisoners marching in front of him. It was this spirit of individual enterprise combined with fearless bravery that made the 29th so remarkable a formation.

The next stage was easier, and both objectives were consolidated by the Worcesters in spite of numerous casualties due to sniping. But in the gaining of the ground staff work had played an important part. A Stokes mortar had been attached to the Worcester support companies, and on two occasions, near Namur Crossing and Pascal Farm, its timely fire at about 300 yards range had contributed to

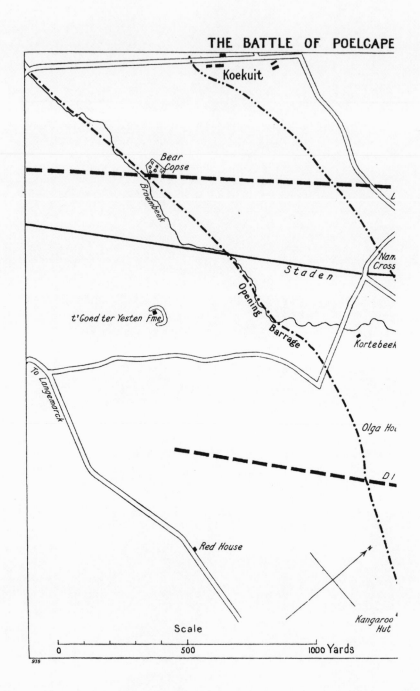

THE BATTLE OF POELCAPE

Koekuit

Bear Copse

Broembeek

Staden

Nam Cross

t'Goed ter Yesten Fme

Opening Barrage

Kortebeek

To Langemarck

Olga Hou

D I

Red House

Kangaroo Hut

Scale

0   500   1000 Yards

935

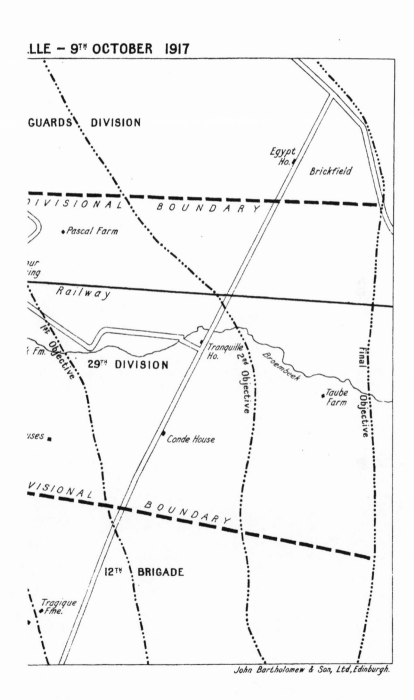

GUARDS DIVISION

Egypt Ho.

Brickfield

DIVISIONAL BOUNDARY

Pascal Farm

our ring

Railway

1st Objective

Fm.

29TH DIVISION

Tranquille Ho.

2nd Objective

Broembcek

Final Objective

Taube Farm

ses

Conde House

VISIONAL BOUNDARY

12TH BRIGADE

Tragique Fme.

make the enemy come out from their dens and surrender. The historian of the Guards Division says that the N.F.L.D. were somewhat behind their own advance, but it cannot have been a very serious menace. There is no doubt that a determined attack by the Irish Guards greatly aided our men, on whose left front a large hostile force were collecting. But the N.F.L.D. were able to report that they held their final objective at the appointed time, and more cannot be expected. Once there, they were subjected about noon to a counter-attack, but drove it off. Another in the evening caused a retirement of 200 yards. The *History of the Guards Division* says that the Irish Guards had to retire as their flank was exposed. The N.F.L.D. say ditto, adding that the Hampshires (the reserve battalion) regained the ground. The broad fact remains that the objectives allotted to the division were substantially gained, and the weary N.F.L.D. could return on the night 10th–11th, after relief by men of the 17th Division, feeling that they had once more done their bit. During the consolidation a few Germans, who had eluded the moppers-up, wandered about trying to be taken prisoners in the orthodox fashion. After several unsuccessful attempts at surrendering to various people, who were much too busily occupied, one pair espied one of our wounded limping back. Here was their chance. They went for him, seized him, and bore him back in triumph, one carrying him and the other steadying him with his hand. They may have thought that the British murdered their prisoners. On the other hand, it may have been one of the symptoms of a lowered *moral*. Padre Swallow had particularly noticed the dejection of the enemy seen in mass. The fight seemed to be out of them. But for the Russian *débâcle*, the Italian collapse, and the dreadful weather, the war might have ended in 1917.

This was Colonel Fuller's last battle as G.S.O. 1. 29th Division. On 11th October he was appointed B.G.G.S. III. Corps, and very glad the 29th were that he should be there, as the sequel will show. It was the custom in the 29th for the closest touch to be maintained between staff and troops. The staff perambulated the trenches, knew every commanding officer and most of the company commanders personally. They were accordingly in a position at any moment to advise whether the troops were fit to go on or not. Constant personal contact awoke confidence in brigades and battalions, and confidence opened " the daylight of honest speech " upon many vital questions. Much valuable information filtered back to divisional headquarters concerning suitable targets for

artillery and such like. A and Q branch functioned under Lieutenant-Colonel L. H. Abbott like clock-work, thanks to those towers
of strength, the regular quartermasters of the divisional units,
without whose efficient co-operation the best-laid plans of the Q
staff might have been in vain.   When the 86th were relieved in the
early hours of the 11th, Brigadier-General Cheape sent his staff-
captain back with orders to provide, by hook or by crook, some sort
of hot meal for the men at Elverdinghe, which was their entraining
place.   Sure enough a savoury and appetizing stew awaited the
whole brigade.   Sundry guardsmen joined in the feast, for there
was enough and to spare, which took place at a spot called Crocodile
Pontoon.   Months afterwards, when Cheape and his staff-captain,
Captain Robert Gee, V.C., were recalling the incidents of the action,
the brigadier suddenly asked how in the world Gee got his hands
on such a lavish supply of fresh meat.   He then was informed that
the stew was composed of the choicest parts of mules, a whole
team of which had been killed hard by by shell fire.   He and his
servant had cut up the meat for the stew from them.

The losses of the division were severe.   In two months battle
casualties amounting to 206 officers and 4,530 other ranks were
incurred.   To this total must be added wastage by sickness, 44
officers and 860 other ranks.   Casualties about 1,000 were also
attributable to the initial period of holding the line from the end of
June to the 21st July.   The grand total was much the same as at
Arras, where in the operations 278 officers and 5,744 other ranks
became casualties, and the sick wastage amounted to 28 officers
and 822 other ranks.   Altogether between the 10th April and the
10th October the 29th Division's casualties amounted to 644 officers
and 13,792 other ranks.   On the other hand they did not fail to
deal very faithfully with the enemy.   Of the 9th October Ludendorff has written : " The front held better than on the 4th, though
considerable breaches were made." . . . " The expenditure in man-
power of the Fourth Battle of Flanders was extraordinarily high.
There was a shortage of troops on the West."   It is known that
two German divisions intended for Italy went " west."   Colonel
Headlam mentions in his *History of the Guards Division*, on page
287, that it was an estimate current at the time, that the Guards
and the 29th between them put out of action no less than six
German divisions, and expresses the opinion that there would
appear to be no exaggeration.   Cambrai was still to follow in the
same year.   And yet the divisional commander has stated that in
his opinion the *moral* of the troops was never at a higher standard

than when they came out of the line in West Flanders.   It was as though they had absorbed the counsel given to Aeneas, " *Tu ne cede malis sed contra audentior ito !* "

They did not leave the slum land of the war without the meed of appreciative and congratulatory messages.   On the very day of the Battle of Poelcappelle, as the action on the 9th October is officially termed, Lieutenant-General the Earl of Cavan, command-ing the XIV. Corps, sent the following : " My heartiest thanks and congratulations to you (*i.e.*, General de Lisle) and all ranks.   A very fine finish to your noble work in Flanders."   General Sir Hubert Gough, who commanded the Fifth Army, of which the XIV. Corps formed part, wrote on the 14th the following valedictory message :
' During the Third Battle of Ypres the 29th Division have set a fine example.   Their work in preparing for battle has been uniformly excellent, their minor operations have been successful, and during the general engagements of the 16th August, the 4th and 9th October, they have still further enhanced their great reputation. Their departure from the Fifth Army is a loss both to the Army and myself.

" Please convey to all ranks my deep appreciation and gratitude for all they have accomplished since their arrival in June in what was then the Ypres Salient.

" I wish every one good fortune and continued success."

CHAPTER IV

THE BATTLE OF CAMBRAI

THE Battle of Cambrai ranks as one of the most thrilling episodes of the whole war. Tanks at last came into their kingdom. The notion that the Hindenburg Line was impregnable was exploded. Within two months of its collapse Ludendorff's trusted officers had told him, in reply to special questioning, that no special danger lay in tanks, and that such a thing as tank panic (*Tankschrecken*) was unknown. Yet, helter-skelter, masses of Germans on 20th November bolted, flinging away equipment, much as the Romans first fled from Pyrrhus' elephants. The Hindenburg Support Line, in spite of its well-chosen situation on the reverse slope, with its 50 yard belt of wire specially laid out for defence by machine guns, fared no better than the front system. Five thousand and more surrendered in the course of a few hours. The German guns ceased firing in an hour and a half. Hundreds of French civilians were rescued from the oppressor, and, almost delirious with joy, walked and talked and thought as free men. It looked as though the last line of the German defence, which, if strongly wired, was still incomplete, would fall on the very same day. This line, known as the Marcoing–Masnières–Beaurevoir line, was, so far as the 29th was concerned, all on the eastern side of the Scheldt Canal. And then the whole affair seemed to die of inanition. The failure of the cavalry to pursue the retreating enemy, due, no doubt, as regards the crossing of the canal, to the destruction of a bridge, undoubtedly disappointed people at home. The dashing raid of the Fort Garry Horse was a fine feat of arms but a mere minor episode. The disappointment and the tense concern about the continued battle on the western flank of the salient was succeeded by alarm, on the news of the 30th November leaking out. The nation lived on its nerves till the final news of the squaring of accounts came in. It then learned that a serious disaster had been averted by the stubborn spirit of certain of the troops engaged. There was a timely and powerful counter-thrust by the Guards in co-operation with tanks through and beyond Gouzeacourt. There were desperate encounters along the northern flank of the great salient formed through the initial successes. Bourlon Wood will be remembered as long as the Empire survives. But at no point was the strain greater or more continuous than that borne by the troops at the farthest point of penetration beyond, in and around Marcoing, Masnières, and Les Rues Vertes, where the 29th Division were holding the line. The aim of this chapter is to tell how the division came to be in the battle, how it fared as it fought its way to the " nose of the bullet," and how it bore itself in the first of the two great defensive fights, as the result of which it can claim to have been supreme in defence as in attack. In *Sir Douglas Haig's Command*, in a note on page 403, Colonel Boraston remarks : " The story of the great fight the 29th Division put up on 30th November has yet to be written. It held out against immense difficulties, thanks to skill and valour unsurpassed perhaps by any division during 1917." The following account is based on statements of eye-witnesses and participators only, and is an attempt to describe the great fight.

The 29th Division, now reinforced by 85 officers and 1,614 other ranks, most of whom were represented by the newly arrived 1st Guernsey Light Infantry, which had not yet been in action, left Proven on the 16th October 1917, and proceeded to Basseux, 6 miles south of Arras, for rest and training, prior to joining the III. Corps (Lieutenant-General Sir William Pulteney) for the coming attack of Cambrai by the Third Army, commanded by a former corps commander of the 29th, General Sir Julian Byng, now Lord Byng of Vimy.

On this occasion a full month was allotted for this purpose, a longer period than usual, but not too long in view of the heavy casualties sustained at Arras and Ypres. The Basseux area was ideal for training purposes, and marked progress was made. Its similarity to the area of the operations to be narrated was so marked that indoor exercises could be carried out on hectograph maps of the Cambrai district and then practised with the troops on the training ground.

The first ten days were spent by the troops in platoon and company drill combined with the training of specialists, such as machine gunners, Lewis gunners, Stokes mortar detachments, bombers, etc. At the conclusion of this first period, each brigade

group was inspected by the divisional commander in a full ceremonial parade. The troops paraded in line of close columns, then
formed a hollow square for the presentation of decorations won in
Flanders. After re-forming line the units marched past, and
finally advanced in review order. But in the main the training
was directed with a view to regaining power to manœuvre—*i.e.*,
fire and movement and initiative in all commanders.

It must not be supposed that the 29th were run on the principle
of all work and no play. Otherwise, why should the Field-day
of the 87th on the 12th November, directed by Colonel Ellis of the
Borders, have been followed on the 13th by the cross-country run,
in which the R.I.F. proved themselves the fleetest of foot and
soundest of wind ? Nor, if that had been the rule, would the terrific
brigade final between the R.I.F. and the K.O.S.B. (who seldom
were far off a football final) have been witnessed by so many
distinguished generals and other officers, who can testify to the fact
that on November 16, 1917, after twenty minutes' extra play, ten
minutes each way, the " Skins " emerged victorious by 2 goals to 1.
Many officers and men had been granted well-earned leave, and
returned in splendid fettle for the ordeal. Altogether, when the
moment for departure came, the 29th marched off from their billets
by brigades to the station at Boisleux-au-Mont as fit a fighting
force as any in France. The 87th were the first brigade to entrain
on the 17th between 6 and 9 p.m. for Péronne. The journey lay
through the scarred battlefield of the Somme, untrod for the greater
part by the men of the division, but with names that were as familiar,
through being the scenes of suffering and triumph of comrades of
other units, as those of their own villages or streets at home. Cour-
celles-le-Comte, Achiet-le-Grand, Irles, Miraumont, Grandcourt, had
figured in dispatches. Some might even remember the days when
the church spires of some of these quondam villages of the promised
land could be seen from observation points in the sector held in 1916.
But Beaucourt-sur-Ancre and Hamel and Albert must have roused
many memories of other days and other comrades. Nor was the
journey for those whose duties took them by motor or machine-gun
transport over less classic ground, for the route taken was through
Bapaume and Le Transloy, to say nothing of Sailly-Saillisel. One
officer paid a pious pilgrimage to a hideous little cellar where he
had thankfully passed a week in February 1917. Péronne itself
had been for three months prior to the great retirement of the
enemy beleaguered by the III. Corps, of which the division was to
form part. And that nothing should be wanting to give confidence

to the troops, the B.-G.G.S. III. Corps was their tried and trusted guide, philosopher, and friend C. G. Fuller, who had been for more than two years G.S.O. I. of the division. There may seem to be here an undue stressing of somewhat impalpable and elusive matters, but it must be kept in mind that only the highest state of mental as well as bodily health could have brought the troops through the trials of the ensuing fortnight. Training, sports, and *moral* pulled the troops through, and in the nurture of the last the Somme memories must have played a part.

The second period of ten days was allotted to company and battalion manœuvre combined with long marches across country in full fighting equipment. This meant a dead weight of between 50 lbs. and 60 lbs. to be carried. During the last period of ten days, these marches were increased as the troops took part in brigade and divisional schemes framed as far as possible to resemble the coming operation against Cambrai. On the final day's training, a practice operation on a large scale on the 15th November, Lieutenant-General Sir William Pulteney, the commander of the III. Corps, the Chief of the General Staff, Lieutenant-General Sir L. E. Kiggell, and the Commander-in-Chief, Field-Marshal Sir Douglas Haig, were spectators.

Sir Douglas Haig expressed general approval of the appearance of the troops and of the system of training, and was most complimentary on the work of the division in Flanders.

The following day a General Staff officer from G.H.Q. (Lieutenant-Colonel Greig) visited headquarters to ask if it was thought the troops of the division had sufficient endurance to last out till the night of the 21st November. As secrecy was the essence of success in the coming concentration, the troops would have to march on three consecutive nights, and on the morning of the 20th November, the day of attack, they would have six miles to march to the place of assembly with full fighting kit. There they would be expected to advance three or four miles, and grave doubts were held at General Headquarters as to whether the troops would be capable of consolidating and holding the ground won. After the severe training from the 17th October to the 15th November, the divisional commander was able to assure the Chief of the General Staff that there was no cause for anxiety so far as the 29th was concerned, and that they would hold any ground they gained until the night of the 21st.

When it is realized that the 29th was not relieved until the 5th December, fourteen days beyond the time they were expected to reach the limit of endurance, it must be admitted the confidence of the commander in his troops was not misplaced.

Much credit for the success of the operation was due to the secrecy maintained by those who, of necessity, were made cognizant of the general plan of attack.

During the first week of November, an advanced party proceeded to the III. Corps area with a view to making all the necessary administrative arrangements in connection with the attack. Nevertheless, no trustworthy information in respect to the destination of the 29th Division reached the Basseux area. On the other hand, rumours increased in numbers as the day for action approached. Throughout all these discussions on the subject, there is no doubt that a very strong feeling prevailed that the division was intended for Italy, and when that stage of the training arrived, wherein the passage of a water obstacle was made the main feature of all field days, little doubt remained as to the veracity of the rumour that the Piave was the river in question.

Concentration in secret was greatly assisted by four days of fog, when enemy aeroplanes could not observe, but two successful enemy trench raids against a unit in the V. Corps to the north, and a unit to the south of the III. Corps, might have enabled the enemy to realize that an attack was imminent, although when the attack came off, it did so as a complete, nay, staggering surprise, as Ludendorff himself admits.

On the 19th November, divisional headquarters moved to a quarry by a mill, known as Quentin Mill, about a mile east of Gouzeaucourt, and troops moved into position that night. The scheme of the attack was original and effective.

At dawn on the 20th November the III. and V. Corps were to attack without any previous artillery preparation, but the six divisions were to be preceded by a mass of tanks equipped with fascines so that they could cross the widest trenches. In the III. Corps the 12th (Scott), 20th (D. Smith), and the 6th (Marden) Divisions were to attack in line with the objectives of the Hindenburg Line and the support line about a mile to the north of it. When these were in our hands, the 29th was to advance from its position in reserve and capture Masnières, Marcoing, and Nine Wood, and was then to cross the canal and occupy the line of trenches lying to the north of the two villages known as the Beaurevoir Line. Five divisions of cavalry were then to break through and cut off Cambrai from the east, and the V. Corps was then to exploit the situation north-west as far as the river Sensée.

From Péronne the division marched five and a half miles to Moislains, where it rested on the 18th. On the night of the 18th–19th it moved on another five miles on the average to the villages near Fins—viz., Equancourt and Sorel-le-Grand, and to Dessart Wood a mile north-east of Fins, which contained eight battalions and more than 100 camouflaged tanks. Still, it appeared that the secret concentration of troops, tanks, and guns had escaped the vigilance of the enemy. The sector of the front was one of the quietest in the live parts of the whole Western theatre. Possibly behind the broad belts of wire and the massive chalk parapets the garrison were taking life easy. On the part of the British no effort was spared to avoid noise, exposure, or confusion. Road and track junctions had been carefully picketed. The allotted areas for assembly had been measured, assigned, and taped out. Movement was restricted as far as possible to the hours of darkness. The advance of the 29th, which began between 1 and 2 a.m. on the morning of November 20, was carried out without a hitch. The 87th, which led, reached the point of assembly at 3.30 a.m. The only audible sound was the chug, chugging noise of the tanks, 378 of which had been allotted to the III. and IV. Corps. The 86th and the 88th were in position in ample time for zero. Meanwhile the divisional artillery had started from the Orville–Authieule–Amplier area on 12th November in the evening and moved by night to the Treux–Dernancourt area, and on the following night to Hennois Wood, where they came under the orders of the III. Corps. To quote Colonel Johnson, " The vehicles were concealed in the wood ; horses were tied up to trees in odd groups ; no lights were allowed. For real discomfort this camp—or rather bivouac —would be difficult to surpass. The wood was surrounded by a wet, muddy field. The weather was wet for part of the time and bitterly cold all the time. No fires were allowed, and the very few tents supplied were worn out, leaked badly, and had no floor boards." Two nights later the 15th Brigade R.H.A. moved into action under the orders of the C.R.A. 6th Division, and the following night—i.e., the 18th–19th—the 17th Brigade R.F.A., so far not already in action, came into action under the C.R.A. 20th Division. They returned to the orders of the C.R.A. 29th Division as soon as that unit was ordered to advance.

At 6.10 a.m. the tanks started. It was one of the most dramatic moments in the war. At 6.20, from concealed guns which had only just registered, there burst a torrent of smoke, gas, and high-explosive shells. And all this in an autumn mist so thick that one could only see 100 yards ahead. It is recorded by the 2nd Royal Fusiliers that they marched on a compass bearing of 40° till they passed through the 6th Division, who had captured and were holding the Hindenburg Line. The assaulting three divisions of the corps attacked with the barrage, and the 29th moved forward quickly to allotted positions in the old front line, which was reached about 7.30 a.m. The feeble counter-barrage did little damage, and soon ceased. Prisoners were soon seen in masses.

While the headquarters of the S.W.B. were waiting in our front line for the signal for the division to advance, an interesting family gathering took place. The commanding officer, Lieutenant-Colonel G. T. Raikes, was examining the country in front when he was joined by his brother, Captain W. T. Raikes, the divisional machine-gun officer. They had not been long discussing the situation when a tank arrived and disgorged yet another brother, Captain D. T. Raikes, commanding a section of the tanks supporting the division in the attack, and the council of war was thus increased to three. Some family !

Soon after 10 a.m. the bugle sounded G, and the three brigades advanced towards their objectives preceded by twelve tanks, four being assigned to each brigade. The machine-guns went forward on the backs of mules, and although there was some hoof-frisking under the stimulus of the gun fire, not a gun was lost or injured, as Captain K. M. Moir has testified.

The orders to the 29th were to wait until information arrived that the leading divisions had gained the Hindenburg Support Line, timed for 10 o'clock. Owing to fog an aeroplane could not act, and it took two hours for information to reach the 29th Divisional Head-quarters that we had gained the Hindenburg Line. To have waited for news of reaching the second objective would have rendered the pursuit by the 29th abortive owing to want of time. At 10.30 a.m. therefore, the three brigades were ordered to advance, the 88th Brigade (Nelson) on the right moving north-east against Masnières, the 87th Brigade (Lucas) in the centre due north against Marcoing, by the east slopes of the Couillet valley, and the 86th Brigade (Cheape) north-north-east by the west slopes of the Couillet valley against Nine Wood, a copse at the top of a ridge overlooking Marcoing, and a mile to the north of it. There was no divisional reserve, as the 29th had three distinct and widely separated positions, to attain each of which would require a full brigade. But a pursuing force is frequently entitled to take extraordinary risks, and in this case there was no choice. The two brigades on the flanks moved in diamond formation with a battalion at each point, so that if the leading battalion was unable to advance, the flanking battalions by continuing to advance would automatically turn the flanks of the defenders. This manœuvre proved most successful. All the brigades advanced through the broad lanes torn by the tanks through the forest of barbed wire. The 16th Battalion Middlesex Regiment, acting as advanced guard to the 86th Brigade, was held up by heavy machine-gun fire from a chalk quarry in front of Nine Wood, a place essential to the safe holding of Marcoing, but the 2nd Royal Fusiliers on the right, and the Guernsey Light Infantry on the left, pushed in and took the quarry by reverse fire with hardly a check, the latter battalion receiving their baptism of fire in the course of this flawless manœuvre. In addition to many prisoners, 26 machine guns were captured there. The centre brigade adopted the square formation, the two leading battalions finding their own advanced guards. After the garrison of the quarry had been thus disposed of, Nine Wood was captured with hardly a check, and outposts pushed on to Noyelles-sur-L'Escaut, a village about a mile to the north-west of the top of the spur, and lying, as its full name tells, on the (left) bank of the Scheldt.

The advance of the 86th, well supported by tanks and a certain modicum of artillery fire, was effected without special incident apart from the Quarry, although far from being a walk over. The objectives, Nine Wood and Noyelles, were captured by 1 p.m., and an attempt made by men of the Royal Fusiliers to cross the canal by the bridge near the Sucrérie. It was found, however, that the bridge over the river Scheldt was destroyed. As the Scheldt came between our troops and the canal, the attempt to cross the canal had to be abandoned. Sources of trouble were the outskirts of Marcoing and the cross-roads a quarter of a mile south-west of Nine Wood (*alias* Bois des Neuf). The failure of the 51st Division to capture Flesquières had stiffened the resistance at this part of the fight. Noyelles was not abandoned without repeated counter-attacks, and our men were in and out on several occasions. On the occasion of the last of these, about 4 p.m., Brigadier-General Cheape boarded a tank commanded by Captain Harcourt and proceeded, accompanied by a company of Lancashire Fusiliers, down the main street. The sight of the tank crashing over two street barricades and clean over a machine gun and its crew was too much for the 200 or so Germans who temporarily held the village, and they hurried away. So far forward were the troops by about 11 a.m. that the brigadier asked the liaison officer to summon the cavalry.

These, however, did not appear for three hours, too late to develop the attack northwards. To the infantry, and some of them had served in the cavalry, it seemed as though, there being no canal to cross here, a vigorous dash would have secured Cantaing and cut off the retreating troops and guns of the enemy, who was withdrawing from Bourlon Wood. Whether the feeling of disappointment was justified or not, has, however, little relevance to the purpose of this tale, which is to follow the fortunes of the 29th.

Meanwhile, the 87th in the centre progressed steadily (and like the 88th, without any artillery help), and with a certain degree of caution, as prisoners stated that Marcoing was held by three battalions. Some troublesome machine-gun fire was met with at Marcoing Copse, half a mile south-east of the village, and a certain number of casualties occurred, but the advance continued, and it was soon seen that any resistance this side of the canal was more apparent than real. The K.O.S.B., the leading battalion on the left, on capturing Marcoing, secured only 50 prisoners. The rest had fled, and yet it was evidently a place of great importance. Valuable assistance was rendered to the K.O.S.B. by tanks in this well-fought action. Nor did the K.O.S.B. forget their instructions regarding bridgeheads. Leaving two companies to mop up the village, Colonel C. A. G. O. Murray sent on the two others to capture the main bridge over the canal. Thanks to the intrepid advance of Major B. T. Wilson, R.E., in front of the infantry, this bridge was saved from destruction in the nick of time. It had been mined, but the engineers were up in time to cut the leads. As soon as the bridge was in our hands, the Borders, under Lieutenant-Colonel A. J. Ellis, D.S.O., came sweeping through to attack the third and last line of the German system of defence. It was at this time that a check was threatened by a well-posted machine gun. The Germans were evidently regaining their heads and hearts. But it was not for long. Sergeant Spackman, of the Border Regiment, dashed across to the far side, for he had located the danger. Single-handed, and with great tactical skill, he worked round the gun by short rushes from cover to cover, shooting down the detachment in his advance. He shot all but one man, who abandoned his gun and bolted. By this intrepid act Sergeant Spackman cleared the way for those of his comrades, who did not cross by the lock bridge at the little Château of Talma, north of the village, to cross the canal. For this dashing exploit Sergeant Spackman won the twenty-first V.C. for the 29th.

Now for the S.W.B. and R.I.F. on the right.   It will be evident to the reader that, when mention was made of firing at Marcoing Copse, it would principally affect the right half of the brigade.   It was the S.W.B. under Colonel G. T. Raikes, D.S.O., who met with and overcame this opposition.   They continued their march towards the river and the canal, which at this point are almost contiguous. About two-thirds of the two miles of distance between Marcoing and Masnières, in the direction of Masnières, is a lock.   This lock the S.W.B. seized, and, crossing by it, formed a bridgehead on the farther side.   Hard behind them came the R.I.F., but, by the time they came up, a machine gun, firing from a building on the far side, made any attempt to cross futile.   It was then that the initiative and bravery of their commanding officer, Lieutenant-Colonel Sherwood-Kelly, C.M.G., D.S.O., once more restored the situation. He ran under fire to a tank, with which he returned, and the fire of which he directed against the building.   He himself at the head of his men then crossed the lock-bridge, followed by his leading company.   Opposition then collapsed, and the remainder of the battalion passed over in safety.   Although it is out of the order of events, it may be stated here that the same officer, on the same day, covered another company through a belt of wire, using a Lewis gun himself.   His final exploit on that day was personally to lead a company against the defenders of some sunk gun pits, between Masnières and Marcoing, which resulted in the capture of 46 prisoners and 5 machine guns.   The *Times* correspondent, in giving his account of this record of gallantry, speaks of " his coolness and nonchalance which were the inspiration of the whole battalion." His arm bore four wound stripes, and his last wound in the lung, as we know, would have entitled him to be permanently invalided. For these exploits he was subsequently awarded the V.C., the twenty-second won for the division.

Although the 88th is mentioned last, it was the first to meet with serious opposition.   The Essex, under Lieutenant-Colonel Sir George Stirling, were the point of the diamond, and the first to strike trouble near a strong place, the Good Old Man Farm on Welsh Ridge, about 250 feet above the Scheldt, and close behind the Hindenburg Support Line, and not yet cleared of Germans. The flanking battalions, the Worcesters on the right under Lieutenant-Colonel C. S. Linton, D.S.O., and the N.F.L.D. under Lieutenant-Colonel A. L. Hadow, C.M.G., on the left, soon came to the rescue in the manner intended by General de Lisle, and 150 prisoners were taken and resistance crushed.

On the left flank the Newfoundland Regiment had considerable trouble. A less efficient battalion might well have found the opposition too great, but the men of this unit always took a lot of stopping. One company was held up for a time by bursts of machine-gun fire from a flank which could not be located. Moreover, there was a derelict tank in that direction. In the end an officer worked round the tank to discover where the fire was coming from. He reached the tank and found the sole survivor was firing at our own troops. His face had been half shot away, and he was almost mad, but in spite of the pain and blood he continued to fire at any one he could see. His feelings, when he realized that he had failed to distinguish friend from foe, can be better imagined than described.

But three-quarters of an hour had gone, and the enemy during this respite partly organized the defences of Les Rues Vertes (henceforth " L.R.V."), a suburb of Masnières, and separated from it by the river and canal. It cannot be too strongly emphasized that Masnières, lying in a hollow beyond the awkward barrier of the canal, and overlooked by the enemy from Crèvecœur, and close to the formidable Marcoing–Masnières–Beaurevoir line on the rising ground to the north-east towards Rumilly, was a bad place to have to hold, as the sequel will show. Its communications were all open and regularly shelled. However, back to the 88th, who were nearing it ! The Worcesters had as their immediate objective a lock 700 yards due east of the southern end of L.R.V. This they seized, and then they formed a bridgehead out of one company. Another company was sent north along the farther bank of the canal to outflank the defences. This manœuvre was entirely successful. But misfortune was impending. The iron bridge on the main road to Cambrai was down, and with it a precious tank. No more could cross by that route. Many military hopes were wrecked and submerged with it in the Canal de l'Escaut. The Worcesters felt the pang of a more intimate loss, for Colonel Linton had fallen, a grievous deprivation in the anxious circumstances in which the battalion and brigade found themselves. But in itself his death was a great loss to the 29th. Acting Lieutenant-Colonel K. A. Johnston, officer commanding the Hants, the battalion in reserve at the back corner of the diamond, grasped the situation at Masnières with military instinct, and diverted his men to the south-east, past the lock by which the Worcesters crossed, to a lock nearer Crèvecœur. By this lock the Hants crossed without opposition, and with them and the Worcesters, Colonel

Johnston pressed the attack on Masnières with two companies, besides attacking and capturing Mon Plaisir Farm and a section of trench in the Beaurevoir line east of the northern end of Masnières.

Meanwhile the Essex on approaching L.R.V. were met by heavy fire from the enemy in possession, but soon dislodged them, and by 1 p.m. reached the bank of the canal, to find that the stone bridge was down, as already mentioned. As the barrier of the canal proved to be impassable, and as the efforts of the brave officers and men of the old 44th are all recorded in an admirable and still inexpensive little book (Burrows, Southend-on-Sea), we can pass on to the N.F.L.D. The open country seems to have been less in the minds of the Germans than the villages. But the N.F.L.D., on reaching the canal lock on the left edge of Masnières, met with stubborn resistance. After a severe combat the bridge was won, but, as the final objective, the Beaurevoir line, was beyond reach, a defensive flank was dug, linking up with the 87th Brigade.

From a coign of vantage General Lucas had been an eye-witness of much of the earlier part of the 29th's operations, which might have been a field day on Salisbury Plain : the 86th with their tanks moving up the slopes and capturing Nine Wood, and his own Borders moving up the slopes towards the Beaurevoir line in extended order, just as a mass of Germans were hurrying from the opposite quarter towards the same goal. As the mist closed in on the combatants, it seemed as though the Germans would win the race, and this proved to be the case. It was the 107th Division, fresh, in every sense, from Russia, just arrived in the very nick of time to save the Mas–Beau Line. In many ways the Germans had the luck that day. And then the mist swallowed up the combatants. Most terrible and significant of all was the sight of the hold-up of the 51st at Flesquières, with a tank in flames on the edge of it, and some six or eight others round about also on fire. Incidentally, it may be mentioned that the tanks cut all telephone wires, so that no communications came from the front for a considerable time.

87th Brigade Headquarters then moved to Marcoing, where the battalion headquarters were already ensconced, and attention was directed to discovering how the attack on the Beaurevoir line and the north-western suburbs of Masnières had succeeded. Great results were not to be expected from a few tired battalions (the R.I.F. had had a *rencontre* of considerable asperity 1,000 yards north-west of Masnières and taken some prisoners *en route*) and one tank, confronted with a wired and entrenched position about a mile away. On the extreme left a company of the Borders captured a portion of the hostile trenches and 19 prisoners. As it could not be supported, it was ordered to retire. This order was carried out with masterly skill by alternate platoons. Not a prisoner escaped. It was a very fine example of " fire and move-ment " in retreat.

Elsewhere all efforts failed, and a bridgehead line of trenches was dug from the canal north of the Talma Château to the canal at the outskirts of Masnières, manned from left to right by the Borders, R.I.F., and N.F.L.D.

The net result from north to west was that the 86th had reached their objective at Noyelles, the 87th had two battalions confronting the final objective and two in reserve in Marcoing. The 88th had captured three-fourths of Masnières, and had three battalions across the canal and one in and around L.R.V. Rain had begun to fall early in the afternoon. It was a nasty, cold winter's night. The men had no blankets, but, though dog tired, they had plenty to do with pick and shovel. The only continuation of the offensive on the 21st November consisted of an attack at noon by the 87th, assisted by 16 tanks, against the Beaurevoir line, now strongly held and ready to repel. The volume of German machine-gun fire was immense. Armour-piercing bullets riddled a number of the tanks, knocked out the crews, and indirect fire caught the troops as soon as they reached a certain height. The S.W.B. and K.O.S.B. suffered many casualties. Next morning it was found that the S.W.B. had hardly any officers left, and Captain Ewbank of the Borders was lent from brigade headquarters. They had been set a hopeless task. After consultation with two tank company com-manders the G.O.C. 87th deprecated a renewal of the attempt on the next day, unless he had 32 tanks *without* or 16 *with* drastic artillery support. Neither condition could be complied with ; the army cancelled the attack, so exit the cavalry.

On the right the 88th mopped up the remaining Germans in the catacombs of Masnières and cleared out the suburbs. The whole village was now ours for what it was worth.

Up north the 86th, and notably the 2nd Royal Fusiliers, bade a fine farewell to Noyelles. They repelled three counter-attacks between 11 a.m. and nightfall, and after much street fighting remained victors in possession of the conquered territory. That evening the 6th Division took over the Noyelles sector, and hence-forth the 29th occupied the two-brigade front Marcoing–Masnières–

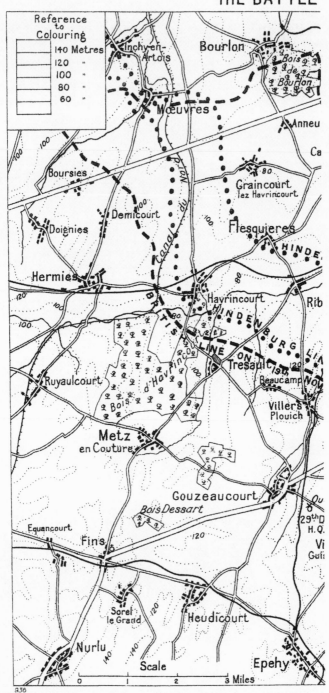

THE BATTLE

Reference
to
Colouring
140 Metres
120 "
100 "
80 "
60 "

Inchy-en-Artois
Bourlon
Bois de Bourlon
Mœuvres
Anneu
Ca
Boursies
Graincourt
lez Havrincourt
Demicourt
Flesquieres
Doignies
HINDE
Canal du Nord
Hermies
Havrincourt
Rib
HINDENBURG LINE
BRITISH LINE ON
Ruyaulcourt
Bois d'Havrincourt
Tresault
Beaucamp WON
Villers Plouich
Metz en Couture
Gouzeaucourt
Bois Dessart
29th D H.Q.
Equancourt
Fins
Vi Gui
Sorel le Grand
Heudicourt
Nurlu
Scale
Epehy
0   1   2   3 Miles

9.36

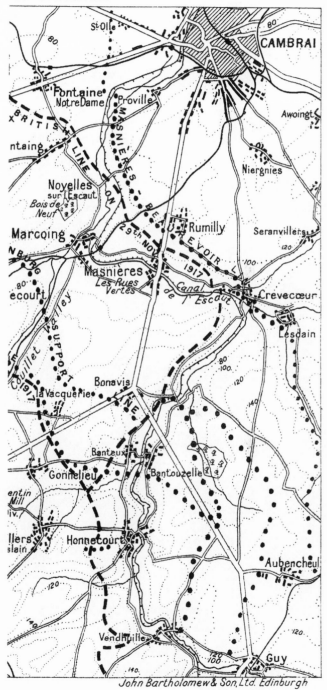

St Olle

CAMBRAI

80

80

Fontaine
NotreDame

Proville

Awoingt

X BRITISH

ntaing

LINE

Niergnies

Noyelles
sur l'Escaut
Bois de
Neuf

Marcoing

Rumilly

Seranvillers

120

29th NOV

NB G

80

100

Masnieres

Les Rues
Vertes

Canal
de l'Escaut

Crevecœur

ecourt

Lesdain

EVOIR L

1917

Bonavis

80
100

120

la Vacquerie

140

1917

NE

Banteux

Bantouzelle

Gonnelieu

entin
Mill

liv.

llers
lain

Honnecourt

Aubencheul

120

140

Vendhuille

120

Guy

120
100

140

John Bartholomew & Son, Ltd. Edinburgh

L.R.V., one brigade always being in reserve in the cellars of Marcoing. These are the three names with which it will be for ever associated.

So ended this well-thought-out offensive, which resulted in a signal defeat of the Germans, but failed to achieve the very important result hoped for. How nearly it succeeded we now know. It is easy to criticize after the event, but there is little doubt that historians of the future will attribute failure to gain the full advantage of the victory at Cambrai in 1917 to the want of " weight behind the spear."

Perhaps the notable feature of this operation lay in the sustained endurance of the troops prior to, during, and subsequent to the attack. There had been no night's rest for three nights previous to the battle, and a night in the train had been followed by three night marches, some of the units doing as much as 12 miles in a night. On the actual day of battle the 29th Division marched 10 miles to the canal, carrying 60 lbs. of equipment. They fought till dark, and then consolidated a position 5,000 yards long by 1,500 deep.

Before describing the interlude (which has its lighter side) between the first and second acts of the mighty drama, just a word about the civilians rescued by the 29th. Over 100 were found in Noyelles and 414 in Masnières. Their appearance was pathetic, their gratitude touching. Their goods had been commandeered. They had been fed by the charity of neutrals.

The following account of the feelings and experiences of the keeper of the lock just east of Masnières on the great day, related by him to Second Lieutenant G. W. P. McLachlan of the 2nd Hants, gives a glimpse into the other side of the picture. Our bombardment at first suggested little, but panic began to show itself among the troops in Masnières. With the crackle of musketry and machine-gun fire and the noise of the tanks, the excitement of the French became intense. When the Germans were seen to be running back everywhere, and those who were billeted in the lock-house said good-bye and took themselves and their kit, not towards the foe, but—towards Cambrai, the strain on the worthy man was almost unbearable. Hope vanished in delight as khaki-clad men of the Essex hove into view over the sky-line. The incredible was true ; the impossible had happened. The warmth of the feeling for the 29th Division and for the 88th Brigade is still as great as ever. Their children are brought up in the faith, and a huge bronze caribou standing proudly on the Cambrai road is a perpetual reminder of the limit of the 29th's advance, and of the men, in particular, who had come the longest journey of all in that division, to rescue them from the cruel and detested invader, who had bullied and starved them for three long weary years.

The Interlude

The next week passed off without striking incident. There were six 6-inch Newton mortars in Masnières by the 24th, but only two were still in action when hostilities were resumed on a big scale. The 15th R.H.A. near la Vacquerie on the right, and the 17th R.F.A. in the Couillet valley, up which the 86th and 87th had marched on the 20th, guarded the divisional front. In the Couillet valley was also the 232nd Army F.A. Brigade. But there was an insufficient mass of guns and too wild a type of weather for accurate shooting on the part of heavies and mortars to warrant a fresh push forward. An attack planned for the 26th was cancelled on the 25th after consultations between the brigadiers concerned, the C.R.A., the G.O.C., and the corps commander. Working in a rotation of short periods in the front line, the work of fortification was pressed on with great energy. Otherwise life began to settle down to much the usual trench existence. Rations and parcels arrived regularly. There was actually a light railhead in Marcoing. Incorporation with the rest of the conquered area was in full swing. The divisional canteen established itself there and satisfied the insatiable craving for cigarettes. The Germans had left plenty of beer and wine of excellent quality, besides much sausage-meat, Delikatessen, Pumpernickel, etc. It is greatly to the credit of the troops that there was no excess and no drunkenness. On the 22nd the men could be seen (presumably the K.O.S.B., the counter-attack battalion at that date) strolling jauntily about collecting souvenirs and examining the first captured German garrison town they had so far met with. Marcoing had been the headquarters of a battalion and of a regiment, and contained engineer and ordnance stores. It has always been averred and believed that General von Kapelle's " gala " kit, iron cross, etc., etc., was found, and is " somewhere out of France," a fate shared by some imposing oil-paintings doubtless by " Kunstprofessoren " of fame in the home of " Kultur." It was not a bad time at first for the troops in reserve, but the firing about the north flank of the salient was disquieting, and it was patent to everybody that they were not relieved because there was nobody to relieve them. The weather became gusty, and rain and occasionally snow fell. On the 23rd German field guns registered, and from that day onwards both the " M.s." were under almost continuous shell fire. A valuable machine-gun officer of the 86th Machine-Gun Company fell in the person of Second Lieutenant A. H. Hosegood, who had done particularly well in the Monchy salient in April and May. The cellars and the wonderful catacombs which had sheltered the Germans on the 20th and part of the 21st were the only refuge, but it is wonderful how tired men will sleep in the most comfortless, crowded, and ill-ventilated surroundings when they can look back on 5,000 yards of new trenches dug, stepped, revetted, and wired. As railway construction was being pushed forward in the wide funnel of conquered ground, and Gouzeaucourt was in process of being rebuilt to provide a lodging for the reserve brigade of the Marcoing–Masnières sector, it seemed to the man at the front that those in authority expected the Germans to acquiesce in the general situation. The general feeling therefore was that we were there for the winter, and the main concern of the 29th was when were they going to be relieved. The G.O.C. was under no misconception regarding the weakness of the southern flank of the salient, and indeed made representations through corps regarding the 20th Divisional front's thinness ; but as the centre of gravity shifted to Bourlon, it looked to those in authority as though an undeniable risk had been amply justified and the weak southern flank of the salient could be put into a state of defence at leisure.

The Counter-attack

" On the Masnières front the 29th Division, composed of English, Scottish, Welsh, Irish, Guernsey, and Newfoundland battalions, although seriously threatened as the day wore on by the progress made by the enemy farther south, where their battery positions had been taken in reverse, most gallantly beat off a succession of powerful assaults and maintained their line intact."

So much for the 30th November.

" On the 1st December fighting continued fiercely on the whole front. . . . Severe fighting took place also at Masnières. During the afternoon and evening at least nine separate attacks were beaten off by the 29th on this front, and other hostile attacks were repulsed in the neighbourhood of Marcoing. . . . With the Bonavis ridge in the enemy's hand, however, Masnières was exposed to attack on three sides, and on the night of the 1st–2nd

December our troops were withdrawn under orders to a line west
of the village."

" Next day (*i.e.*, 2nd December) the enemy renewed his
attacks in great force on the whole front from Gonnelieu to Marcoing. . . . North of La Vacquerie repeated attacks made about
Masnières and Marcoing were repulsed in severe fighting, but
the positions still retained by us beyond the Canal de l'Escaut
were extremely exposed, and during the night our troops were
withdrawn under cover to the west bank."

These quotations from the official dispatches summarize
succinctly the main work done by the 29th in defending their
comrades Bourlon way, and, in effect, the Third Army. What
follows in amplitude is more of the nature of an answer to " how ? "
than to " what ? " The scene of the fighting to be described is
confined to the little quarter-circle of bridgehead front between the
Masnières–Cambrai road and the canal lock, by which the Hants had
crossed on the 20th, the village and environs of L.R.V., and a line
running up towards the Good Old Man on Welsh ridge in the
Hindenburg Support System and thence back north to Marcoing.
Excluded to all intents and purposes is the bridgehead west of
Masnières and the Cambrai road and enclosed by the sharp bend
of the canal.

On the 30th November the 88th Brigade were in reserve in
Marcoing. So were the K.O.S.B., the reserve battalion of the 87th,
who were holding the " bend " sector with the Borders on the left,
the R.I.F. on the right, and S.W.B. in support. The left sector
therefore contained two brigades.

The 86th occupied the Masnières or right sector with outposts
at Mon Plaisir Farm and the lock. The battalion, whose left rested
on the Cambrai road and faced Rumilly, was the 1st Lancashire
Fusiliers under Major T. Slingsby, M.C., and on their right the 16th
Middlesex under Lieutenant-Colonel J. Forbes-Robertson, D.S.O.
In support were the 2nd Royal Fusiliers under Major J. S. Hodding.
In the catacombs, out of which the last remnant of the Germans had
been extracted on the 21st, were the Guernseys under Lieutenant-
Colonel A. H. S. Hart Synnott, D.S.O., who was well backed up in
his arduous labours by Captain Wilson of the 16th Middlesex. The
brigade had relieved the 88th on the night of the 28th–29th, and were
the first to come into action. By 5 a.m., or shortly after, the whole
of the troops were standing to, ready for emergencies. As early as
7.30 movement was descried near Crèvecœur. By 8.40 it was
definitely reported that the two battalions in the line were being

heavily attacked, and that the brigade on the right were falling back. General Cheape was more concerned about his right flank than his front. He immediately sent half the Guernseys to L.R.V., and warned Captain Gee, his staff-captain, then in L.R.V., to inform the G.O.C. 87th of the situation, obtain help from him, and warn a detachment of Royal Engineers in L.R.V. By a most regrettable accident Major Deardon, the brigade-major of the 86th, had been recently wounded, and his place was taken by Captain Innes of the K.O.S.B., who proved himself a very worthy successor. Innes was sent off to warn the S.W.B. on the west of Masnières. Once there he manned all the bridgeheads west of Masnières. On his return Captain Innes reported Germans close to Marcoing, which it will be remembered lay two miles west of Masnières. The situation was now clear. The enemy was attacking on both sides of the Scheldt and its canal, and the anxious thought arose that, if he were at Marcoing, he would probably be nearer L.R.V. than was pleasant to contemplate.

However, the opportune arrival of Captain Gee in *propria persona*, wounded but triumphant, brought the good news that L.R.V., though once lost, had now been regained. The part that gallant officer played in that heroic recovery won him the V.C.—the twenty-third won for the division. In the opinion of his brigadier and G.O.C. he saved the brigade and possibly the division. There was every risk of the division being surrounded, and Colonel Kelly was not joking when, pointing at the masses moving up from Crèvecœur, he shouted to Captain Oliphant of the K.O.S.B., for the last year the versatile and efficient intelligence officer of the 87th, " You'll be eating brown bread in Germany to-night." This personal incident is therefore of the essence of the battle, and I give it in the words of Captain H. C. O'Neill, to be found in his excellent work, of which I have made frequent use, *The Royal Fusiliers in the Great War*. Captain Robert Gee belonged to that distinguished regiment.

" The 2nd Royal Fusiliers had come back into support on 28th November as counter-attack battalion ; and when the German assault began Y and Z Companies were lying about the sugar factory at Masnières, W was in the quarry, and X off the Cambrai road. Masnières was heavily shelled from 2 to 5 a.m., and at 6.15 the battalion stood to arms. At 7 a.m. the German attack from Crèvecœur made such rapid progress that the battery positions were taken in reverse, and the southern flank of Masnières was uncovered. X and Z Companies were quickly brought across the canal by the lock bridge near the sugar factory to form a defensive flank as far as the old brigade rear headquarters in Les Rues Vertes, while two platoons of X Company were sent to help in the street fighting. For the Germans had not only penetrated the suburb, but had even captured the ammunition dump. The troops, in point of fact, were called upon to defend a position which virtually had already been lost.

" Into this picture it is difficult to fit the achievement of Captain Gee, who won the V.C. for multiplied acts of daring that seem, on calm reflection, to outshine the inventions of writers of fiction. At 8.50 a.m. the position in Les Rues Vertes seemed to be lost ; and the amazing thing is that it was not abandoned. No one exactly knew where the Germans were, but they appeared to be everywhere, and certainly in the most inconvenient places. Captain Gee, who was then at brigade headquarters, was ordered by telephone to form a defensive flank with servants and headquarters details. He at once sent Captain Loseby with six men to get into touch with the right flank. Taking four signallers and two orderlies with him, he then set out to get a grip of the situation. But at the first corner firing was heard. A little farther on the Germans could be seen. With four of the men he opened fire, while the other two seized whatever came first—chairs, tables, etc.—to form a barricade. The enemy were held off for about five minutes, and then a Lewis gun came up, and there was time to breathe. The second house beyond the barricade was the brigade ammunition dump, full of small-arm ammunition, bombs, etc., and Captain Gee determined to get to it. He knocked a hole through the wall of a house on his own side of the barricade and crawled through to the first dump, only to find both dump men dead and the quartermaster-sergeant missing. He then climbed a wall to the bomb store, and was immediately seized by two German sentries. He had a bayonet (or rather an iron shod [ED.]) stick with him and a revolver, but he could not reach the latter, and in the struggle he killed one of the sentries with the stick while an orderly shot the other. He got back to the road again with a better realization of the desperate nature of the struggle. Some 30 or 40 men had now arrived. Half of them were sent to Captain Loseby, others were set to the task of building another barricade ; and with the six remaining, he recaptured the bomb store and cleared three houses. Two companies of Guernsey Light Infantry now arrived from brigade headquarters. These were sent to the uncovered flank, posts were established on the three bridges across the canal, and a strong company were sent to the outskirts of the village with orders to build a barricade and link up on the left.

" After this a bombing party was organized to set about clearing the houses on the Marcoing road. At this point the Germans' nerves appeared to wear thin, and they ran from house to house as the bombers got to work. Captain Gee, seeing that this part of his task appeared to be approaching completion, began to attend to the supply of ammunition and bombs to the troops across the canal and at the bridges. He then worked up to the château and through a hole in the wall into the brewery yard. The Germans had already left ; and it was evident that when the houses on the other side of the Marcoing road were cleared the village would again be in our possession. This task was handed on to a small party, and Captain Gee went up to the roof of the château to take stock of the position. The Germans were to be seen digging-in about 100 yards clear of the village. He at once got a supply of bombs, and with the help of another orderly he put the machine-gun team out of action and captured the gun. Another machine gun was in the house near the Crucifix. A Stokes gun was ordered up, and Captain Gee now saw that there were posts all round the suburbs.

" At the end of the village the men were still being troubled by a machine gun, and there were also numerous snipers at large. For a moment he had to take refuge in a shell hole ; but it was necessary to order up a Stokes gun before dark to deal with the machine gun, which was situated in a corner house. So he made a dash for the barricade, reaching it across the open in safety, but was caught in the knee by a sniper as he jumped the barricade. He had had four orderlies shot at his side, had been a prisoner for a few minutes, and had come through almost unprecedented risks. He wished now to carry on, but was ordered back to have his wound dressed."

It may now be stated briefly, if a digression can be pardoned, that the main attack on the north side of the canal broke entirely before the iron resistance of the Lancashire Fusiliers and the Middlesex, who that day lived up to the regimental name, " the Die Hards." If anything, on a day when all fought and none failed and there is nothing to discriminate, the latter battalion had the more fiery trial in the canal sector, which more directly faces Crèvecœur. Inspired by Colonel Forbes-Robertson, who, although temporarily blinded, was led round, cheering and directing the movements, particularly at the canal lock 700 yards south-east of Masnières, the Middlesex did not let the enemy get closer than 100 yards. The outposts also held out, and at the end of the day's fighting not a trench had been lost and great slaughter inflicted on the enemy.

But it is necessary to return to the broken flank and the perilous situation on the British side of the canal. Captain Innes had not exaggerated. About 8.30 a.m. reports reached Brigadier-General Lucas of Germans advancing in extended order over Welsh ridge in the direction of L.R.V. and Marcoing, where his headquarters were. General Cheape's message had evidently not got through, and it was not before 9.30, or so, that the seriousness of the situation emerged. There was only just time to turn out the headquarters personnel and man the south-eastern defences of the village, to enable the K.O.S.B. and the 88th to deploy and advance to the attack. The defences consisted of a sunk road, from which a deadly fire was poured on to the attackers. The little band, not content, advanced to the attack, took eight prisoners, and drove the remainder back. It was while gallantly supervising this timely and valuable operation that Captain Ewbank fell, a great loss to his battalion, brigade, and division, in all of which his sense of duty, trustworthiness, and courage were fully appreciated.

A little mixing-up of these hurriedly deployed units was bound to occur. Colonel Murray had headed for the northern slopes of Welsh ridge, and the K.O.S.B. were thus on the extreme right. Next them were the Hants ; next them the Worcesters. Then came the Essex, and on the left wing the N.F.L.D., who found touch with the S.W.B. on their left by the evening, when they lined the eastern end of the sunk road between Marcoing and L.R.V. They knew generally what was expected of them. Generals Lucas and Nelson had indeed received written orders, just as the men were turning out, from the G.O.C., through Colonel Moore the G.S.O. 1., to advance east at 10 a.m. But it seems as if the tactical instinct of the troops had led them to take the course in any event. For they were off before the actual orders could be explained to them. "All units," says General de Lisle, "working independently by platoons, advanced to the east instinctively, acting in accordance with the careful training they had received in ' Fire and movement.' The outskirts of the town were at once cleared, and the advancing Germans driven back 2,000 yards beyond the right flank of the 29th at L.R.V. These five battalions then linked up the 5,000 yards gap between this village and the left of the 20th Division, which had fallen back to the Hindenburg Support Line. This performance was the more creditable in that platoons and companies were mixed and that all units worked *without any orders and without control.* This time the brigade-major (Captain J. K. McConnell, 20th Hussars) rode on a barebacked transport horse up and down the line, but, in his own words, there was no need to interfere, for the general line and direction was perfect, and the accuracy of the ' fire and movement ' was as good as in a practice manœuvre."

On the right contact was obtained with the 20th Division, and the line now faced south-east from L.R.V. to the north-eastern spurs of Welsh ridge. With darkness things settled down into a fair defensive flank, but General Lucas reported he had no further reserves. The net result of the day's fighting was that the 29th held their own Masnières–Marcoing sector intact, and had formed a new line to join up with the next division on their right. The casualties were very heavy, and Captain McConnell was slightly wounded, and Captain P. Cuddon took his place. The 86th, surrounded on three sides, was in a precarious position.

Meanwhile, why had Colonel Moore come up at 9.30 a.m., and why did the G.O.C. direct an attack to the east ?

To enable this question to be answered, we must start the day afresh, this time five miles behind the front, at divisional headquarters, in the quarry at Quentin Mill near Gouzeaucourt. For some days, gunfire had been audible along the south-eastern front, but even the most wary found it difficult to believe that the Germans, after two and a half years on the defensive since the Marne, were going to launch a really dangerous attack without giving clearer warning. Something, it was agreed, was impending, and the line was none too strongly held on the southern side of the salient. On the morning of the 30th November the hostile gun fire, although heavier than usual, did not appear to indicate that an attack was imminent, and the general, who kept early hours, his A.D.C., Captain Nickalls, the G.S.O. II., Captain A. T. Miller, D.S.O., and Captain Croome, G.S.O. III., were finishing breakfast peacefully at 8 a.m., when a rude interruption disturbed the calm of the morning pipe. Some shells began to burst in the quarry, and a voice called out that the C.R.A., Brigadier-General E. H. Stevenson, D.S.O., was severely wounded in the knee. This was indeed the case, and he was carried into divisional headquarters. A few minutes later rifle fire at close range told its own tale to ears that had heard it in South Africa. Moreover, shells of a creeping barrage were now falling between the quarry and Gouzeaucourt, and the ground there was perfectly open and exposed to fire from the ridge. In the direction of the enemy, in the grey light of the morning the chalk downs were covered with men walking back. It was not unlike Epsom on a race day. It was evident that it was a question of flight through the barrage or capture. At the call of the G.O.C. all who could, chose the former alternative. General Stevenson had to be left behind in charge of an orderly, also wounded. It is satisfactory to be able to record that though the wave of hostile forces passed through and far beyond the quarry, it receded later before a masterly counter-attack by the Guards, and the C.R.A. and his orderly were rescued early on the following day. Captain Croome and several men were killed, to every one's deep regret, but the other officers reached Gouzeaucourt unhurt. They had run grave risks. In addition to the barrage, there was a machine gun sweeping the road, supplemented by rifle fire. Worst of all, three low-flying aeroplanes fired on all, who stopped for breath in shell holes. So close to the ground were these planes, that the faces of the firers could clearly be seen, as they leant over at the aim, or hunted for targets. A good many of those in that hurried flight were killed or captured, including the mess-waiter and some servants and cyclists. Many of the fleeing host were unarmed ; many didn't seem to want to use their rifles. One Lewis gunner had the unanswerable defence that he had no more ammunition. Captain W. J. Robson and three troopers of his regiment, the Northumberland Yeomanry, attached to the 29th as dispatch riders, sacrificed their lives in a superb but forlorn attempt to stop the enemy. " A gallant action to go straight at the Boche like that, when everybody else was going the other way," writes an eye-witness. With which sentiment every Borderer and every Briton will agree.

It is curious, but so hurried and short-lived was the German occupation of Gouzeacourt that nearly all the headquarters officers' kit was eventually found intact. Two stolid Suffolk lads of the R.A.M.C., then in Gouzeaucourt, finding themselves cut off but as yet unobserved, locked themselves into a cellar and said nothing about it. In the afternoon they emerged as cool as cucumbers. History does not say whether they smoked cigarettes while in hiding.

Gouzeaucourt was upside down with confusion. It was five miles behind the brigades on the Marcoing–Masnières line, and the troops there had to be warned. At all costs the 88th must protect the flank from L.R.V. to Welsh ridge. Colonel Moore, G.S.O., had returned from an early round of the line in a much damaged car. He was sent back post haste to give the orders to Generals Lucas and Nelson, as already recounted. Captain Nickalls was sent off in a car to warn the 20th, 6th, and 55th Divisional headquarters.

On his return Captain Nickalls organized the defence of the northern outskirts of Gouzeaucourt with the help of the transport personnel of the Durham Light Infantry and the West Yorkshire Regiment, and prevented the Germans from gaining a footing there. For his gallant action there Captain Nickalls was awarded the M.C. That done, the G.O.C. directed his attention to the defences of the straggling town of Gouzeaucourt. He was fortunate in discovering a company of Royal Engineers of another division. These he placed under Lieutenant-Colonel Biddulph, his own C.R.E., in the southern end of the town. As is well known, Gouzeaucourt was to all intents and purposes captured, and had to be recovered by the Guards. But it was the centre and northern part that the Germans took. The southern flanks, near which were two 8-inch guns, held out against them all the time. This post was reinforced later on by some men from the transport of the Durham Light Infantry and of the West Yorkshire Regiment under the adjutant of the latter and the quartermaster of the former. They did most excellent work.

Having reported the situation to the III. Corps, General de Lisle hurried off on foot to find out the situation at the front.

A curious feature of this day of excitement and surprises was the contrast between the calm and ignorance of one valley as opposed to the confusion and alarm of another. North of Gouzeaucourt, towards Villers-Plouich, the men working on the railway might have been at Albert. A number of the engineers working there were Americans. They were unarmed, but went into action —possibly the first organized body of Americans to do so—with picks and shovels. By the end of the day every survivor was armed with a Mauser rifle and a bayonet. The sight, which met the eyes of Major W. Raikes, officer commanding machine guns, and Captain Maurice (" Tim ") Healy, O.C. " unfits "—*i.e.*, 29th Divisional Reserve Company—on the main road between Sorel-le-Grand and Gouzeaucourt, was one long block of traffic, in places jumbled into inextricable confusion by the bursts of shells fired from a long-range gun. The stragglers, who poured in, showed no alarm. If they could be re-equipped, they were ready to fight. An officer of a certain standing (not of the 29th) " was shouting to somebody at the telephone, ' Tell them we will hold Welsh ridge to the last man.' Whose last man was not quite clear. I saw no signs of the officer's own command unless, indeed, he was O.C. stragglers."

The situation began to clear up. It was now realized that on something like a ten-mile front, from Crèvecœur at the bend of the Scheldt to Vendhuille on the same river, the Germans had broken through our front system, captured from south to north Villers-Guislain and Gonnelieu behind our original front line, and the Bonavis ridge, which had been won on the 20th November with the help of the tanks after the sanguinary struggle at Lateau Wood. La Vacquerie was threatened, the 20th Division was pushed back, and the Germans filtered through to the very edge of Marcoing. By the afternoon it looked as though the worst was over, but it was thanks to very gallant conduct on the part of certain troops that this result was brought about. The opportune drive of the Guards which cleared Gouzeaucourt and Quentin Mill, and swept up the heights to the east, is told elsewhere. The arrival of a brigade of cavalry was " the most welcome sight I saw all the war," says an eye-witness. But there was enough gallantry on the part of 29th men behind the actual front to fill, and more than fill, the space available in this volume.

First and foremost come the exploits of the divisional artillery. It is not often that the personnel of artillery have the opportunity of displaying individual acts of gallantry other than those connected with serving their guns in difficult circumstances. On the 30th November, however, the artillery showed that it could not be surpassed in individual acts of bravery. The following is an extract from the *War Record of the 29th Divisional Artillery* :—

" It was apparent about 09.00 (*i.e.*, 9 a.m.) that the enemy had broken through on the 20th Division front, south of the St. Quentin Canal. Considerable bodies of infantry of this division were now retiring through the 15th and 17th Brigade gun positions, and the enemy infantry was seen advancing over Welsh Ridge, close to the positions of the 17th Brigade.

" One battery of the 232nd Army Brigade was forced to abandon its guns, so the personnel was withdrawn, carrying away sights and breech-blocks.

" The 92nd and D/17 Batteries each ran a couple of guns out of their emplacements and engaged bodies of enemy on Welsh Ridge with open sights. Major Stanford, commanding 92nd Battery, having been wise enough to secure a Lewis gun for his battery, brought this Lewis gun to bear on the advancing enemy himself. Captain Booth also was busy with another Lewis gun which he commandeered from the retiring infantry.

" The fire of the 13th and 26th Batteries and of the two remaining batteries of the 232nd Army Brigade was directed on large numbers of the enemy seen approaching Masnières from the direction of Crèvecœur. At the same time Lieutenant-Colonel Burne, commanding 15th Brigade R.H.A., with the consent of the G.O.C. 86th Infantry Brigade, switched off to cover a gap on our right, and telephoned to the 17th and 232nd Brigades to ask them to cover the whole 29th Division front.

" Meanwhile, at the request of the G.O.C. 86th Infantry Brigade, Majors Eden and St. Clair, commanding the Warwickshire and B Batteries respectively, tried to stop the infantry retiring from Bonavis ridge, whilst the G.O.C. 86th Infantry Brigade made dispositions to cover his flank, which was now completely in the air. The infantry, however, refused to stop, saying that they had orders to retire to the Hindenburg Support Line. On this being reported to the G.O.C. 86th Infantry Brigade, the 15th Brigade was ordered to hold the gap with its guns. Lieutenant-Colonel Burne sent out flank observers and turned intense searching and sweeping fire on to the line of canal crossings from Crèvecœur to the lock east of Mon Plaisir Farm, where enemy cavalry and infantry were crossing.

" By 9.15 a.m. all the retreating infantry had retired through the guns of the 15th Brigade, and the batteries were left ' high and dry ' with no infantry in the vicinity.

" About 10.40 the leading lines of the enemy infantry came into full view of the 15th Brigade batteries. These lines were followed by small columns and machine guns. All guns of the 15th Brigade engaged the enemy with direct laying, and kept them off till about 11.10, by which time parties had worked round the flanks and were within 40 yards of the guns, firing kneeling at the gunners.

" Lieutenant-Colonel Burne then ordered withdrawal of the wounded, and the rest of the personnel with breech-blocks and sights, to the Hindenburg Support Line. L Battery remained in action to cover the retirement of the others, inflicted much damage on the enemy, and prevented heavy casualties occurring to the withdrawing personnel, who had to move up hill, heavily laden, in full view of the enemy for about 600 yards. The L Battery personnel then followed the others.

" The infantry holding the Hindenburg Support Line were not enterprising, and resisted Colonel Burne's efforts to persuade them to advance and recapture the guns, but eventually supplied an officer and 20 men with a Lewis gun to accompany him, two other artillery officers and eight N.C.O.s and gunners, to the left flank

of the gun positions.   This party took up a position covering the
former 15th Brigade Headquarters and wireless station, did a lot
of execution amongst the enemy, and enabled the headquarters
party to burn all maps and secret documents.   By 14.00 (*i.e.*, 2 p.m.)
the enemy had worked round the flanks, and the whole party withdrew to the Hindenburg Support Line.

" Meanwhile, the 92nd and D/17 Batteries assisted to hold the
enemy in check between Marcoing and Couillet Wood till about
11.30, when the 29th Division counter-attacked, with the support
of the guns of the 17th Brigade, drove the enemy back from Les
Rues Vertes, and established a line of defence."

The following letter from the late gallant Lieutenant-Colonel
E. R. Burne, R.A., to Major J. N. Diggle is a contemporary document of rare interest and importance :—

" You left just in time not to have lost all your kit.   We
eventually emerged with just what we stood up in.   A most thrilling
day, and we fought the Hun by ourselves for over an hour and a
half after those fellows on our right had come through us and gone
back.   We had to keep the gap as long as we could for the sake
of our division, who fought like tigers.   Great targets, masses of
Uhlans, etc., finishing up with columns of infantry at from 200
to 40 yards range.   Then I held on to a trench with the help of
a few infantry I could pick up.   My headquarters were captured
and recaptured, and we finally held it till ammunition ran out.   As
you can imagine, it was in parts a good show, and in parts not such
a good show.   I can't say much more, but the Hun main effort,
with ten fresh divisions, was stopped, though there were anxious
moments in our rear.   Our headquarters had a bit of a doing.   My
servant, groom, doctor, vet, both horses, and others, including the
R.S.M., gone West.   The batteries fought splendidly and escaped
fairly lightly owing to the way they stuck to it."

Small wonder when they were led by an officer of that spirit.
The 29th Divisional Artillery War Record also tells of the full
use Lieutenant R. W. Gascoyne-Cecil, O.C. X/29 Trench Mortar
Battery, made of his one mortar in the defence of Masnières and
his untimely death while fighting as an infantry officer later on in
the day.   It was an end worthy of a son of the noble and patriotic
house of Salisbury.   The other mortar had poured bursts at intervals
into L.R.V. until it was unfit for use.   Both mortars finished their

career by honourable burial in the canal, and the detachment joined
the 86th Brigade in the defence of the canal as infantry.

A private of the Royal Fusiliers just off leave was found trudging
along by Welsh Ridge to join his battalion in Masnières. An officer
told him it was hopeless to try and find his unit, which was probably
out of Masnières by this time, and with a wave of his hand indicated
a party of Germans in the low ground. All the man said was that
he would find his regiment where he left it; he then used a short,
unprintable expression conveying his disgust with the situation, fixed
his bayonet, and moved off in the direction of Masnières. One
wonders whether he ever got there. It was of such that the 29th
were composed.

Right in the rear a worthy M.M. was won by a veteran " unfit "
of sixty-two. How he got to France was a mystery, but as he
kept his health, and was only rebuked for disregard of his personal
safety, when in charge of salvage parties in Flanders, he had no
difficulty in staying there. This was Company Quartermaster-
Sergeant H. Sumner of Liverpool, who on the morning of the
30th was making his way with a salvage party towards Marcoing
when an excited artillery officer rode by, carrying a breech-block,
and at once ordered him to take his men back to Sorel. This, of
course, he had to do, but he gave a chance to five of his men to
slip off to Marcoing, where they acted as runners to the G.O.C. 87th
for the next two days. In order to get back to Sorel he had to pass
through the bottle neck under very heavy shell and machine-gun
fire. Not bad for sixty-two !

On the following day—i.e., the 1st December—the Germans
renewed their attacks on the Marcoing-Masnières position. But
the 29th, although weary and at less than half strength, hung
doggedly on. On the previous day a corps message had exhorted
them to " hang on at all costs." This is just what they were
doing. The length of line had been doubled, and the strength
of the brigade nearly halved by losses. The most intense shell fire
poured all day long into Marcoing. But it was Masnières and
L.R.V. that suffered most. There, four serious and four minor
attacks—minor only by comparison—were driven off in hand-to-
hand fighting. The two outposts of the 86th were driven in and
gone beyond recall, but as long as the canal crossings were ours
or covered by machine-gun fire under the competent leadership
of Major W. Raikes, and the bridgehead held, the loss of Mon
Plaisir was in itself not serious. The conduct of the 86th must
have been magnificent, remarked General Lucas at the time, and

it is not his way to fling about superlatives. The Commander-in-Chief wired to the G.O.C. 86th Brigade, expressing his gratitude to him and his brigade. The first attack at 7.45 a.m. was preceded by a most intense barrage of half an hour's duration. Captain Roberts and his machine-gun company, firing from a sugar factory, did tremendous execution among dense masses of the enemy caught in enfilade. Possibly 500 fell, and the German Red Cross were kept busy for the rest of the day. In the defence of L.R.V. the Stokes team and Captain Latham Brown of the 2nd Royal Fusiliers distinguished themselves. On the Cambrai road Lieutenant Corder did splendid work with a trench mortar barrage. A later attack on a huge scale took place after 2.30 p.m. An unprecedented barrage—" like nothing I have ever seen in France between 1914 and now," said General Cheape—broke out and laid Masnières and L.R.V. low. It lasted altogether for an hour and a half, but the last quarter of an hour was devoted exclusively to L.R.V. When the hellish din at length ceased and stock was taken of the situation, there was danger that the canal bridge nearest on the eastern side to Masnières would fall to the enemy, who had crept forward under the shelter of the barrage. Men were sent to deal with this party, and then the brigade-major (Innes) and a few Guernseys counter-attacked, and by dexterous revolver shooting and bayonet work cleared another party out of L.R.V. Captain Innes and his orderly, Private Martin, K.O.S.B. killed four and captured five Germans between them. " It was a real good show."

The Guernseys were joined by Captain Booth, R.A., who led them along the street south-west, capturing five of the enemy and clearing all the north end of the village ; he then proceeded with his party to clear the southern portion. On reaching the main Cambrai road a party of at least 20 was encountered. As it was now dark, Captain Booth went right up to within five yards of them to see who they were. On being challenged, they were found to be Germans armed with bombs, which they threw, wounding Captain Booth. The command of the party then devolved on Captain Craib, R.A., who, after ten minutes' hard fighting, drove the enemy back. It was due to the efforts of these two officers that the enemy finally retained only that portion of Les Rues Vertes which lies to the south of the main Cambrai road, and that the Advanced Dressing Station in the brewery, from which a large number of our wounded were finally evacuated, remained in our hands. Captain Booth unfortunately succumbed to his wounds.

The strength of the troops of the 29th in action had been reduced by 50 per cent. during these two days' fighting, and the extent of line held had been increased 100 per cent., from 5,000 to 10,000 yards of front. The resisting power of the 29th, therefore, was only 25 per cent. of its original strength; moreover, there was no reserve for the division, nor was any available in the III. Corps. It was therefore necessary to shorten the line by giving up the town of Masnières and " blunting the salient," so as to save 5,000 yards of front. Though this meant more fatigue to tired troops to dig the new line, and how tired they were no one can realize, who had not seen them, it provided a small reserve for emergency.

Towards the evening of the 1st December an incident, which Major W. J. Rice, R.A.M.C., has contributed, rivals the thrills of fiction. There was an advanced dressing station in a cellar at Masnières, in charge of which was Captain Fagan, M.C. The Germans were then in the village and made impossible Captain Fagan's task, which was to evacuate wounded men to the British lines, only a few hundred yards away. At the head of the stairs stood a sentry with rifle loaded and bayonet fixed. An orderly arrived at the top of the stairs with a cup of steaming coffee and invited the German sentry below to partake of it. Fritz yielded to temptation, deserted his post, went downstairs, took the coffee and, unwarily, a seat. In a moment he was seized from behind, disarmed and searched. Ultimately the sentry and some wounded Germans were left when Masnières was evacuated. By the brilliant presence of mind of the R.A.M.C. personnel concerned, all the British wounded were safely removed under cover of darkness.

It was as clear as day that the 86th could not stand another day like the 1st December, to say nothing of the 30th November. It was with full knowledge and approval of those in authority withdrawn, without accident or casualty. The wounded were evacuated. Not a sound was made. Next morning the Germans continued to shell Masnières and L.R.V., being still under the impression that they were occupied by us. The 86th then retired from the battle of Cambrai through the R.I.F. and S.W.B., weary, and thinned to breaking point, but covered with imperishable glory. It was after 3 a.m. when the brigadier and his acting-brigade-major bade farewell to Marcoing at 87th Brigade Headquarters. A glance at the map will show that the withdrawal from Masnières considerably shortened the line of the 88th, which now rested on the canal just east of the lock west of Masnières. Marcoing copse was still ours. Meanwhile the bridge-head in the Marcoing bend was contracted by the R.I.F. withdrawing its right

flank to the canal in touch with the 88th. These movements necessitated more digging by tired troops, whose relief was long overdue.

The 2nd December brought no large scale attack. Marcoing
was heavily shelled at intervals, and one direct hit in the mouth
of brigade headquarters dug-out killed four and wounded nine. The
R.I.F. easily repulsed hostile patrols. Word came that the 87th
were to be relieved by the 16th Brigade of the 6th Division. In
the end it was only the relief of the Borders and R.I.F. which was
effected, and it had dire consequences for the S.W.B. Such relief
as there was, was completed smoothly and expeditiously by 2 a.m.,
and brigade headquarters and the two battalions retired in two
hours to the Hindenburg Support Line south of Ribécourt.

The strain of this exhausting rearguard action on Brigadier-
General Nelson, then in a trench some 700 yards south-west of
Marcoing, was intensified, although a most keen and sympathetic
eye could glean nothing from his cheery wink on the 3rd except
dogged optimism and the power to endure even worse things. His
left was flanked by troops new to the position, who knew neither
its strength nor its weakness. It was possible that the necessity
to hang on, if not to the whole bridgehead, at any rate to the canal
bank, might not appeal so strongly to the newcomers as to those
who had, so to speak, lived themselves into the position, and knew
instinctively that for the divisions on the northern flank, unless
the whole line came back, Marcoing was of vital importance, while
its loss threatened complete destruction to the 88th and the attached
battalions. It was an awful moment when, on the morning of the
3rd, a heavy bombardment, affecting both sides of the canal, broke
out. The S.W.B. were practically annihilated ; on the 30th November their trench strength was 540, but on relief on the night 3rd–4th
December only 80 of all ranks could be mustered. One of the most
serious losses to that battalion was the death from wounds of
Major H. G. Garnett. Troops of the 6th Division stationed east
of the canal, in the bend formerly held by the 87th, were driven in,
and the left flank of the S.W.B. was thus exposed to a continual
and destructive enfilade fire from machine guns. It was a machine-
gun bullet that killed Garnett. The indefatigable medical officer
of the battalion, Captain Blake, R.A.M.C., saw to his burial that
night on the field of battle. The N.F.L.D. were nearly as badly
mauled. An isolated bit of trench previously held by them was
taken by the enemy, but in the main the line held firm, the net
result being that it touched the canal a little west instead of east
of the lock before mentioned. Things then quieted down, and at

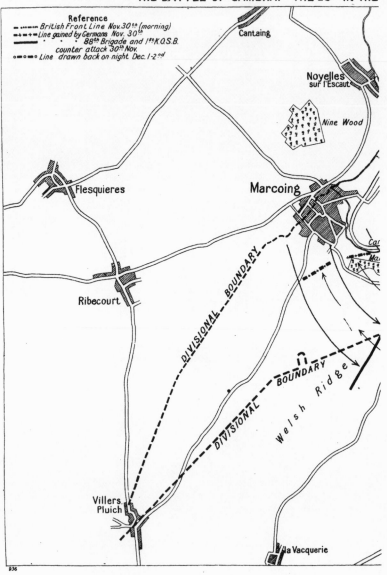

Reference
British Front Line Nov.30th (morning)
Line gained by Germans Nov.30th
88th Brigade and 1st K.O.S.B. counter attack 30th Nov.
Line drawn back on night Dec.1-2nd

Cantaing

Noyelles sur l'Escaut

Nine Wood

Flesquieres

Marcoing

Ribecourt

DIVISIONAL BOUNDARY

DIVISIONAL BOUNDARY

Welsh Ridge

Villers Pluich

la Vacquerie

936

THE COUNTER ATTACK   NOV.30ᵀᴴ DEC.5ᵀᴴ 1917

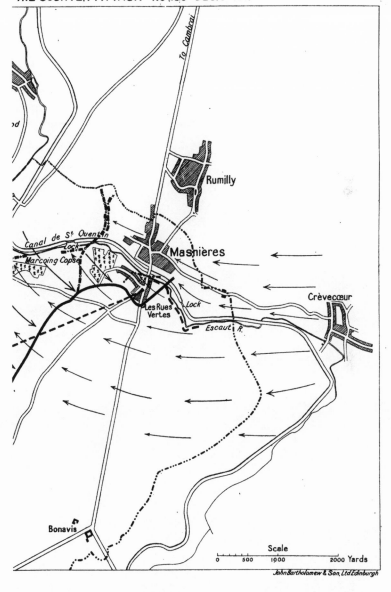

To Cambrai

Rumilly

Canal de St Quentin

Lock

Marcoing Copse

Masnières

Crèvecœur

Les Rues
Vertes

Lock

Escaut R.

Bonavis

Scale

0   500   1000   2000 Yards

John Bartholomew & Son, Ltd Edinburgh

night the remnants of the S.W.B. withdrew their wounded and themselves to Ribécourt. That night the line ran behind the south-west corner of Marcoing Copse.

Local opinion in the 29th was to the effect that but for the gallantry and initiative of Colonel Rosher, officer commanding one of the units of the 16th Brigade, things might have been even worse—in fact, a complete catastrophe. That officer, at a critical hour on the 3rd, collected as many men as he could lay hold of and posted them in the bend north of the canal to cover the bridges. By so doing he probably saved the situation.

The following story of an unknown warrior of the S.W.B. is characteristic of the fighting spirit of the 29th. When at about 11 a.m. the heavy bombardment was opened by the enemy and the front trenches were overrun, concentrated rifle and machine-gun fire was opened from our support trench to prevent the enemy from advancing farther. An officer in the trench was shouting for ammunition to be collected and passed along, when a shell hit the parapet of the trench and mortally wounded the man next to him. Although unable to speak, and almost unconscious, he managed to hand his bandolier to the officer and then died.

Such an example of the true fighting spirit deserves to be recorded, and it is my informant's lasting regret that in the heat of the action he was unable to ascertain the gallant fellow's name.

The German counter-attack was fizzling out. Some admirable staff work had cleared up the position at Marcoing and, after a comparatively peaceful day, the night of the 4th–5th saw the relief of the 88th and K.O.S.B. at dawn. As the whole army front fell back on to the Hindenburg Support Line the same night, it meant that a last dig-in on an outpost line was squeezed out of the 88th and K.O.S.B. That battalion was under orders to catch the train at Etricourt at midday on the 5th, a feat out of the question for many. But a good-sized body did follow Colonel Murray on this sixteen-mile march on the top of fifteen days of marching, digging, and fighting.

What follows is from the pen of General de Lisle :—

"On the night of the 4th, in accordance with the Army Order to shorten the line, the 29th withdrew from the canal to the Hindenburg Support Line, and when this had been occupied the division was relieved by the 6th Division. The troops crawled back slowly. Officers and men were gaunt, emaciated, and miserably weak, but filled with pride in themselves and in their comrades. They knew

that but for their stubborn resistance the flood from the east would
have passed over the gun positions of the artillery firing to the
north-west, where Bourlon Wood was being as heavily attacked.
They knew how necessary their sacrifice was to the remainder of
the Third Army, and they offered themselves without a murmur,
but they were desperately tired.   On being relieved, one brigade
commander (Brigadier-General Nelson, commanding the 88th
Brigade) collapsed and for three days was unconscious.   He did
not fully recover for six months."

After so terrible an experience, troops want time to recover,
time to get over their horror, the loss of comrades, etc., but the
great healer is the knowledge of having done their duty.   When
Brigadier-General Nelson awoke from his three days' collapse and
the division commander told him why he found himself in hospital
and not in his foul-smelling dug-out, he said : " I don't care what
happens to me now ; I have commanded the most wonderful troops
in the world, who have fought the best fight any man can see and
live.   I feel my career has been crowned."

It was this inward satisfaction that pervaded all ranks, though
they bitterly resented the rumours prevalent that the 29th had
given way before the weight of the German attack—a resentment
which was not entirely dispersed even by the message of high com-
mendation from all higher commanders, including the Commander-
in-Chief.

SPECIAL ORDER OF THE DAY
by
Major-General Sir BEAUVOIR DE LISLE, K.C.B., D.S.O.,
commanding 29th Division.

I wish to express to the troops of my division my high
appreciation of their gallant conduct and resolute determination during the operations from November 20 to December 4,
1917, and to convey to all ranks the following messages received
by me.

From Lieutenant-General Sir W. PULTENEY, K.C.B., K.C.M.G.,
D.S.O., commanding III. Corps.

" The corps commander would like to place on record his
deep appreciation of the fighting spirit of the 29th Division.
The magnificent defence of the Masnières–Marcoing line at

a most critical juncture and the subsequent orderly withdrawal reflects the highest credit on all concerned.

" In the fifteen days in which your division has been in
action on this front all ranks have displayed an endurance
which is beyond praise.

" He would be glad if this could be conveyed to your
troops."

From General Sir JULIAN BYNG, K.C.B., K.C.M.G., M.V.O.,
commanding Third Army.

" I would like to express to all ranks my sincere appreciation of the services which have been rendered to the Third
Army by the 29th Division.

" Both in the attack on November 20, 1917, and in their
defence of their sector on the 30th November and subsequent
days, the division has more than maintained its splendid
reputation.

" I ask you to accept my warmest congratulations."

From Field-Marshal Sir DOUGLAS HAIG, K.T., G.C.B., G.C.V.O.,
K.C.I.E., Commander-in-Chief, British armies in France.

" Please convey to General de Lisle and men of the 29th
Division my warm congratulations on the splendid fight successfully maintained by them against repeated attacks by
numerically superior forces. Their gallant defence of Masnières
throughout two days of almost continuous fighting has had
most important results upon the course of the battle, and is
worthy of the best traditions of the British army."

CHAPTER V

" A gulf profound as that Serbonian bog,
Where armies whole have sunk."

THE 29th received a parting gift from the enemy in the shape of
a shower of shells on and around the railway track on which they
were—well, not quite speeding. One engine was struck and over-
turned, and delay was thereby caused. But it's a long journey
that has no terminus, and in due course divisional headquarters
settled down in Cauroy in the familiar Arras rest area, the battalions
being dotted about at such pleasant spots, normally, as Lucheux,
Liencourt, Grand Rullecourt. But the weather was cold, snow
often fell, and a good roof meant more than pretty country. On
the 6th December, when the weary warriors were still sleeping
off the fatigue of their recent ordeal, and were indifferent alike to
" fire " or " movement," word came round that on the 9th all must
start for Hazebrouck to join the Second Army. Probably the
arrangements had been made on the hypothesis that the relief of
the 29th was to take place on the 21st November! As the relief
was a fortnight overdue, a move on the 9th was out of the question.
General Headquarters saw reason, and a week more was spent
resting and training. On the 8th the various brigade and battalion
commanders read out to their units the orders quoted in the last
chapter. On the 10th the G.O.C. went home on a month's leave,
and Brigadier-General Lucas reigned in his stead. The R.I.F.
were still minus Colonel Sherwood-Kelly, in hospital at Tréport,
after a collapse from over-strain, when the fight finished. Sir
George Stirling was acting for Brigadier-General Nelson as
officer commanding 88th Brigade. Some ceremonial parades were
held. For instance, on the 18th the K.O.S.B. received a short
eulogy from the acting G.O.C. for what was unquestionably their
finest five days' work in a noble war career.

By the 16th the drafts sent to replace the 5,400 casualties sustained at Cambrai had been received, if not absorbed, and the division moved northwards, marching *via* Hesdin on the Canche, Warmin, etc., to the Wizerne area, a few miles from St. Omer. Snowy conditions made the long march a rather trying experience for the troops. Some cars were actually held up. Altogether it was very Christmaslike, and by the time the men had settled down and eaten on Christmas Day an excellent dinner, they were in that cheery mood which made a visit from the VIII. Corps commander, Sir Aylmer Hunter-Weston, a complete success. The general had never ceased, and does not cease, to take an interest in the old 29th, and this was a very special occasion. In high military circles the value of the fight put up by that division at the canal was thoroughly appreciated. Moreover, it had come into the VIII. Corps once more, and so was under the orders of its first leader in battle.

The period at Wizerne was spent in training, and in spite of adverse weather, battalions and brigades carried out some excellent manœuvres. To some it may seem strange that in the intervals of operations during a great campaign so much attention to training was necessary. It must be remembered, however, that in the 29th the average casualties amounted to 100 per cent. every six months. New men and new officers were continually arriving, and could only be properly " absorbed " during these rest periods. This process of absorbing depended on mutual confidence between officers and men, the selection of the most suitable as leaders of sub-units and as specialists. The qualifications of individuals, officers and other ranks, could be arrived at only during training ; and when battalions and companies had absorbed the new drafts, it was vitally important that units should learn to work as a team. This art can only be learnt at manœuvres where situations likely to occur in face of the enemy are practised with blank ammunition.

Then it was a case of " back to the slime " and the region of uncouth names, which needed very little alteration by a R.A.M.C. wag to serve suitable names for the casualty-clearing stations near Proven. Mendinghem, Bandaghem, Dosinghem are good English, and also colourable place names for West Flanders.

On January 18, 1918, the 29th took over the Passchendaele salient. This sector had not materially altered since captured in October. The defences consisted of shallow slits without communications and without wire. The dead of friend and foe still lay unburied, and supporting lines or reserve positions did not exist. It was not a pleasant situation, but the only solution was hard work to put the sector in a proper state of defence and in a sanitary condition.

The outlook was unpromising. At this time the staff of the division had been almost completely changed. Of the four brigadier-generals, three were new since the Cambrai fighting. The three general staff officers and the C.R.E. were also newly appointed.

However, all went well. The new officers quickly acquired the spirit of the division, and in Brigadier-Generals Jackson of the Borders, Freyberg, V.C., of the 63rd Division, and Johnson, R.A., the 29th had the good fortune to receive three very exceptional leaders.

The work of preparing defences was exceptionally arduous. The whole area had been churned up by shells into craters which were full of water, and in some places these craters were over-lapping and the soil like a morass, so before any digging was possible, extensive draining had to be undertaken.

On the 12th February, the 29th handed over the sector to the 8th Division (Heneker) and moved back to the rest area at Steenworde. Prior to being relieved, the 29th lost that excellent battalion, the 1st Royal Inniskilling Fusiliers, which was sent to join the 16th Irish Division. The 1st Essex also left the division on the reduction of brigades to three battalions, a measure necessitated by the want of drafts to fill up the losses incurred in France in 1917. To fill the cup of bitterness of separation, the 16th Middlesex shared the fate of the 5th Royal Scots. They disappeared and were disbanded. They had done right well by their regiment and division. The three weeks in the rest area were spent as usual in ceremonial parades, lectures, and manœuvres, and the 7th March found the 29th again holding the Passchendaele salient, which by now was more capable of defence.

It was well known that the Germans had concentrated a large striking force in the Western Front with a view to making one last bid for victory. Though the Intelligence Branch were confident that this great attack would be directed against the right of the British line, all formations had to prepare for subsidiary attacks, as the Germans were tapping all along the line to discover any weak places, and to mystify us as to the real point of their proposed attack. Though the defences at Passchendaele were by no means ideal, they were now capable of defence, and the German minor operation on 11th March on a two-battalion front collapsed in front of the opposition of the 2nd S.W.B. and the 4th Worcesters. The only Germans who crossed our wire came in as prisoners.

On this day Major-General Sir Beauvoir de Lisle left the 29th to command the XIII. Corps after having commanded the division since June 1915, and a few days later Major-General Douglas Cayley, who had led the 88th Brigade so long, arrived to take over the command.

The suddenness of the parting took the division's breath away. The 29th without de Lisle was difficult to imagine. They had got to know one another, and had broken the ice. They saw the heart behind the reserve, the method behind the fatigues and practices. If the general had the ordinary human capacity of being afraid, he had discovered some wonderful way of concealing it. For no one had ever seen him different in his manner when in a hot place from what he was on parade. He was a man who gave his confidence very slowly. The confidence in him was equally no mushroom growth. Once established, it went on growing and growing. The mere announcement, at one stage of the Lys fighting, that he had taken over the XV. Corps, in which the 29th were then serving, was enough to stimulate the *moral* of those who heard it. The news was passed along : " de Lisle's our corps commander. It's all right." There is also the yarn, apocryphal possibly, but symbolically true of the "Tommy," who, after answering questions as to who his divisional brigade and battalion commanders were, with the usual "Dunno, sir," was asked, "Well, you must know this. Who's your company commander ? " The answer was affirmative, immediate, and explicit—" de Lisle." Strange but true ! There were many sad hearts in the humblest ranks at parting from a stern disciplinarian and martinet. They knew him, for he would turn up at times when things were none too comfortable in the line. The sight of him conferring with company officers and the commanding officer, dressed in his tin hat with the same regulation gas mask they all wore, was a reassuring spectacle for the garrison in the trenches or isolated posts. Nor could the general leave his division without emotion.

The following farewell order was issued by General de Lisle, whose departure was sudden, and who was unable to visit the units. Before leaving his headquarters he was received by a guard of honour of an officer and 12 men from every battalion, and on his way to Poperinghe the 86th Brigade turned out spontaneously from their reserve camp and lined the road, an act that deeply affected their old commander.

SPECIAL ORDER
by
Major-General Sir BEAUVOIR DE LISLE, commanding
29th Division.

On being removed from the command of the 29th Division after nearly three years, I wish to express to all ranks my high appreciation of their distinguished services during this period, and to thank them for the loyal support they have given to me at all times.

During this time the work of the 29th Division has been beyond all praise.

The division has been congratulated by both Commanders-in-Chief, and all army commanders and corps commanders under whom it has served.

Some of its achievements will be quoted in military history by future generations, but the highest honour it has hitherto won is the fact that in the past three years this division has never lost a trench that it has not immediately regained, and no unit has ever failed to do its duty.

I find it difficult to express my regret at leaving a body of troops of which I am so proud and which I have loved so well.

I regret that time does not admit of my visiting each unit to bid farewell, and I must do so in this Special Order of the day.

BEAUVOIR DE LISLE,
Major-General.

YPRES, *March* 11, 1918.

PART II—THROUGH TRIBULATION TO VICTORY

CHAPTER I

THE LYS

" Our backs are to the wall."

IN March 1918 Major-General Sir Beauvoir de Lisle, on promotion to the command of a corps, gave up the command of the 29th Division, which he had held for nearly three years. Under him the division had fought continuously with the greatest gallantry, and had been brought to a very high state of efficiency. His loss was much felt by all ranks. He was succeeded in command by Major-General D. E. Cayley, who, as a battalion and brigade commander, had done very nearly the whole of his service in the war with the 29th Division, so that he, if any one did, knew and appreciated the splendid spirit which this division had ever shown at all times and in all circumstances of victory or failure.

At this time the division was in the VIII. Corps, commanded by Lieutenant-General Sir Aylmer Hunter-Weston, the original commander of the division in the Gallipoli campaign, and was holding the Passchendaele sector of the defences north of Ypres. No one who had not seen this sector at the beginning of 1918, after the continuous fighting and bombardments of the previous summer and autumn, can conceive the scene of appalling desolation and destruction which the countryside afforded. It was almost an impossibility to dig trenches in that water-logged ground, so that approaches to the front line could only be made over duck-board tracks, many of which were fully visible to the enemy and in consequence by day were scarcely usable, and by night were under constant artillery and machine-gun fire. The truth is that our advance in the previous autumn had stopped short by a few hundred yards of where it should have reached, with the result that our forward system was under close direct observation of the enemy. In addition, the line held was a very pronounced salient, so that fire could be brought against it from flanks and almost from the rear. Few of those who underwent them will forget the discomforts and general beastliness of this time. It was a bad preparation for sudden and strenuous exertion in battle. The enemy were, or were soon to be, fully engaged farther south in the battle for Amiens, so that on the whole the sector was a quiet one, though a continuous and steady artillery fire was kept up on communications. One or two hostile raids were attempted without success, and were repulsed with loss on different occasions by the 2nd S.W.B. and the Royal Guernsey Light Infantry. Our expectation at this time was that on any day at the shortest notice we would be withdrawn and put into the Amiens battle ; and our fear was that we should be put into the battle piecemeal and in a hurry, with no chance of getting straight after leaving these horrible trenches. This is indeed what happened, but it was to stem the new German offensive on the Lys, and not farther south, that our efforts were required.

On 9th April, as a result of a heavy and successful German attack on the Armentières front, the division was ordered to move at once to the XV. Corps, at that time commanded by General du Cane, on that front. The brigades were taken straight from the line without rest. The 87th Brigade, commanded by Brigadier-General G. H. Jackson, embussed that night at Poperinghe, followed by the 86th (Brigadier-General R. Cheape) on the next morning, and arrived about Neuf Berquin (between Merville and Estaires) in the course of the next day, the 10th. The 88th Brigade (Brigadier-General B. Freyberg) were still in the trenches and not yet relieved. It was a fortnight before we saw them again. The divisional artillery (Brigadier-General R. M. Johnson) was left behind in its old positions.

The divisional commander arrived in the Lys area early on the morning of the 10th, and found a considerable state of confusion and uncertainty as to the situation. All roads were much congested and blocked with refugees flying before the German advance. Many pitiful scenes were witnessed, as the people in this part had been living in comparative peace since the autumn of 1914, and had never thought it likely that they would again be overwhelmed by war. Their rage against the Portuguese was intense, and the divisional commander on more than one occasion saw unfortunate soldiers of that nation being violently assaulted by women.

At this time the enemy was still held on the line of the Lys, except that he had effected a crossing at Bac St. Maur farther to the left, and was moving towards Steenwerck. It was reported that we had a force about La Crèche advancing to oppose this movement. The 86th and 87th Brigades were moved across in the afternoon to clear up the situation in this direction, and to join hands if possible with the La Crèche force. It was hoped that the crossings of the river at Merville and Estaires would be firmly held, so that our right flank would be secure. But they were captured by the enemy during the night. It resulted that, as no touch was obtained with the La Crèche force, which appears never to have got properly under way, the two brigades were more or less isolated with both flanks exposed. A rearguard action therefore had to be fought.

The enemy attacked strongly on the morning of the 11th, and a gradual retirement was made in the direction of Doulieu. Casualties were heavy as position after position was turned. After a comparatively quiet night, the retirement was continued on the 12th, under constant hostile attacks, through Bleu to a position about Vieux Berquin. There was very little artillery available to cover the infantry retirement, which made the task of keeping off hostile attacks all the harder. Apparently there was a big dump of ammunition in Bleu, which was exploded by a lucky shell after we had evacuated the place, and this explosion materially delayed the enemy's advance at a critical time when units were in considerable confusion.

It was on this day that Lieutenant-Colonel J. Forbes-Robertson, D.S.O., who was commanding the 1st Battalion Border Regiment, began the series of exploits which gained him the V.C.

The following graphic account of Colonel Forbes-Robertson's deeds is from the pen of Captain J. C. Ogilvie, who writes :—" At dawn on the 11th April the regiment found itself grouped in a number of small farms in front of the Meteren Becque, after an all-night movement at right angles to the Neuf Berquin–Estaires road, which had added considerably to the topographical confusion present in most of our minds on this new and very uncertain front. The country was a confusion of small farms and fields enclosed by overgrown hedges, scattered areas of dense wood, and divided by heavily treed roads. The day opened in perfect stillness and dense fog, but out of the fog arrived the Boche with trench mortars and machine guns mounted on lorries. Every farm was subjected to intense fire at close range. Colonel Forbes-Robertson, realizing the critical state of affairs, mounted and rode alone from farm to farm, utterly regardless of his personal safety, and organized an effective defence.

That done, he rode out to the left, where he found the flanking battalion already in retirement, having lost its entire headquarters staff
and most of its officers.   Taking command of the whole situation he,
personally, and in full view of the enemy, organized a slow fighting
retirement in the general direction of Bleu village and Doulieu.
By nightfall the troops under his command had only lost some
900 yards of ground.   In the darkness the light from the burning
farms showed the Germans to have passed our undefended right
flank, and to have entered Neuf Berquin.   On the left, everything
was indefinite as, in spite of repeated personal reconnaissances,
Colonel Forbes-Robertson had been unable to gain touch with any
British troops.   During the night he personally guided the remainder
of his troops to a line in and around Bleu village, where dawn
of the 12th found us once again under direct close range trench-
mortar and machine-gun fire.   Here the remainder of the two
battalions, some 150 all told, remained until the night, and here the
heaviest fighting of the three days took place.   The mud and
wattle farm buildings gave no protection, and all through that
day Colonel Forbes-Robertson rode round from building to building
encouraging and directing each man individually.

"Between Bleu and Vieux Berquin was an open space of 800
yards, constantly swept by machine-gun and rifle fire.   Across this
Colonel Forbes-Robertson rode, and back across it he walked, his
horse having been shot under him, with the cheering news that a
company of Irish Guards was holding on in Vieux Berquin.   It was
the first cheering news that we had had for two days, and it gave
all of us renewed strength.   That night Colonel Forbes-Robertson
again spent superintending and guiding a personally conducted
retirement to the railway cutting in front of Mont de Merris, where
the Australians found him at dawn with the survivors of his two
battalions.

"During three days and nights of constant infantry and machine-
gun fighting, Colonel Forbes-Robertson by his wonderful soldiering
had, with a handful of troops, retired a distance of 6,000 yards, and
brought the German advance on that particular front to a standstill.

"Had it not been for the extraordinary gallantry, the cheery
leadership, and the compelling personality of Colonel Forbes-
Robertson during those days and nights of confused fighting, it is
difficult to conjecture what might have happened.   His superb
courage and dogged optimism, his apparent omnipresence, and his
undoubted control of the very difficult situation, bound to his
person all the troops he had collected under his command.   On

MAJOR-GENERAL D. E. CAYLEY, C.M.G., D.S.O.

foot and on horseback, he personally directed every step of the retirement. There was no sending of orders ; he carried them himself. Time after time he was ' missing ' for varying periods, only to turn up again, having been prowling round one or other of the undefended flanks. Those of the division who were privileged to know him will readily understand the cheering effects of feeling lost and turning round to see old Forbes trudging up to you leading a wounded, half-foundered horse, and to hear his cheery voice swearing and laughing, bringing news of how ' this ' company was doing, and how So-and-so was getting on ; a quiet ' pow-wow ' on the whole situation, and off he went to the next post, leaving the finest feeling of confidence and companionship behind him."

Could there be a finer tale of gallantry ? No V.C. earned in the war was better deserved.

General Jackson, who commanded his brigade, adds a note. " Forbes had been dull and morose all the morning, but brightened up as things got worse. When they were really bad, he brightened up a lot, borrowed a horse (not his own, as he considered his old dun mare too good to risk), and said to one or two of his headquarters, ' The time has now come for me to take a hand.' "

By the night of the 12th the two brigades had got back to a line about Vieux Berquin, with their right on the Hazebrouck-Estaires road, and their left about the Bailleul railway in front of Strazeele station by Lyndé Farm. This position was consolidated, and held all next day, the 13th, against numerous attacks, though their flanks, especially the left, were uncovered by the retirement of other troops. Meanwhile the 1st Australian Division, which had come up from the south, had dug a trench line from the Forêt de Nieppe to Meteren. After nightfall the two brigades were withdrawn behind this line, and their stupendous ordeal of three days and nights of continuous fighting against a strongly superior enemy was ended. The fighting strength of these two brigades after the battle was found to be not much over 500 men.

A few incidents of the battle are worth recalling. On the night of the 13th a good many did not receive the orders for retirement. Lieutenant-Colonel G. T. Raikes of the 2nd S.W.B. (who hurried back from leave and joined in the middle of the battle) and Lieutenant-Colonel Wilson of the 2nd Royal Fusiliers, found themselves with a party with no one on their flanks. So word was passed down the line that in an hour's time the order would be given to " left turn," when every man would rise, turn to his left, and follow the man in front of him. The plan worked all right, and at the end of the hour a snake of men were trailing across what was then Boche country, headed by the two commanding officers, with a servant and another man as advanced guard. Without further adventure or mishap the whole party got themselves safely behind the Australian line.

The following was another incident of the same nature. Captain Lockwood, of the Lancashire Fusiliers, with a handful of men, held the extreme right of the divisional line. As related above, after nightfall, their task being accomplished, the division was ordered to withdraw. But the orders failed to reach this party. A critical situation arose, as it was discovered that the enemy were on both flanks and in the cemetery not a hundred yards to the front. But in the absence of orders Captain Lockwood determined to hold on, which he did, keeping the enemy back till all ammunition was exhausted, and inflicting considerable losses on them. He realized then that a retirement was necessary, and most skilfully withdrew his whole party, including several wounded men, behind the Australian line, which was reached just before dawn.

In another part of the field the bulk of the London Field Company Royal Engineers had been detached on the evening of the 10th towards Merville. When the enemy crossed the river there that night, this party found themselves completely isolated. But there was no thought of sudden retirement, to get themselves out of their difficult position. On the contrary, they took up a position to prevent the Germans debouching from Merville, and held them up for a considerable time. When eventually forced back, after severe casualties, they continued to fight a rearguard action on their own for the next two days, suffering and inflicting severe losses. All the officers but one of this gallant company were killed or wounded, and well did it earn the three Military Crosses and three Military Medals awarded it.

There were, of course, a good many lighter incidents during the battle. One related by Brigadier-General Cheape is as follows.

During one of the nights of the battle, while digging in, they heard the Germans killing a pig in a farm through which they had recently retired. A patrol was sent out, and, completely surprising the Germans, " jumped " the farm, and left several dead Germans to keep company with the dead pig. History does not relate what happened to the pig.

A familiar face, especially in the 86th Brigade, was that of Captain Harding, the quartermaster of the Royal Fusiliers, who had been with his battalion during the whole war. On the evening of

the 12th, when the battle seemed to be at its most desperate, and
the line had got to Vieux Berquin, he suddenly appeared right up
in the firing line with his transport and rations, apparently quite
unconcerned, and bucking every one up by his cheerfulness and by
the food he brought to his beloved battalion. It really was a
wonderful feat of energy and initiative on his part to find the
battalion as he did, and doubtless the thought that they were being
well looked after was the greatest encouragement to the men in the
difficult time they were going through.

Major W. Raikes, second in command of the 29th Machine Gun
Battalion (which did magnificent work all through the battle),
provided a comic element. He had had many adventures in
the three days, and fallen into various ditches, wire fences, etc., so
that he was caked with mud and almost without clothes before the
end. However, he managed to find a pair of French *poilu's* trousers,
and eventually came out of action and reported himself to the
divisional commander clothed in them and not much else except
mud.

The 87th Brigade had to change their headquarters seven times
during the battle, being shelled out in most cases. On one occasion
the brigadier and his brigade-major, Festing, who were the last of
the headquarters party to leave, had to retire through the back
window of the farm they were occupying, taking the telephone with
them, as the Boche was just entering the front yard. They were to
be seen trying to move across country, hedges, and deep ditches, in
an apparently leisurely manner, though really in a desperate hurry
to get clear.

On one occasion Colonel Forbes-Robertson helped his battalion
most materially by the matter-of-fact way in which he organized
an issue of beer to the men in a hamlet through which they were
retiring. The business was organized in a few minutes, and, as can
be imagined, the idea of the thing, as much as the actual beer, had
a wonderfully steadying effect on his men. It should be added that
he himself with his headquarters party and a Vickers gun or two
covered the battalion while the issue was going on, so enabling
every one to drink his beer undisturbed.

An Advanced Dressing Station had been established in Vieux
Berquin in the school, on the 11th April, in charge of Major Fiddes,
R.A.M.C. Captain M. F. Healy, who was commanding the Divi-
sional Employment Company, writes as follows :—

" In a very few minutes the principal rooms were cleared out
and fitted up for hospital use. On one side we put a waiting room

for stretcher cases, and a treatment room on the other side of the
court ; also two rooms for sitting and walking cases. The wounded
began to come in pretty thickly after a short time. But cars began
to fail, and at one time we had 40 stretcher cases without any means
of evacuating them."

After great trouble, largely on the part of Captain Healy himself,
this problem was solved.

" On the 12th the Boche decided to choose the school as a target.
A whole battery of 5.9s opened on us by volleys. Anything from
thirty to fifty shells came over in bunches of four or five at a time.
The houses on either side were totally destroyed, all our windows
were blown in, splinters rained down all around us. Major Fiddes
decided to get out. Quietly and coolly four men took each stretcher
and started to cross country towards Strazeele station. The sitting
cases were carried, the walking cases were helped. Stores were
coolly packed up by the R.A.M.C., the final touch of swank being
supplied by one man, who produced a brush and swept out the
room. He might have spared his pains, for as fast as he swept
the falling shells scattered the dust again. Thanks to this excellent
coolness we all reached Strazeele station without hurt."

Captain Healy mentions that wine was there in abundance at
the hand of every man, but not a man was so much as flushed with
drink, and all seem to have contented themselves with a voluntary
ration of about half a glass a man. This was a particularly creditable performance.

The dressing station was moved that night to Pradelles, and on
the morning of the 13th to Rouge Croix.

" Here we established ourselves in a farm deserted by all except
a very old man, whose one anxiety was to know exactly when it
would be necessary to turn loose the animals (apparently their own
instinct was to carry them away from the Boche). We all wanted
eggs and milk, so I gave the old man 50 francs as an indemnity,
which, to his credit be it said, he did not want to take. I think the
old chap considered he had made a good bargain, but he reckoned
without his host. Later on in the day a scavenging party arrived
from some French troops in the vicinity, and in the most shameless
way they took every hen in the place, cut its head off, and walked
off with the carcasses. The old man seemed quite indifferent, but
I suppose he considered this better than letting the Boche get
them.

" We remained till the 14th, when, the division having been
relieved, we packed up. We came out with the knowledge that

every wounded man who had succeeded in getting as far as a Regimental Aid Post had been safely evacuated, though in four days it had been necessary to change the site of the dressing station four times. Roads were choked with on-coming guns and troops and retreating refugees ; ambulances were scarce and casualties were heavy. But coolness and courage were plentiful, and succeeded in adding a very fine page to the record of Royal Army Medical Corps devotion during the present war."

Meanwhile, not so far to the north of Estaires the 88th were heavily engaged. They had been relieved in the Ypres area by the 123rd Brigade of the 41st Division on the 9th–10th April, and had reached St. Jans-ter-Biezen, about 3 miles west of Poperinghe, partly on foot and partly by train, only to learn that the situation did not admit of rest and billets, but, on the contrary, that they must start at once for Bailleul and the Lys. At first it was thought that their destination was the 29th, then engaged in the battle of Estaires. On reaching Bailleul they learned they were under orders to reinforce the 34th Division, commanded by Major-General Sir Lothian Nicholson, K.C.B., C.M.G., then fighting a rearguard action in the course of the retreat from Armentières towards Bailleul.

The 34th had been deeply involved in the Somme fighting of the great German offensive of March 1918, and had suffered more than 3,000 battle casualties. By the end of the Battle of Bailleul (in which they, along with the 88th, were now engaged) the division was so depleted in strength that it temporarily ceased to exist.

When the 88th, after a brief period under orders of the G.O.C. 25th Division, came under Sir Lothian's orders at 11 a.m. on the 11th April, the 34th had been compelled through sheer weight of numbers and exposed flanks to fall back astride the road and the railway, which connect Armentières with Bailleul. At Nieppe, on the road, an attempt at a stand was made, but the tired Northumbrians, as sturdy a lot as ever left the banks of the Tyne, who formed two of the three brigades of the 34th (the remaining brigade being composed of two service battalions of the Royal Scots and the 11th Suffolks), were unable to hold their ground owing to " enemy progress in the Ploegsteert sector," and were obliged to fall back through the 88th, who held a line between Steenwerck station and Pont d'Achelles, 2,000 yards north-west of Nieppe.

On the morning of the 12th fighting waxed severe. Pressure on the left flank, occupied by the Monmouths, caused two companies of N.F.L.D. to be summoned from reserve to fill a gap. The line then

held by the brigade was 5,000 yards wide, an unusual extent even
for a strong brigade. And this was a weak one. All along this
thinly held line a fierce bombardment rained. On the right the
Worcesters and the Hants on the left of them held tenaciously to
their position between La Crèche and Steenwerck station. General
Freyberg specially mentions their steadfastness on this critical
occasion. On the left the Monmouths, weary after digging in four
times in twenty-four hours, a heavy task even for pioneers, were
pushed back until supported at first by one and later by a second
company of N.F.L.D. As the afternoon wore on the enemy made
a determined attack in overwhelming force and engulfed a platoon
of N.F.L.D. under Lieutenant Moore, but not before the timely
face to the flank directed by that gallant officer had taken heavy
toll of the Germans and extracted the sting from the attack.

About 6 p.m. Captain C. S. Strong led a counter-attack with
the two reserve companies of the N.F.L.D. The men responded
with the ardour of those who, since the beginning of February 1918,
had been entitled to say that they belonged to the " Royal " Newfoundland Regiment. His Majesty King George V. had been
pleased to allow the Newfoundland Regiment to prefix Royal,
in token of the " magnificent bravery of all ranks." The situation was steadied at De Seule, three-quarters of a mile north-
west of Pont d'Achelles. Unfortunately Captain Strong was
mortally wounded.

The historian of the 34th Division pays handsome tribute to
the services of the Monmouths under Lieutenant-Colonel J. Evans,
whose total strength at the end of the day was only 4 officers and
150 other ranks, and proceeds : " The situation was undoubtedly
very critical for some time, till the dashing attack of Colonel Woodruffe's men [Colonel Woodruffe was O.C. R.N.F.L.D.] had restored
the situation." That night the R.N.F.L.D., after digging and wiring
a new trench in company with the 23rd Northumberland Fusiliers,
moved back into reserve.

The 13th was less eventful for the rank and file. It was one of
anxiety for the brigadier commanding the 88th on account of the
risk of being at any moment left high and dry and cut off. The
last exploit of the R.N.F.L.D. while in the 29th illustrates the class
of peril. Just about the approach of evening Captain John Clift,
in charge of a company, noticed that the enemy were already
in force on a road north of and roughly parallel to the Armentières
road. This threatened a turning of the whole brigade position. In
the words of Lieutenant-Colonel John Shakespear, C.M.G., D.S.O.,

etc., this company "caught a column of Huns in mass astride the de Broeken road, and gave a good account of them. The other companies of the R.N.F.L.D. joined in the fray. A gap having occurred between D and C companies, Captain Clift, calling to him men of the Northumberlands, closed it and held up the attack twenty-five yards from his line. Thus the advance of the enemy at this point was stayed at about 9 p.m., and the efforts of the Boche to close the pincers in which he thought that he held General Nicholson's forces failed, and during the night they slipped away."

After a period of suspense, at 10.15 p.m. the brigadier received orders to withdraw to the Ravelsberg ridge just east of Bailleul and dig in a new line. This order was carried out in perfect order.

The remainder of the 88th's tour in the line was spent in incessant fighting and relieving and being relieved in cold and often snowy conditions in or in front of Croix de Poperinghe, north of Bailleul, until on 21st April it was relieved by the French, when they took over the Kemmel defences. The 88th bade farewell to their friends in the 34th and returned to their comrades in the 29th, well knowing from the terms of the G.O.C.'s message to General Freyberg that they would be right welcome home.

During the course of their fighting General Freyberg had sent the following message to his own division, dated 18th April : " We are still in and fighting hard ; we have lost a goodish number of officers and other ranks. We all want to get back to the division as soon as possible. I don't think we have disgraced the Red Triangle."

To which a reply was sent :—

" Well done, 88th. Am doing all I can to get you back."

Their services are best summed up in the following Special Order issued by General Nicholson :—

The G.O.C. 34th Division wishes to place on record his great appreciation of the services rendered by the brigade during the time it has been attached to the division under his command. The steadiness of the brigade when covering the retirement from Nieppe, the stubborn resistance put up during the retirement to the Bailleul-Crucifix Corner line—which undoubtedly saved a serious situation—are exploits of which the brigade may well be proud. Throughout the period the steadiness, gallantry, and endurance of all ranks has been worthy of the highest traditions of British infantry ; and the G.O.C. 34th Division is proud to have had such troops under his command.

At the same time the divisional commander received a private note from General Nicholson, specially praising the personal services of General Freyberg.

The machine-gun section had been indefatigable, and the officers had shown initiative of a high order. The smartness of the deployment on the 10th had extricated the 121st Brigade R.F.A. from an awkward situation. These gunners most gallantly supported the 88th through the subsequent fighting, and were of inestimable value. "There is no doubt," wrote one who knew, "that this brigade formed a rallying-point, on either side of which the defence of this part of the front pivoted."

On the whole, the battles of the Lys, the second great defensive operation in which the 29th were engaged, may rank with the defence of the Cambrai salient.

As a result of the battle, owing to their heavy losses and to the impossibility of replacing them speedily, the Royal Newfoundland Regiment and the Royal Guernsey Light Infantry were withdrawn from the division. Both battalions were a great loss, but especially the former, who had done brilliant service in the 88th Brigade for nearly three years. When it came to fighting, there was no one to surpass them in the division.

The Guernsey Light Infantry had only joined the division in the previous autumn, but had made a reputation for themselves in their first battle, the Battle of Cambrai.

The places of these two battalions were taken by the 1st Royal Dublin Fusiliers, who went to the 86th Brigade instead of the Guernsey Light Infantry, and the 2nd Leinster Regiment, who replaced the Newfoundlanders. The Dublin Fusiliers had only left the division in the previous autumn, on the reconstitution of Irish divisions, so that they may be considered as coming back to their real home. The Leinsters were new to the division.

As a general comment on this Battle of the Lys, it has to be admitted that our men were much handicapped by a want of training in open warfare. The enemy had been undergoing such training during the whole previous winter, whereas nearly every available man of ours had to be utilized in holding the line. The result was that the enemy proved himself much more skilful in the open than our men, who felt themselves outmatched in this respect, and for that reason had perhaps more success than he should have had. But as regards the share of the division in this battle, the greatest credit is due to the men for splendid resistance. This was shown clearly in the daily situation maps of those days, when the division was daily indicated as forming a marked salient towards the enemy, their resistance being really greater than that of adjoining troops, and their retirement in many instances being caused only by the retirement of other troops on their flanks.

Congratulatory messages were received after the battle from the Commander-in-Chief, from Sir H. Horne, commanding First Army, from Sir Herbert Plumer, commanding Second Army, and from Lieutenant-General de Lisle, commanding XV. Corps.

Sir Douglas Haig's words were :—

" By the gallant action north of the Lys in the early days of the Lys battle, the fine fighting record of the 29th Division has been well maintained."

It is interesting to record that at one period of the battle, when French troops were coming up to relieve the pressure, the division shared headquarters for a day in a farmhouse with the 133rd French Division, commanded by General Valentin.

After a short period for reorganization and absorbing of rein-forcements, the division, on the 27th April, took over the line from the 31st Division from the Forêt de Nieppe to the Hazebrouck–Bailleul Railway. The division remained in the line till 22nd June, two brigades being in front and one in reserve. Constant work went on, strengthening the position against a threatened German renewal of the offensive. As we saw later on, when we advanced, the fullest preparation for such an attack had been made.

A number of raids were carried out at various times to improve the line and obtain identifications of the troops opposite us. The most successful was an attack by portions of the Royal Fusiliers and Royal Dublin Fusiliers on the morning of the 3rd June, which resulted in the capture of 33 prisoners, advanced our line to the Plâte Becque, and took Lug and Ankle Farms.

The 1st Australian Division on our left were setting us a splendid example all this time by the individual enterprise of men holding the line. They were frequently in the habit of crawling out at any time of day or night, through the high crops, and surprising and capturing German posts, till a regular reign of terror was established on their front.

We suffered at this time from a very bad epidemic of influenza, and many officers and men were affected, the principal symptom appearing to be acute depression, which temporarily led to lack of enterprise. We had another handicap, too, during part of the time. A large number of gas cylinders were established in our line with the intention that the gas should be released on the first favourable opportunity. The cylinders were established well behind the front line, so that the necessity arose of evacuating the front trenches every night, as it would have been impossible to hold them when the gas was released. Every morning, therefore, just before dawn, these trenches had to be reoccupied, with no certainty that in the course of the night the enemy had not already taken them. This procedure went on for more than a week, and was most wearying and harassing to the troops in front. Eventually, as the direction of the wind refused to become favourable at night, the gas was released by day, probably without very satisfactory results, as the cloud must have been fully visible to the enemy long before it reached their line.

On 16th May the division was at last again complete, as our divisional artillery, to every one's satisfaction, rejoined us from Ypres, where it had remained with the 41st Division since the rest of the division had left there on 10th April.

Colonel Murray, commanding the 17th Brigade R.F.A., has furnished the following description of German shelling, which occurred in May :—

" A beautiful quiet day till 5 p.m., when the Germans began shelling D.17 Battery with a 12-inch howitzer. They kept it up for an hour, at the end of which time the position was completely obliterated. Never was there such a scene of destruction. Before they began, the battery was in a green field with hardly a shell hole in it. When they stopped, there was not a blade of grass to be seen, and the whole field was a mass of craters, 20 feet deep and 30 feet wide. Every scrap of ammunition was blown up, and the guns were thrown about in all directions. The accuracy of the shooting was phenomenal, for, with the exception of a few craters on each side of the field, every single shell fell in the field. One wonders what form of observation was used, for no balloons were up at the time, and we could see no aeroplanes. Yet it must have been direct to obtain such accuracy. There were no casualties, and, strange to say, when the guns had been collected and overhauled they were found to be quite uninjured. Except for the loss of ammunition, the effect of this terrific and accurate bombardment was nil. What extraordinary things happen in this war ! "

When the 22nd June arrived, all hands were delighted to be relieved from the line, as there had been no real chance of getting together after the heavy losses of the Lys battle. Training, especially in open warfare, was vitally necessary, and such training went on continuously and strenuously. But as play is essential if staleness is to be avoided, many sports and games were engaged in. The principal event in that line was a most successful Divisional Horse Show, held on 9th July, at which nearly the whole of the division was present, and many guests, including the army commander, General Sir Herbert Plumer, and the two former commanders of the division, Generals Hunter-Weston and de Lisle. The turnouts for the various events were most excellent, the judging in consequence being a difficult business. The final event was competition between the drums of the different units, who gave a most stirring display. General de Lisle was the judge of this event, and gave the award to the 1st Royal Dublin Fusiliers. Colonel Wright, commanding the Army Service Corps in the division, was largely responsible for the great success of the show.

The divisional troupe, under the same officer's fostering care, was giving a very good show at this time, and playing to crowded houses. Their performances and costumes were really excellent, and they gave pleasure not only to the men of the division, but to many others. One especially noteworthy occasion was a gala performance at St. Omer, when all women workers in the neighbourhood, from principal matrons to ambulance drivers, were invited, and came in hundreds, appearing thoroughly to enjoy the show.

So a month was spent till, on 22nd July, the division was moved up to the X. Corps near Cassel, with the idea of taking part in an attack to recover Bailleul. This move was made conspicuously by daylight, so appears only to have been of a camouflage nature to attract the enemy's attention to this front, while he was being hammered on the Marne and the Aisne.

A particularly good show held at this time on 31st July was a ceremonial parade of the divisional artillery. It had been impossible to organize one before, as the whole of a divisional artillery was seldom out of the line at the same time. This parade included an inspection by the divisional commander, walk and trot past and advance in review order. The turn out, movements, and bearing of the men could scarcely have been improved .

Early in August the division took over the Merris sector from the 1st Australian Division. This division, thanks to the Gallipoli tie, was always on the best of terms with the 29th. To illustrate the feeling :—

One night a party of Australians who were, let us say, cheerful, fell foul of the military police in one of our villages, and were all for fighting them. However, one of the Australians spotted the Red Triangle badge on a policeman's arm, and fraternization at once took place, the Australians remarking that they weren't going to fight with the 29th Division, and allowing themselves to be arrested without further trouble.

In front of this Merris sector was the village of Outtersteene and a low ridge, which was the last high ground on this side of the Lys.

On 18th August an attack on this ridge, in conjunction with the 9th Division on our left, was carried out. The plan was, shortly, that the 9th Division should begin the business by capturing Hogenacker Mill, the key of the position. This they did brilliantly. The 87th Brigade (temporarily commanded by Lieutenant-Colonel G. T. Raikes of the S.W.B.) then passed behind them and attacked Outtersteene ridge and village with complete success, gaining all objectives and capturing 450 prisoners. The regiments principally engaged were the S.W.B. and K.O.S.B., with the Border Regiment in support. In addition to the prisoners many machine-guns, trench mortars, and three field guns were captured. After the taking of the position, the enemy put down a very heavy bombardment, but in spite of severe casualties, especially to the K.O.S.B., the whole position was maintained.

On the following day the ground to the south of the ridge was attacked by the 86th Brigade, all objectives were successfully gained and held, and a further bag of 180 prisoners brought in.

These attacks revealed the very forward preparations for a German attack on a large scale on this front. Thousands of shells of all calibres up to the largest were found scattered about in small dumps in and immediately behind the front line, so that in the event of an initial success by them, their guns could come up at once and find waiting for them the necessary ammunition, with which to carry on the attack. Probably, however, after the French counter-offensive was started in July, all German idea of an attack on this front was abandoned. But it showed us that all the previous hard work on our defensive positions had not been undertaken without very strong reasons.

After a day or two we were left in fairly peaceful possession of our new positions. These gave us a much more extended view, and to the same extent denied it to the enemy.

The harvest was now ripe, and the country nearly up to the front line was covered by heavy crops, sown in the previous winter, before the German offensive on this front. The division was able to do most useful work for the civilian population in reaping and carrying these crops from the forward area. Many tons were saved, to the great benefit of the local inhabitants, chiefly by the hard work of the Divisional Ammunition Column, under Colonel Spedding, and by the men of the Royal Army Service Corps. There was a good deal of game still in the country. Earlier in the year those in the Forêt de Nieppe had kept themselves supplied with pheasants in spite of the season, and had also shot roe deer. The following note from Colonel Murray, R.A., written about this time, is plaintive :—

" We have had frozen rabbits for three days in succession, and I feel as if I never wanted to touch a rabbit again. With the greatest difficulty I managed to get hold of another cartridge for my gun, so I sent Ratsey out to shoot something for the larder. The brute came back with a rabbit. Said he thought it was a hare—I shall make him eat it."

A few days later a good many large fires were visible behind the Boche lines, so that it looked as if he were destroying stores and was meaning to go farther back. On the 30th August it was discovered that he had left the previous night. Arrangements were made at once for following him up, the 87th Brigade being advanced guard, who pushed on this day for three miles well beyond Bailleul, practically without getting touch of the enemy. In this advance one was able to realize how magnificently our gunners had done in the previous months, and what a very thin time the Boche must have had behind his line. Every road and track ruined by gunfire, and littered with fragments of wagons, and stores, and dead animals ; and all his gun positions plastered with shells. The huge piles of shells all over the country, pre-sumably brought up for the big offensive which did not come off, were a remarkable sight.

On the 31st the 87th Brigade got as far as La Crèche without much opposition. Our front was extended, and the 88th Brigade was brought up on the left of the 87th on this day.

On the 1st September the advance was continued beyond Steen-werck, and on the 3rd Nieppe was captured. The German resist-ance was slight, but the advance was slow, chiefly owing to the officers and men being unaccustomed to working in the open after so many years of trench warfare. But the time was invaluable to all as open warfare training, and all ranks improved daily at the game. Single guns were brought up to help the infantry forward, and assist in driving back machine-gun posts established in farm-houses. They were most successful in this, as were also sections of the machine-gun battalion. Of course, the whole country was strewn with booby traps, and house after house, and cross-road after cross-road went up to heaven as a result of delay action mines. Three of the houses which had been occupied temporarily by the 87th Brigade Headquarters vanished shortly after they were vacated.

In one case an officer chose a very nice-looking shanty to sleep in, and only just in time discovered a cigar box behind the door, ready to fall as soon as the door was closed, the box being attached by wires to a mine under the floor. Perhaps the most ingenious trap discovered was a grandfather clock with shells instead of weights, with the fuses downwards and a bar placed across half-way down to explode the shells as soon as they touched it. The Engineers, being presumed experts in these matters, were kept busy looking for and making innocuous similar contrivances. But on the whole very few casualties resulted from all these traps, as every one became pretty cautious.

On the 3rd September the 87th Brigade was withdrawn, and the 86th took their place. A more vigorous advance was planned for the next day, the capture under a barrage of the line Hill 63 to Ploegsteert by the 88th Brigade on the left and 86th on the right. Hill 63 was the dominating position, so, to cover the 88th Brigade in its attacks, a strong barrage was arranged. As less resistance was expected on the 86th Brigade front, the barrage there was much weaker.

During the afternoon of the 3rd the 2nd Hampshire Regiment of the 88th Brigade were ordered to drive the enemy from the old General Headquarters line, which was done, and to push on as near the western slopes of Hill 63 as possible, to an arranged forming-up position. The Hampshires at nightfall reported themselves in position, and after dark the 2nd Leinster Regiment were ordered to prolong the line, they had taken up to the left, preparatory to the attack in the morning.

As a matter of fact, the Hampshires had been partially held up and were not quite in the position they had indicated, which was still in German hands. There was a large crater in the road, indicating the right flank of the brigade. This was occupied by the enemy, and was only taken by the Hampshires after a hard struggle in the dark. When Colonel H. W. Weldon, commanding the Leinsters, came up the road towards this crater, he found packed on the road and in adjacent ditches three of his companies, besides many of the Hampshires and a company of the Lancashire Fusiliers from the 86th Brigade, who were to prolong the line to the right. Very heavy German machine-gun fire was sweeping all over the area, which was constantly lighted by hostile flares. In fact, it seemed that the forming up for the attack was impossible as the time was already 2 a.m. However, Colonel Weldon got hold of Captain G. Farrell, commanding his leading company, and directed him to bring his company back in single file, move for 800 yards parallel to but in rear of the originally selected positions (which were still in the enemy's hands) and then push forward till he got into touch with the left of the Hampshires. The remaining companies of Leinsters were ordered to follow and prolong the line northwards. This was done, and eventually the confusion was cleared up. As the situation was fully realized, the barrage next morning was ordered to remain stationary for sufficiently long to enable the troops, who had not reached the intended alignment, to do so. This was done, and in spite of the very great difficulties indicated above, and thanks to the splendid leading of the officers of the two battalions, the attack was launched at the time directed. After it was launched, the difficulties were by no means over, as a belt of uncut wire, estimated as 50 yards wide and apparently quite insurmountable, was encountered, and the attacking battalions had to force their way through this. Most of the casualties occurred here, but by the determination of all the obstacle was successfully overcome. After this it was more or less plain sailing, and all objectives were gained, about 250 prisoners being captured.

The attack of the 86th Brigade towards Ploegsteert was started at the same time, but owing to the weakness of the artillery support, for the reasons given above, was held up without getting very far. The Lancashire Fusiliers and Royal Dublin Fusiliers were the attacking troops from left to right. After Hill 63 had been captured by the 88th Brigade, however, more artillery was available and an attack under a barrage was ordered for the afternoon. This was completely successful, and all objectives were gained. The Dublin Fusiliers, who had had rather a bad time in the morning, were determined to revenge themselves for it, and consequently went forward in the afternoon full of fight. They got well into the Boche with the bayonet at Ploegsteert and slew many of them, so felt their day had not been wasted. Another 100 prisoners were captured in this little affair.

It is interesting to notice that in this attack on Hill 63 there were in the Leinster Regiment three brothers Farrell, commanding three of the four companies, of whom one, Captain G. Farrell, was wounded, and another, Captain V. Farrell, was awarded the D.S.O. for his gallantry and skilful leading at the time the wire obstacle was encountered.

After the battle the following message was received from General Sir Herbert Plumer, commanding the Second Army :—

" Please convey to the 29th Division my hearty congratulations on their successful operations to-day.   The capture of Hill 63 was of the utmost importance, and was brilliantly carried out, as was also the capture of Ploegsteert."

General Plumer's presence amongst us was a continual inspiration to confidence and cheerful optimism.   His frequent visits to the division, to brigades and battalions, always left the recipient of the visit in fresh heart to carry on his job with determination and vigour.

With the exception of a few days in July, since the middle of April the division had been in the XV. Corps, commanded by their old chief, General de Lisle, whose interest in the division was constant and unabated.   We were now to leave him for the final stage of the war.   On the 5th September the division was withdrawn from the line after a most successful time.   They had advanced ten miles since the 30th August, in the face of continued resistance, captured much material and many prisoners, and finally ended up with an entirely successful attack on a very strong position, which had obviously been prepared by the enemy for a long resistance, and thus effectually upset his local plans.

CHAPTER II

THE LAST BATTLE OF YPRES

On 17th September the division moved to the II. Corps, consisting at that time of the 9th and 36th Divisions, and commanded by Lieutenant-General Sir Claud Jacob, in the Ypres area, and took over billets and camps there for the last time. This move was preliminary to taking part in large operations in conjunction with the Belgian army for the final driving back of the enemy in Belgium. A day or two afterwards the division took over the line east of Ypres from the Menin road on the north to Zillebeke Lake, the front from which they were to attack. As a result of our recent most successful operations from Outtersteene onwards, and of the splendid news of the victories farther south, every one was in the best heart and highest state of confidence, and was at last really realizing that very little more exertion would mean final defeat of the enemy and the end of the war. The difficulties to be encountered in an attack were not so much perhaps the resistance of the enemy, as the dreadful state of the country for the first few miles of advance. Indeed, the state of desolation and destruction in all that area is indescribable. Scarcely a moment for four long years that it had not had shells from both sides raining on it. All the natural drainage had been destroyed, so that everywhere the ground was treacherous, and in many places quite impassable from the resultant bogs and marshes. The problem of getting guns forward to support the infantry as they advanced, and all supplies for man, beast, and gun, was likely to prove a difficult one.

The line was held very lightly by a series of posts, so as to keep men as fresh as possible for the attack. Indeed, the posts were so far apart, that it was quite easy for men to walk between them to the front, without realizing that they had done so, as happened in a rather unique incident, related by Brigadier-General Johnson, commanding the divisional artillery.

Two N.C.O.s of the divisional ammunition column sent out by Lieutenant-Colonel Spedding to reconnoitre roads for the advance, passed through our front line without discovering any posts. On seeing a pill-box, one of them, Corporal Shadgett, went inside to inquire the way, but found to his surprise that the occupants were Huns. Luckily, he happened to stand in front of the rifle rack, in which all rifles except one were stacked. That one was being cleaned by its owner at the table in the pill-box. Nothing daunted by the fact that his revolver was not even loaded, Corporal Shadgett drew it and covered the eight occupants of the pill-box, at the same time shouting to his companion, Bombardier Almond, to come in ; which he did, and the Huns at once surrendered and were marched back to Vlamertinghe by the two N.C.O.s and handed over to the prisoners' cage there. For this prompt and gallant action Corporal Shadgett was awarded the D.C.M. and Bombardier Almond the M.M.

The attack was fixed for the 28th September. The weather had been fairly good, and our constant anxiety was that it should remain so, so as to make the physical difficulties of the advance at any rate not insurmountable. The divisional front was from just north of the Menin road on the left, to Zillebeke Lake on the right, the attacking troops being from left to right, 86th and 87th Brigades, with 88th Brigade in reserve. Our objectives were first the high ground astride the Menin road about Stirling Castle, Glencorse Wood, Inverness Copse up to Polygon Wood on the left, and Dumbarton Wood on the right ; all the country, in fact, that had been gained with such tremendous fighting and losses in the previous autumn, and from which a withdrawal had been enforced in the spring, when, as the result of their offensive, the enemy had captured Mount Kemmel. These objectives were assigned to the two leading brigades. When these were taken the 88th Brigade was to go through the front brigades and exploit the success through Gheluvelt and as far as possible in the direction of Menin.

The divisional artillery, after firing the creeping barrage, which would cover the infantry up to the first objective, would then endeavour to get forward to help the further advance.

The heavy artillery, the 77th Heavy Brigade, under Lieutenant-Colonel Walters, after preliminary firing on strong points, would fire a barrage from the limits of the field artillery barrage to beyond Gheluvelt—in fact, up to their extreme range.

Zero hour was fixed at 5.30 a.m., previous to which on the

Belgian front a preliminary bombardment of three hours' duration was to be fired.

On our immediate left was the 9th Division, and on our right the 35th Division, in the XIX. Corps (Sir H. E. Watts).

At the appointed moment the barrage opened. It was perfect, and the infantry were able to advance behind it as behind a wall. A certain number of casualties were caused by over-eagerness on the part of the infantry, who did not always wait for the barrage to lift. The enemy was overwhelmed, and the attack was completely successful, gaining by 8.30 a.m. all the high ground for which in the previous year there had been such bitter fighting. Many prisoners, of course, were taken and many guns overrun. As the attack started the rain began to fall, and kept on persistently, adding most materially to the difficulties of the advance, though, through the keenness and enthusiasm of all, each line was reached absolutely up to time.

An incident, as related by General Jackson of the 87th Brigade, illustrates well the spirit of cheerfulness and confidence with which the men were fighting. It took place at Jackdaw Tunnels (a system of dug-outs near Stirling Castle).

General Jackson writes : " It was raining hard, but we were all at the top of our form because the fight was going so well. A sentry (as I assumed from waggishness) presented arms to me at the mouth of one of the tunnels. Even the 29th did not, as a rule, pay compliments during a battle, so I asked him what he was playing at, and why he did not watch the mouth of the tunnel in case any Boche came up from the dug-outs, which had not yet been searched. He stood aside to let me see, at the same time saying, ' The tunnel is all right.' I saw a German, whom he had bayoneted and pushed into the narrow opening, doubled up like a Jack-in-the-box, to stop any one coming up."

General Cheape, who advanced with his brigade-major, Captain McFeely, took 17 prisoners himself in the first few minutes. During the advance of this brigade, the attack was temporarily held up by a machine-gun strong point near Clapham Junction. Two young subalterns of the Dublin Fusiliers, on their own initiative, got round the flank of the post, jumped into the trench, and pistolled the machine-gunners, thus allowing the advance to continue after the least possible delay.

The 88th Brigade, under General Freyberg, were treading on the heels of the leading brigades, and immediately the lifting of the barrage allowed it, dashed forward in further advance. At the

same time, batteries began to move forward to support this further
advance. The difficulties were enormous, as the main road from
Hooge onwards, up to the crest of the high ground, was quite
impassable for vehicles of any kind. However, an old plank road
to the left of Hooge was found just passable, and so with good-will
and after tremendous exertions, by nightfall five batteries and
sections of three others were in action on the far side of the crest.

Meanwhile the 88th Brigade advanced triumphantly over the
high ground, meeting with little organized opposition. The going
continued very bad, and the rain was pouring down. The 86th
and 87th Brigades were reorganized, and followed up the advance.
General Freyberg was to be seen mounted on a sorry captured
transport horse, at the head of the advance, his steed being urged
on with blows from behind, and his orderly following him with his
red brigade flag. It is rumoured that the beater of the horse was
General Johnson, the C.R.A., who had gone forward to reconnoitre
for his guns !

Gheluvelt was soon reached, or rather the site of it. Nothing
of the village was to be seen except a Boche notice-board—" Ghelu-
veld." It was the 4th Worcestershire Regiment who took the place,
a curious coincidence, considering the famous charge there and
defence of the place by the 2nd Worcestershire Regiment in the far-
off days of the First Battle of Ypres. Our line by midday was
farther forward than it had been since the autumn of 1914. Many
more guns were overrun, some being fought by their detachments
up to the last moment. In one case an 8-inch howitzer battery
was in action east of Gheluvelt ; Captain Hackett of the Worcestershires was leading the advance. When he and his men arrived within
a few yards of the guns, one of them loosed off a final round. No
harm was done, but this so annoyed Hackett that he rushed forward
and beat the nearest Boche gunner over the head with his stick,
asking him " What the —— he meant by loosing off his —— gun
at him ? " This officer, it is interesting to note, had started the
war as a sergeant in Gallipoli, and with intervals away for wounds,
had served continuously with the division, earning the D.C.M. and
M.C. and getting his commission and command of a company.
Eventually, by the evening, the line of the Kruiseik Spur was
reached and made good, an advance of over five miles, which took
us on to classic ground. Nearly a thousand prisoners were captured
and numerous guns of all calibres.

The field ambulances did extraordinarily good work on this day.
In the very early stages of the attack, two motor ambulances could

be seen on the Menin road following close behind the barrage, and picking up and returning wounded men to dressing stations quite regardless of hostile fire. The very important result to the wounded was that they were attended to with the least possible delay.

Here for a day or two in mid-October 1914 the 7th Division had stood facing the surging masses of the haughty invader. Just beyond lay ground untrod by British soldiers since the Napoleonic wars.

The rain persisted, and the problem now was to get supplies up over the three miles of morass to the troops in front. The Engineers and the 2nd Monmouthshire Regiment (the Pioneer Battalion) and all who could be spared from other work, such as the personnel of the trench mortar batteries, were pressed into the service of repairing the roads sufficiently to allow of light traffic. As many guns were forward as it was in any way possible to supply with ammunition. Thanks to the spirit in which all worked, the road improved every hour, but all in front had to depend for the time being on the services of pack transport. It was impossible to move cookers and vehicles carrying greatcoats, so that those in front, in the wet and cold, were not likely to have a comfortable time, especially in the absence of all shelter, except a few habitable, but filthy, pillboxes.

During the night the enemy had been reinforced, so, under the conditions, progress next day was slow but continuous. On this day General Cheape distinguished himself by shooting down a low-flying Boche aeroplane. Seeing this machine coming along, he seized a rifle from a man near him, and as it came over him fired and brought it crashing down. A fine shot !

By the 1st October the centre of the line was advanced to the village of Gheluwé, about three miles from Menin. This was a strong village, and more or less untouched. In addition, as was discovered later, all the houses had been concreted inside, so as to make them proof against anything except heavy artillery, which, of course, owing to the state of the roads, it had been impossible to bring up.

Heroic efforts had been made on the previous days to get the communications right, and, in spite of the dreadful weather, much success had been attained, so that all ordinary transport could now use the main road. Many temporary deviations had to be made to avoid craters and other places, where the road was totally destroyed. The difficulties were not lessened by a division of French cavalry, who, in the absence of decent country on either flank, selected the main road for their bivouacs and horse-lines. They had been sent forward to exploit the success of the infantry, but owing largely to the state of the country and the weather, never got further forward than Gheluvelt. After two or three days they cleared off.

On the 2nd October a strong attack was made on Gheluwé and towards Menin, the divisions on the flanks also attacking. This was only partially successful. A good part of the village was taken by the 2nd Hampshires, but counter-attacks drove us back again to the edge of it. On the previous day the division had suffered a great loss in the death of Lieutenant-Colonel Burne, one of the heroes of the Cambrai defensive fight, commanding 15th Brigade R.H.A., who was killed by a chance shell when reconnoitring to find out the exact positions of the forward infantry.

On the 4th the division was relieved by the 41st Division (XIX. Corps), and was sent back for a few days preparatory to further attacks.

The time from the 28th September had been one of most pronounced success, and it is certain that the success would have been even greater had it not been for the continuous rain and consequent vile conditions. As General Jacob said in the course of a congratulatory order which he published : " When it is remembered that in 1917 it took over three months to gain the high ground and how costly these operations were, it redounds greatly to the credit of the 29th Division that not only did they capture the ridge, but also the ground far beyond, in less than twenty-four hours. It was a great achievement, and I offer all ranks my heartiest congratulations and thanks for all they have done." *

During the period before the next attack, some troops were quartered in Ypres in which an occasional shell from an extreme range still fell. One of the very last of these hit and killed Lieutenant-Colonel Beatty-Pownall, Border Regiment, who was in command of the K.O.S.B. He had done most gallant service in the previous months at Outtersteene and elsewhere. He was a great loss.

THE BATTLE OF COURTRAI

We again went into the line on the night of the 5th, the 86th taking over trenches, or rather scratches, farther to the north, opposite Ledeghem. Our next attack was to be from this position.

---

* It was amusing, therefore, to read in the *Times*, in its account of this battle, words to the effect : ".The Twenty-ninth Division, famous principally for its theatrical troupe, which performed in London," etc., etc.

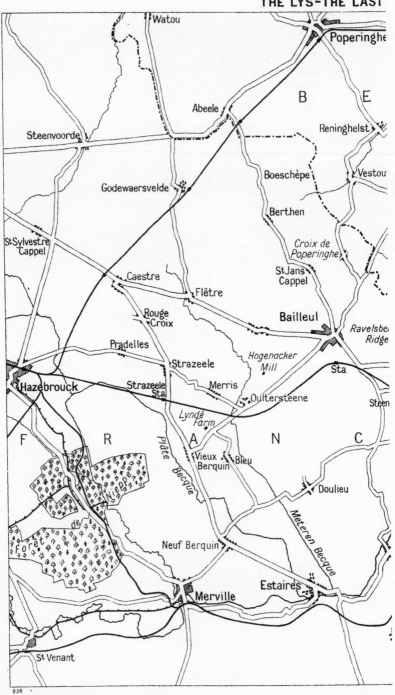

Watou

Poperinghe

Abeele

B E

Steenvoorde

Reninghelst

Boeschèpe

Vestou

Godewaersvelde

Berthen

St Sylvestre
Cappel

Croix de
Poperinghe

Caestre

St Jans
Cappel

Flêtre

Rouge
Croix

Bailleul

Ravelsbe
Ridge

Pradelles

Hogenacker
Mill

Strazeele

Sta.

Hazebrouck

Strazeele
Sta.

Merris

Oultersteene

Steen

Lyndé
Farm

F R A N C

Vieux
Berquin

Bleu

Nepp

Plate Becque

Doulieu

de

Meteren Becque

Forêt

Neuf Berquin

Estaires

Merville

St Venant

956

BATTLE OF YPRES

Vlamertinghe
Ypres
Menin Road
Glencorse Wood
Polygon Wood
Inverness Copse
Zillebeke Lake
Hooge
Stirling Castle
Zillebeke
Veldhoek
Gheluvelt
L G I U M
Dickebusch
Dickebusch Lake
Zandvoorde
tre
Locre
Mt. Kemmel
Kemmel
Wytschaete
Messines
Wulverghem
La Douve
Warneton
Neuve-Eglise
Hill 63
rg
De Broeken
Bois de Ploegsteert
Ploegsteert
la Crèche
Pont d'Achelles
werck Sta.
Nieppe
Quesnoy-sur-Deule
E
Steenwerck
Houplines
La Lys R.
Armentières
Erquinghem
Perenchies
Sailly sur la Lys
Bois Grenier
Fleurbaix
Lomme
Laventie

Scale
0   1   2   3   4   5 Miles

John Bartholomew & Son, Ltd. Edinburgh.

All was ready by the 14th.   The attack was to be made by the 88th
Brigade on the right, and the 86th on the left, with the 87th in
reserve, and was timed for 5.35 a.m. (dawn).   In the absence of
regular trench lines, the forming up previous to the attack was
difficult, as tapes had to be laid out for the troops to form up on.
(Incidentally these tapes were engineer stores, and apparently
highly valuable, as General Jackson was much put about a few days
before when he was asked at Gheluwé to return the tapes his brigade
had formed up on for the advance from Ypres!)   The officer
commanding Leinster Regiment, Lieutenant-Colonel Weldon, after
seeing to this job for his battalion, walked back to his headquarters
about 600 yards in rear.   There he discovered his brigadier a reek-
ing mass of filthy black slime.   General Freyberg had walked head
first into the farmyard pond in the dark.   The odour was so un-
pleasant that the interview was limited to the very briefest narrative
of facts, and a hasty advance again on Colonel Weldon's part to the
danger zone.   " Anything rather than a continuation of that dreadful stink ! " he writes.   As General Freyberg remarked next day,
" It was bad enough to fall into the mess, but worse to have every
one avoiding me."
     Ledeghem itself was a tough-looking proposition, a well-built,
nearly untouched town of considerable size.   Some buildings on the
outskirts, including the railway station, had been taken a day or two
beforehand, and from them the initial attack could be supported by
close machine-gun fire.   The morning of the 14th opened beautifully
fine, but in the low-lying country about Ledeghem there was a
decided fog.   We were using a good many smoke shells in the
barrage, so that the fog was artificially thickened until it became
too dense to allow of easy movement for the attackers.   It, however,
effectually blinded the defenders, so that all their advanced machine-
gun posts were rushed and captured with ease.   We had got beyond
the zone of concrete pill-boxes, so that there was nothing in the way
of defences which could not be dealt with by field artillery.   However, one handicap, of which we had had no previous experience,
existed, and that was the presence of the inhabitants.   Promiscuous
shelling was bound to cause casualties among them, so that great
care had to be exercised.   The Huns, for no other name does justice
to the Germans in this operation, were not so particular, and on
evacuating a locality, though knowing that the villages they had
abandoned were full of women and children, they proceeded to blow
them to pieces as soon as they were out of them.   In consequence,
as we advanced, our men witnessed many distressing scenes of killed

and wounded women and children.   The effect was to spur them on, if it were possible, to even greater exertions than they were already making, finally to beat such a cruel and unchivalrous foe.

To continue the account of the battle itself.   The Lancashire Fusiliers of the 86th Brigade were specially detailed for the clearing of the town of Ledeghem, itself behind the advance.   This was effected about 7 a.m., over 150 prisoners and many machine guns being captured.   One building gave a good deal of trouble, but was gallantly captured by Captain Dunn, of the Lancashire Fusiliers. He proceeded with a lance-corporal and two men to tackle this house, which was strongly held, a large number of the enemy being in the cellars.   These were inclined to show fight, but after Captain Dunn had dispatched two or three with his revolver, the remainder were so impressed by his determined attitude that the whole garrison surrendered.   Two of his men were wounded, but the number of prisoners taken in this house alone was 74, the number of machine guns being five.   A D.S.O. was awarded Captain Dunn for his gallant work.

Meanwhile the advance of the two brigades continued, and all opposition was overcome in spite of stout resistance at various points.   Battery after battery of guns was overrun and captured. One hostile battery was caught by our barrage fire as it was limbering-up to retire, and most of the horses were killed, the battery falling complete into our hands when the advance reached it. Unexpected obstacles in the form of broad bands of wire entanglement were encountered, but only temporarily held up the advance.

It was an interesting fact that the battalions of the divisions working on the flanks of the 29th Division were units who had served long and brilliantly at one time in the division.   On our right was the 36th (Ulster) Division, and their left-hand battalion was the 1st Royal Inniskilling Fusiliers, who had done most of their war service in the 87th Brigade.   On our left was the 9th Division, whose right-hand battalion was the Royal Newfoundland Regiment, who had only left the 88th Brigade in the previous April.   So we felt that our flanks were in good hands.

The fog was certainly most confusing, and General Cheape relates how he found himself with a small party leading his brigade, having overrun many Germans.   His party actually shot the horses of and captured many German guns which were attempting to retire past them.   His brigade suffered a great loss during the advance by the death of Lieutenant-Colonel A. Moore, D.S.O., commanding the Royal Dublin Fusiliers, who was killed by a fragment of shell while talking to his brigadier.

On the right the 88th Brigade, headed by the Leinster Regiment, made splendid progress. Two acts of most conspicuous courage were done on this day by men of this battalion, for which V.C.s were awarded. Private M. Moffat got his chance when the advance of his company was held up by a fortified farmhouse. He, seeing the situation, at once dashed forward single-handed in the face of very heavy fire, worked round to the back door of the house, and broke it in. He shot the first two of the enemy who came against him, and forced the surrender of the remainder—3 officers and 27 men. Nothing could have been more gallant and timely than this action, which cleared the way for the rest of the battalion. Private Moffat then took charge of his prisoners, and about 100 more, took them back by himself and handed them over to the provost-marshal, returning at once and resuming his place in the firing-line. His was the 26th V.C. won for the division.

Sergeant J. O'Niell, who had gained the Military Medal in the attack on Hill 63, also performed acts of the greatest gallantry, which did not, however, in themselves, earn for him the 25th V.C., but only in conjunction with other acts of supreme bravery per- formed a few days later. On this occasion, near Moorsele, he showed the greatest gallantry in leading a small party against a battery in action, capturing it and all its men, and by so doing most materially helped forward the attack.

Some of these, and other captured guns, were turned against the enemy. For instance, the headquarters of the Leinster Regi- ment were established that night in the late headquarters of a German battery, with the guns close by. The men of this regiment turned the guns round, cocked them up as high as they would go, and with immense satisfaction loosed them off in the general direction of the enemy, fortunately without accident to themselves. As one man was heard to remark : " Begob ! it was a gunner I was meant to be."

Immediately the firing of the barrage was finished the 15th and 17th Brigades of Artillery went forward into close support of the infantry. The 77th Brigade of Heavy Artillery was again with the division, and had assisted most materially in covering the advance. They also got some of their lighter guns forward as soon as the situation allowed of it. This brigade had been of most splendid assistance to the division since 25th September, and con- tinued to be so till they left us about 21st October. The total advance during the day had been over 6,000 yards ; at least fifty guns were captured and over 1,000 prisoners.

The two leading infantry brigades, thanks to the fog and the fighting, were temporarily in a state of considerable disorganization, units being much mixed up. During the night they were reorganized, and by next morning, having held all the ground gained, they were again ready for anything. Their services were not, however, required at once, as the battle next day was carried on by the 87th Brigade, which had been in reserve.

To every one's great comfort we were now in the land of un-destroyed houses, so that all ranks at night had good roofs over their heads and slept in comfort.

During the day a very large number of inhabitants had been encountered. These were collected as much as possible outside the danger zone, fed and generally looked after as far as circumstances would allow. The feeding and care of all these extra mouths was a great added responsibility to the division, especially considering the still dreadful state of the communications behind us. But it was done with the greatest goodwill, and our efforts received the thanks of the Belgian authorities.

On the morning of the 15th, then, the 87th passed through the other two brigades to resume the advance. The earlier stages of the attack were carried out under cover of a creeping barrage, which started at 9 a.m. The advance went forward steadily and systematically all day, all strong points being dealt with as they were reached. A very formidable belt of wire entanglement over 20 yards wide was encountered and overcome. The villages of Salines and Heule were captured and the line advanced a good three miles nearly to Cuerne just short of the river Lys. There was a further considerable bag of prisoners and guns.

The most successful bit of fighting was on the extreme left of our line, really in the line of the division on our left. The S.W.B. were the battalion responsible for the success. Heule Wood, which was well to the left of our ground, had been light-heartedly reported captured and held by our left-hand neighbours. As a matter of fact they had not yet nearly reached it. So when the S.W.B. came along, expecting a clear run, they found this wood full of Huns and machine guns on their flank. The platoon com-manders on the flank at once tumbled to the situation. The leading left platoon commander on his own initiative at once put his men at the top far corner of the wood ; the next platoon commander put his men at the wood itself. The company in support at once moved up to help, and between them the wood was successfully cleared. It was later handed over to a subaltern of the other division, who expressed himself as quite annoyed at having his wood taken for him. However, he had to be content with the thought that the taking of the wood for him not only helped the 29th Division along, but also enabled his own people to get forward without undue delay. The officers chiefly concerned in this skilful and successful bit of fighting were Captain C. Dutton, M.C., Second-Lieutenant A. Glover, M.C., Lieutenant C. Hardy, and Second Lieutenant A. Pritchard. The two former obtained immediate awards of bars to their Military Crosses, and the two latter were awarded the Military Cross.

After firing the barrage the artillery gave the closest support to the infantry, B Battery R.H.A. and the 92nd Battery R.F.A. going forward with them.

On the next day, the 16th, the 87th still carried on, and took the line to the river Lys between Courtrai and Harlebeke. The divisions on our flanks had also reached about this line, thus completing a most successful series of operations.

A pause was here necessary to allow of preparations being made for forcing the passage of the river. All bridges had been destroyed, and the river was a formidable obstacle 30 yards wide and 8 feet deep. In addition the hostile bank commanded our bank at very close range.

The division on our left managed to get a few men over the river on the night of the 16th. But the movement was premature, and they could not maintain themselves and had to be extricated the following night. The operation of withdrawal owed its success largely to the co-operation of the 2nd Hampshire Regiment of the 88th Brigade, this brigade having just taken over the front from the 87th Brigade. In absolute silence pontoons were rowed across the river, containing a covering party of this battalion. If the movement had been detected it is certain that a heavy barrage would have been put down on that part of the river. Under the protection of this covering party the men on the far bank, including a good many wounded, were safely got back, and finally the covering party itself got away undetected. The success of this small under-taking was very largely due to General Freyberg himself, who was backwards and forwards across the river, personally seeing to every detail of the evacuation.

By the 19th all preparations for the crossing had been made and material collected for bridges. Immediately after dark on this night work on two footbridges was begun under cover of men who had been ferried across. These bridges were completed with only slight opposition, and the 88th Brigade began to cross. By dawn they were all over and lined up on the opposite bank, ready to advance. It was a very great relief that no covering bombardment for the operation was necessary, as the houses near the river were full of inhabitants.

At 6 a.m. the advance commenced behind a barrage fired by all batteries, who had previously established themselves in positions to cover the crossing. The attack went ahead most successfully and ground was continuously and steadily gained.

Immediately the infantry were across the river the Royal Engineers began the construction of a pontoon bridge, the Monmouthshire Regiment being engaged at the same moment in making the approaches to the bridge. By very fine work this bridge was completed by 8 a.m., and the artillery, having finished firing the barrage, at once began to cross. The bridge was not under direct observation of the enemy, so that its position was not spotted at once. The morning, too, was rather misty, so that aeroplane observation was not feasible. Later on, however, when the mist cleared, its position was discovered, and it was kept under continuous long-range fire, but never suffered a direct hit.

The country over which the attack proceeded was thick with inhabitants, and here another slight but unexpected obstacle to progress arose, as the people were most insistent that the advancing troops should come into the farm-houses for coffee and refreshments. Probably a good many men did snatch a snack this way (a pleasant interlude in a battle), but the advance was in no way checked.

It was here that Sergeant O'Niell of the Leinster Regiment put a finishing touch to the gallantry which gained him his V.C. He had heard that a brother of his, serving in the 36th (Ulster) Division, working on our right, had been killed the previous day, and in consequence he can only be described as "seeing red." He appears, therefore, to have continually dashed ahead of the advance (in the early stages through our own barrage), and again and again to have been the first man of his battalion into any farm or village on their front. His example was most inspiring, and he seemed to bear a charmed life. Giving no quarter and asking none, he single-handed cleared several houses, first at Staceghem and later on in the day at Esscher, both considerable villages and strongly held. He seemed to inspire the enemy with terror wherever he went, so that several times they fled before him, abandoning their machine guns. No man could have exhibited greater bravery, and no man by his example could have helped his battalion forward more than did Sergeant O'Niell on this day.

The 88th Brigade had had a most strenuous time, having been up all night crossing the river, so that at about noon, when they had advanced over and made good some two and a half miles of country, they were brought to a standstill.

The 86th Brigade in support had crossed the Lys as early as possible by the pontoon bridge, and were close up. They had doubled across the bridge by platoons, shells bursting in the water on either side. It was a Sunday morning, and many noticed how, in spite of the battle, all church bells in Courtrai and Harlebeke were ringing. Incidentally, the principal church in Courtrai had a peal of chimes, and one of the first tunes they played on them after the town was occupied by us was " Tipperary " !

Considerable difficulty was experienced in declining the hospitality of the inhabitants. But the brigade managed to evade this, and following up, passed through the 88th and took on the attack, which then went ahead with renewed vigour towards the high ground about St. Louis and the Wolfsberg, very important positions, as they were the last that overlooked the valley of the Lys on our front. These were attacked and successfully gained by evening and consolidated, touch being obtained with the divisions on our flanks. The total advance on this day had been about five miles, with the capture of about 300 prisoners and a few abandoned guns. The 87th Brigade, in reserve, had crossed the Lys during the day, so that the whole of the fighting strength of the division was now east of that river.

On the afternoon of the next day the 86th Brigade made a further short advance under a barrage and captured the strong position of Banhout Bosch. On the following day, the 22nd, a further general advance was planned towards the Scheldt. The 87th Brigade were the attacking troops for the division, with objectives towards Ooteghem. The front was wide and the country very difficult and open, defended by machine-gun posts in the numerous farms. The attack was only partially successful, but an advance of a mile was made, 150 prisoners and many machine guns captured. This was the last day of actual battle for the division, and it was signalized by one of the bravest deeds in the whole history of the division.

. In all our actions the 29th Machine-Gun Battalion, under the command of Lieutenant-Colonel Meiklejohn, * D.S.O., as brave an

* See page 95.

officer and as stern a disciplinarian as one would wish to see, had done wonderful work in helping forward attacks, consolidating positions won, and assisting in their defence, so it was only appropriate that an officer of this battalion should win this last distinction for the division. Lieutenant D. S. McGregor was the officer. He was in command of a section of machine guns attached to the right flank platoon of the Border Regiment, who were to attack. In the assembly position he concealed his guns on a limber under the bank of a sunken road. Immediately the troops advanced they were subjected to intense enfilade machine-gun fire from a hill on their right front. Lieutenant McGregor went forward fearlessly into the open to locate these hostile guns, and, having done so, realized that it was impossible to get his guns forward either by pack or by hand without great delay, as the ground was absolutely open and swept by a hail of bullets. Ordering the teams to follow by a more covered route, he went to the limber, got into it, and ordered the driver to leave cover and gallop forward. This the driver most pluckily did, galloping down about 600 yards of absolutely open road under the heaviest fire into cover beyond. (Private W. G. Harris was the name of this brave driver.) The driver, horses, and limber were all hit, but Lieutenant McGregor succeeded in getting his guns into action, effectively engaged the enemy and kept their fire down, and so allowed the infantry to resume their advance.

With the utmost bravery he continued to expose himself in order to direct and control the fire of his guns, until about an hour later this very gallant officer was killed, while observing fire effect for the trench mortar battery. His great gallantry and supreme devotion to duty were indeed the admiration of all who saw them, especially of the officers and men of the Border Regiment, who were so helped by them. He was awarded the V.C., the twenty-seventh and last bestowed on the division during the war, and the driver, Private Harris, the D.C.M.

On the following day, the 23rd, the division was withdrawn, and to their great regret left General Jacob's corps, with which they had had so brilliant and successful a time. They went back to a few days' comfort at Roubaix and the neighbouring big towns.

Of course in the last few days talks that a cessation of hostilities was imminent were flying about everywhere. It was probable, however, that the passage of the river Scheldt would have to be forced before this event happened. So on the 7th November the division took over a line about Bossuyt on the left bank of the river, preparatory to making the attempt. The river was a formidable obstacle, sixty yards wide, and very deep, so that the forcing of it looked to be a difficult business, especially as our bank was overlooked at short range by commanding heights on the enemy's side.

However, on the 9th, the attack having been planned for the following day, the enemy retired and was at once followed up by the 88th Brigade, who were holding the front. They improvised footbridges, and were across early in the day, advancing as far as Celles by evening, without getting into touch with the enemy. It was with difficulty that pack animals with rations followed them, having to be ferried across the river, till bridges, which were all destroyed, could be repaired. No vehicles or guns could cross till this was done, which was not till late on the following day. Much destruction had been caused to the roads by the retiring enemy, and all cross-roads, railway, and road bridges had been blown up, so that the question of supply was likely to be a difficult one.

The advance was resumed by the 88th Brigade on the 10th to beyond St. Sauveur. A squadron of the 7th Dragoon Guards, under Major Chappell, joined them this day. This squadron had come by forced marches many miles to catch up, and horses and men were much exhausted.

During the day news was received that at 11 a.m. on the following day an armistice would come into force, the opposing sides to remain on the ground on which they found themselves at that hour. Orders were therefore issued to General Freyberg, commanding the advanced guard, to push on his cavalry at once and endeavour to seize the bridges over the river Dendre at Lessines. These orders did not reach him until 9.30 a.m. on the 11th. He at once saddled up his attached squadron and in spite of the exhaustion of the horses galloped down the Lessines Road, taking no notice of the fire of the German outposts. The distance was ten miles of hilly road. The squadron, led by General Freyberg in person, arrived at the outskirts of Lessines a few minutes before 11, and, though fired on, immediately rushed the town and seized the bridges, which had been prepared for demolition, so preventing their destruction. Three officers and 100 men were taken prisoners in the town, being completely surprised and unable to escape across the bridges. A good many more were taken on the far side of the river, but were let go again, as it was now obviously after 11 a.m. We had no casualties, but a few horses were hit. The dashing brigadier was just missed by a bullet which hit his saddle. The scene in the town must have been astonishing when the cavalry arrived. The inhabitants in a moment turned against their German oppressors, stoning and hooting them. The prisoners had to be protected from their fury. Our troops, on the other hand, were almost over-whelmed with the enthusiasm of their welcome. It is credibly reported that all, from the general downwards, were warmly kissed by many pretty girls, decorated with flowers, and treated to as much wine and beer as they could wish for. The burgomaster came out in state, and on the spur of the moment arranged an elaborate breakfast in the Town Hall, where with much speech-making and enthusiasm he entertained as many as possible.

This striking little success was indeed a very fitting grand finale for the division, and for it General Freyberg gained a second bar to his D.S.O., and Major Chappell a D.S.O. It had an amusing sequel, as the Germans protested to the Armistice Commission that the prisoners had been captured after the whistle had been sounded. It is true that we had not synchronized our watches with theirs, but we were able to prove entirely satisfactorily that the whole trans-action was completed by 10.59 a.m. So some hundred men had to go back and help to restore the roads they had been destroying.

The division, after this, was concentrated about Flobecq and Lessines, being transferred again to General Jacob's corps. To our great joy and pride we found that we were chosen as one of the two British infantry divisions (the other being the 9th) selected to lead the advance into Germany. With the 2nd Cavalry Division (Pit-man) a day ahead, we began our march on the 18th November. For convenience of movement and billeting, the division marched in four groups on two parallel roads, the two rear groups, as a rule, taking over billets evacuated the same morning by the leading groups. The joy of the inhabitants at our coming was a thing none of us will ever forget. The whole people behaved as if a real and very heavy weight had been taken off them, so that they could hardly keep on the ground, but had to be constantly dancing and singing.

The following experiences of the Rev. Kenelm Swallow, C.F., who accompanied the billeting officer as interpreter in advance of the troops, is of interest :—

" This march was probably the sternest test of sheer endurance, as apart from bravery, that the division ever encountered. Food and smokes were short all the way, the men were filthy and covered with lice, and utterly worn out. The marches were very severe—anything up to twenty miles a day, the roads bad, and the weather usually appalling. The food-supplies for some twenty thousand men depended upon one pontoon bridge across the Scheldt. I happened to be crossing this bridge on the occasion when it collapsed. It was crammed with heavy general service wagons drawn by mules. The whole structure groaned and cracked, and eventually sank into the river, the wagons, etc., just getting to the other bank in the nick of time.

" A young second lieutenant and myself and the four N.C.O.s who made up the battalion's billeting party were the first Englishmen the inhabitants of most of the previously occupied Belgian villages had seen in their lives. Many villages were quite unaware of our nationality or our purpose. As soon as this was realized, we received tremendous ovations. It was very difficult to get on with our job of arranging the billets, owing to the numerous invitations to eat and drink in every house we entered. The curés especially were noteworthy in this respect. In one case I remember how an old curé fished up bottles of champagne from the bottom of his well, where he had stored them all through the war, in anticipation, he told us, of this great day of days. The champagne was consumed with due appreciation in the Headquarters mess. Another became so hysterical with delight as to go into his church and fetch the sacred candlesticks off the altar for the adornment of our mess table in his parlour.

" Most of the villages had bands—very bad ones. On the arrival of the battalion (the S.W.B.), it was met about half a mile outside the place by the local band, who escorted it in with great pomp. Then, as a rule, the entire civilian population assembled in the central spot of the place to witness the local burgomaster or maire greet the commanding officer as if he were royalty, while the band played the British National Anthem. One town printed florid placards of welcome. One of them, which I still have, reads :

WELCOME
TO THE ALLIÉS ARMIES

**HONOUR AND GRATITUDE
TO OUR VALOUROUS DEFENDERS**

LET US GLORIFY OUR HÉROS

HOURRA FOR THE LIBERTY

LESSINES, Le 11 Novembre 1918."

So through Enghien to Tubize, where we halted a couple of days. While there, on 22nd November, the great honour fell to us of furnishing two companies, made up of detachments from all the infantry units of the division, at the state entry of the King and Queen of the Belgians into Brussels. It was a marvellous day, not only from the weather point of view, but from the overwhelming enthusiasm of the whole people. The King took the salute in front of the Chamber of Deputies, where the Allied detachments—Belgian, British, French, and American—marched past him. It was a stirring show, and no part of it finer than the 29th Division detachment, led by General Freyberg, V.C., on horseback, with his eight wound stripes. It was an historic occasion, and the significance of it was emphasized by the stirring reception and welcome the people gave us.

During our march the civic receptions accorded to the senior officer who was billeted in any town were at times a little bit trying to the recipients, however much they were appreciated. As an example, the reception of the divisional commander at Braine l'Allend, where we arrived on 23rd November, will suffice.

Shortly before his arrival the town council hurriedly met and voted 500 francs for entertainment. As he rode into the town he was escorted by cheering crowds to the Hôtel de Ville, where, at the entrance, he was met by the burgomaster and all the leading citizens. An enormous bouquet and a small Belgian flag were presented by a small girl (whom he kissed), and then an adjournment was made to the Council Chamber, where the 500 francs was found to have been laid out in wine. Many speeches of welcome and replies were made and many healths drunk. The Livre d'Or of the town was produced, and in it the divisional commander wrote his name, noticing that the last name before his was that of the famous and patriotic Cardinal Mercier, sometime in 1908.

After that an adjournment to the Grand Place, where the town band was playing, and round it all the people were dancing. The band at once struck up our National Anthem, and kept it up for at least ten minutes, during which time the general had to stand rigidly at the salute ! At last they finished, and the director of music of the town, a fine old man of eighty years, came forward and was introduced. He said they had had no music for four years, and how happy they were to be able to begin enjoying life again. Most of the people, and all the children, then came up and shook hands with the general, who at last was able to escape to his billet, an historic house, in which the Prince of Orange had spent the night previous to the Battle of Waterloo. The dancing and music still went on, and was kept up till nearly midnight, many soldiers, not to mention officers, taking part. Indeed, the general, looking out of his window, was pained to observe his A.D.C.s joining in !

The following day the division's line of march took it across the field of Waterloo. It was extraordinarily interesting to compare the very restricted bounds of this battlefield with the enormous areas over which modern battles are fought. From the top of the Belgian memorial the divisional commander took the opportunity of giving a lecture on the battle to as many officers as could be there.

Even up to now, and from now onwards especially, the supply question became exceedingly difficult, as the railways had not yet been repaired, and all our supplies had to come up by lorry from railhead, which, at its farthest point, was nearly 100 miles distant from the head of the column. It was wonderful the way the mechanical transport company worked over narrow and bad roads, chiefly by night. The supply trains themselves were often twenty-four hours late, so that no rations whatever were in hand, and on more than one occasion the rations for the day only turned up a few minutes before the day's march began. It had been impossible to re-equip the division before we started on the march, so that clothing, and especially boots, which suffered much on the *pavé* roads, were getting into a very bad condition. Many men were marching almost without soles to their boots. It was wonderful how they got along. There was practically no falling out, and whenever the troops were met on the road they were seen to be stepping out gaily. The march discipline throughout was excellent, though nearly all the marches were long (some of them over twenty miles) with many steep hills, and the men were carrying their full packs and equipment.

So we continued through Belgium, passing another famous battlefield at Ramillies, crossing the Meuse at Huy, all through the mountainous Ardennes country by Spa to the frontier at Stavelot. The frontier was crossed on 4th December in pouring rain, and Malmédy was the first hostile town to receive us. Naturally, the demeanour of the people changed at once. We were met correctly but sullenly.

To quote Mr. Swallow once more :—

" On December 4, 1918, I actually entered Germany with no

more concern than one crosses a road at home.   Near Malmédy we
came to a place where posts about six feet high, painted black and
white, ran through the fields at intervals of about 200 yards.   This
was the frontier.   Not a soul was to be seen.   There were two houses,
one on either side.   The Belgian house flew colours.   That on the
German side had all the blinds drawn down, like a house of mourning
and death.

" When the battalion reached this point an hour or two later
they marched over playing national and Welsh airs.   Nobody came
out to meet us at the first German village, Widerum.   No one was
to be seen save a few boys and girls.   We came upon these somewhat unexpectedly round a corner, and they fled from us in terror.
All the inhabitants evidently expected that unspeakable atrocities
would be committed.   We found them quiet, homely people, all of
them hating the war, and most of them quite likeable.   The battalion arrived soaked to the skin after a long march in a continuous
downpour ;   hot drinks were waiting for them in every billet, and
the men were provided with fresh clean straw in abundance.   As
we went farther, and came to somewhat larger places, proclamations
in German, bordered in deep black, were to be seen on all prominent
walls.   These gave the Germans the official intimation of their
country's humiliation, coupled with instructions as to how to behave
during the occupation.

" We received throughout every possible assistance from all
town and village authorities, and it was interesting to observe the
accuracy and business-like method which ensured that every burgomaster was in possession of all details affecting the billeting capacity
of his town or village.   These were invariably handed over to me in
my capacity as interpreter of German.

" One of the newly-imposed duties of every burgomaster was to
collect all the arms, offensive and defensive, in his area, and to hand
them over to the British military authority immediately on the
latter's arrival.   For a German to be found in possession of any
arms was a penal offence and liable to severe punishment.   In one
place a tremendous sensation was caused by the discovery of an
inoffensive-looking German, in whose cellar some of our troops found
enough firearms and bayonets to arm the entire town.   When I
found this individual he was in his own kitchen under close guard
of two stalwart and fierce-looking English Tommies with rifles and
bayonets, what time his wife and numerous progeny clung around
his person and wept loudly and long.   It subsequently transpired,
however, that he was the burgomaster himself, who had collected

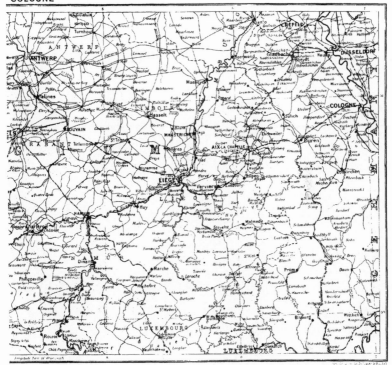

all the arms in pursuance of his duty, and had then found himself under close arrest for daring to have them in his possession ! Needless to say that his sense of outraged justice was soon removed directly the facts were made known."

The country was full of disbanded soldiers in uniform, which they were allowed to keep as long as civilian hats were worn and buttons and badges removed. The order that all men must take off their hats to officers took a bit of enforcing, but with the thoroughgoing German respect for authority, the men soon tumbled to it and obeyed. The country was strewn with signs of the German retirement, derelict wagons, motor cars and equipment of all sorts everywhere. Most units managed to fit themselves out with German cookers to supplement their own, and also an extra wagon or two. All were much struck with the sight of the mass of strategic railways close behind the frontier, and after seeing in addition the enormous training camp at Eisenborn (which might have been Aldershot on a large scale from the surroundings of heather, pine trees, and sand), no one could doubt that the invasion of France through Belgium had been decided on many years before the war.

Fairly drastic steps had to be taken to prevent the inhabitants putting up prices against us. Though there was no exchange question at the time, prices were found to be far lower than in England, and in this rich Rhineland there appeared to be plenty of everything.

So we advanced through beautiful mountain country to the outskirts of Cologne, which was reached on 9th December. Here preparations for the passage of the Rhine on the 13th were busily undertaken, and all ranks determined, as far as lay in their power, to make this historic event a splendid one. Deficiencies of clothing and boots had been replaced. Unluckily the 13th turned out to be a day of storm and pouring rain (what else could be expected on Friday, 13th ?), so the effect of all the hard work of the previous days was rather spoilt.

The division was to cross the Rhine by the Hohenzollern Bridge, the principal bridge in the town, while the Canadians crossed by the New Bridge on the right, and the 9th Division by the Mülheim boat bridge on the left. At the entrance of the bridge, under the colossal mounted statue of the Kaiser, a Union Jack was flying, and here General Plumer, commanding the Army of Occupation, stood to take the salute at 9.30 a.m., when the head of the column arrived. In spite of the rain the sight was most impressive as Artillery, Engineers, Infantry, and Machine Guns filed past to the music of the divisional band and of the pipes of the K.O.S.B.* General Plumer after a time moved to another bridge, and General Jacob, the corps commander, took the salute of the remainder of the division. The column took four hours to pass the saluting point. In spite of the rain the turnout and marching were magnificent.

The march was continued to various small towns about four miles on, from which on the following days our final positions on the bridgehead perimeter, twenty miles north-east of Cologne, were taken up.

It was a country chiefly of wooded hills, villages, and small towns, so proper accommodation for all was difficult to obtain. But eventually, by using schools, factories, and similar buildings, all were comfortably housed. Everything possible was done to make the time pass pleasantly for all ranks. Games and sports of all sorts were organized, and all very quickly appeared to make themselves at home in their surroundings.†

There was interesting and amusing work on the frontier in stopping smuggling into and out of the neutral zone. The ladies, probably relying on their sex, appear to have been the most successful on the whole, but after a good many had been searched and had been found, by special searchers of their own sex, with their skirts and undergarments stuffed with cigarettes, soap, and other forbidden articles, a check was put on their activities. The soldiers and inhabitants got on well together. There was no undue fraternization (though when the units of the division were being replaced by young soldier battalions from home, the police of the new 51st Hampshire Regiment, being boys of under eighteen, did on their first night in Wermelskirchen arrest some of the hoary old veterans of the Leinster Regiment for this offence) ; nor to our credit were there more than the very fewest number of cases of assaulting or attempting to oppress the people.

In other ways the division, which had ever shown so fine a fighting spirit, more than upheld its reputation by the splendid state of discipline which it maintained under trying circumstances. There was nearly universal unrest and discontent about, but it raised no head among us, even though the men were very sorely tried by such procedure as the demobilization out of their turn of

* Nor must we forget the unwonted spectacle of an infantry brigade of English and Irish units preceded by a Highlander playing on his native pipes the martial and cheery air, " The Muckin' o' Geordie's Byre." To these strains Brigadier-General Cheape rode up to and over the bridge at the head of the 86th Brigade.

† It is worth while mentioning that the division won handsomely the interdivisional team boxing competition of the Rhine Army.

men going on leave.   All seemed to realize that demobilization was more than a matter of a day or two, and contentedly waited their turn.   This admirable maintenance of discipline in such circumstances was one of the finest and proudest achievements to the credit of the division, in the whole of its splendid career, proving again, what all soldiers know, that the best fighters among soldiers are the best in every other way too.

Gradually, as demobilization took effect, all units were reduced much below establishment, till finally in March 1919 they were reduced to cadre strength, and sent home for reconstitution.   Their places were taken by battalions of young soldiers from home.

One of the last functions held was an enthusiastic dinner at the Divisional Officers' Club at Bergish Gladbach, at which over 100 officers were present, when the proposal for the formation of an association of officers of the division was made by the divisional commander.   This was carried with acclamation, and steps were taken to inaugurate it.   The membership of the association is now over 500, and the dinners, held twice a year on the dates of the Gallipoli landing and the battle of Cambrai, are great gatherings of old friends, and seem likely to be successful for many years to come. While they last, the memory of the division will be kept green amongst its members.

So the division was disbanded after four years of glorious history. In looking back on this time, the most remarkable thing about the 29th Division seems to have been its splendid spirit of comradeship, which made every officer and man who joined it proud to belong to it.   In good times or in bad, in victory or failure, this spirit was always there.   Men changed, officers changed, but the spirit remained and carried the division triumphantly through all vicissitudes of fortune to the victorious conclusion of its history. While Britain remains its fame should never die.

APPENDICES

APPENDIX I

ROLL OF THE VICTORIA CROSSES WON DURING THE GREAT WAR BY OFFICERS, WARRANT OFFICERS, NON-COMMISSIONED OFFICERS AND MEN OF THE 29TH DIVISION.

Supplement to the London Gazette, August 24, 1915.

HIS Majesty the King has been pleased to approve of the award of the Victoria Cross to the undermentioned officer and non-commissioned officers of the 1st Battalion Lancashire Fusiliers in recognition of most conspicuous bravery displayed :—

No. 1.   Captain RICHARD RAYMOND WILLIS, 1st Battalion Lancashire Fusiliers.

No. 2.   No. 1293 Sergeant ALFRED RICHARDS, 1st Battalion Lancashire Fusiliers.

No. 3.   1809 Private WILLIAM KENEALLY, 1st Battalion Lancashire Fusiliers.

On April 25, 1915, three companies and the headquarters of the 1st Battalion Lancashire Fusiliers, in effecting a landing on the Gallipoli Peninsula to the west of Cape Helles, were met by a very deadly fire from hidden machine guns which caused a great number of casualties. The survivors, however, rushed up and cut the wire entanglements, notwithstanding the terrific fire from the enemy, and after overcoming supreme difficulties, the cliffs were gained and the position maintained.

Amongst the very many gallant officers and men engaged in this most hazardous undertaking, Captain Willis, Sergeant Richards, and Private Keneally have been selected by their comrades as having performed the most signal acts of bravery and devotion to duty.

Supplement to the London Gazette, March 15, 1917.

HIS Majesty the King, etc. :—

No. 4.   Captain (temporary Major) CUTHBERT BROMLEY (since drowned).

No. 5.   1506 Sergeant FRANK EDWARD STUBBS (since died of wounds).

No. 6.   2609 Corporal (now Sergeant) JOHN GRIMSHAW.

On April 25, 1915, headquarters and three companies of the 1st Lancashire Fusiliers, in effecting a landing on the Gallipoli Peninsula to the north-west of Cape Helles, were met by very deadly fire from hidden machine guns, which caused a great number of casualties. The survivors, however, rushed up and cut the wire entanglement, notwithstanding the terrific fire from the enemy, and after overcoming supreme difficulties, the cliffs were gained and the position maintained. Among the many very gallant officers and men engaged in this most hazardous undertaking, Captain Bromley, Sergeant Stubbs, and Corporal Grimshaw have been selected by their comrades as having performed the most signal acts of bravery and devotion to duty.

(The above awards to be read along with those already cited as conferred on Captain R. R. Willis, Sergeant Alfred Richards, and Private W. Keneally.)

Supplement to the London Gazette, August 23, 1915.

His Majesty the King, etc. :—

> No. 7.   No. 8980 Corporal WILLIAM COSGROVE, 1st Battalion Royal Munster Fusiliers.

For most conspicuous bravery in the leading of his section with great dash during our attack from the beach to the east of Cape Helles, on the Turkish positions, on April 26, 1915.

Corporal Cosgrove on this occasion pulled down the posts of the enemy's high wire entanglements, single-handed, notwithstanding a terrific fire from both front and flanks, thereby contributing to the successful clearing of the heights.

Supplement to the London Gazette, June 23, 1915.

His Majesty the King has been graciously pleased to approve of the grant of the V.C. to the under-mentioned officers . . . for most conspicuous bravery and devotion to duty :—

> Lieutenant-Colonel CHARLES HOTHAM MONTAGU DOUGHTY-WYLIE, C.B., C.M.G., Headquarters Staff, Mediterranean Expeditionary Force.
> No. 8.   Captain GARTH NEVILLE WALFORD, Brigade-Major R.A., Mediterranean Expeditionary Force.

On April 26, 1915, subsequent to a landing having been effected on the beach at a point on the Gallipoli Peninsula, during which both brigadier-general and brigade-major had been killed, Lieutenant-Colonel Doughty-Wylie and Captain Walford organized and led an attack through and on both sides of the village of Sedd-el-Bahr on the Old Castle at the top of the hill inland.   The enemy's position was very strongly held and entrenched, and defended with concealed machine guns and pom-poms.

It was mainly due to the initiative skill and great gallantry of these two officers that the attack was a complete success.

Both were killed in the moment of victory.

Note.—Colonel Doughty-Wylie was not a member of the 29th Division.

Supplement to the London Gazette, July 24, 1915.

His Majesty the King, etc. :—

> No. 9. Second Lieutenant GEORGE RAYMOND DALLAS MOOR, 3rd Battalion Hampshire Regiment.

For most conspicuous bravery and resource on June 5, 1915, during operations south of Krithia, Dardanelles. When a detachment of a battalion on his left, which had lost all its officers, was rapidly retiring before a heavy Turkish attack, Second Lieutenant Moor, immediately grasping the danger to the remainder of the line, dashed back some 200 yards, stemmed the retirement, led back the men, and recaptured the lost trench.

This young officer, who only joined the army in October 1914, by his personal bravery and presence of mind, saved a dangerous situation.

Supplement to the London Gazette, September 1, 1915.

His Majesty the King, etc. :—

> No. 10.   Lieutenant HERBERT JAMES, 4th Battalion Worcestershire Regiment.

For most conspicuous bravery during the operations in the southern zone of the Gallipoli Peninsula. On June 28, 1915, when a portion of a regiment had been checked owing to all the officers having been put out of action, Second Lieutenant James, who belonged to a neighbouring unit, entirely on his own initiative gathered together a body of men and led them forward under heavy shell and rifle fire. He then returned, organized a second party, and again advanced.   His gallant example put fresh life into the attack.   On the 3rd July, in the same locality, Second Lieutenant James headed a party of bomb-throwers up a Turkish communication trench, and after nearly all his bomb-throwers had been killed or wounded, he remained alone at the head of the trench and kept back the enemy single-handed till a barrier had been built behind him and the trench secured.   He was throughout exposed to a murderous fire.

Supplement to the London Gazette, September 1, 1915.

His Majesty the King, etc. :—

> No. 11.　Captain G. R. O'SULLIVAN, M.C., 1st Battalion Royal
> Inniskilling Fusiliers.

For most conspicuous bravery during operations south-west of Krithia on the Gallipoli Peninsula, 1915.

On the night of July 1–2, 1915, when it was essential that a portion of a trench which had been lost should be regained, Captain O'Sullivan, although not belonging to the troops at this point, volunteered to lead a party of bomb-throwers to effect the recapture.

He advanced in the open under a very heavy fire, and in order to throw his bombs with greater effect, got up on the parapet, where he was completely exposed to the fire of the enemy occupying the trench. He was finally wounded, but not before his inspiring example had led on his party to make further efforts which resulted in the recapture of the trench.

On the night of June 18–19, 1915, Captain O'Sullivan saved a critical situation in the same locality by his great personal gallantry and good leading.

Supplement to the London Gazette, September 1, 1915.

His Majesty the King, etc. :—

> No. 12.　No. 10512 Sergeant JAMES SOMERS, 1st Battalion Royal
> Inniskilling Fusiliers.

For most conspicuous bravery on the night of July 1–2, 1915, in the southern zone of the Gallipoli Peninsula, when, owing to hostile bombing, some of our troops had retired from a sap, Sergeant Somers remained on the spot alone until a party brought up bombs.　He then climbed over into the Turkish trench and bombed the Turks with great effect.　Later on, he advanced into the open under very heavy fire and held back the enemy by throwing bombs into their flank until a barricade had been established.　During this period he frequently ran to and from our trenches to obtain fresh supplies of bombs.　By his great gallantry and coolness Sergeant Somers was largely instrumental in effecting the recapture of a portion of our trench, which had been lost.

Supplement to the London Gazette, March 10, 1917.

His Majesty the King, etc. :—

> No. 13. No. 9887 Sergeant EDWARD JOHN MOTT, 1st Border Regiment.

For most conspicuous gallantry and initiative when in an attack the company to which he belonged was held up at a strong point by machine-gun fire.

Although severely wounded in the eye, Sergeant Mott made a rush for the gun, and after a fierce struggle seized the gunner and took him prisoner, capturing the gun.

It was due to the dash and initiative of this N.C.O. that the left flank attack succeeded.

Supplement to the London Gazette, June 27, 1917.

His Majesty the King, etc. :—

> No. 14. No. 24866 Sergeant ALBERT WHITE, late South Wales Borderers.

For the most conspicuous bravery and devotion to duty. Realizing during an attack that one of the enemy's machine guns, which had previously been located, would probably hold up the whole advance of his company, Sergeant White, without the slightest hesitation and regardless of all personal danger, dashed ahead of his company to capture the gun. When within a few yards of the gun he fell riddled with bullets, having thus willingly sacrificed his life, in order that he might secure the success of the operations and the welfare of his comrades.

Supplement to the London Gazette, September 14, 1917.

His Majesty the King, etc. :—

> No. 15. No. 13531 Sergeant (acting Company Quartermaster Sergeant) WILLIAM H. GRIMBALDESTON, King's Own Scottish Borderers. (Blackburn.)

For most conspicuous bravery in attack. Noticing that the unit on his left was held up by enemy machine-gun fire from a blockhouse, though wounded, he collected a small party to fire rifle grenades on this blockhouse. He then got a volunteer to assist him with rifle fire. In spite of very heavy fire from the blockhouse he pushed on towards it and made for the entrance, from which he threatened with a hand grenade the machine-gun teams inside the blockhouse. These he forced to surrender one after another.

The extraordinary courage and boldness of Company Quartermaster Sergeant Grimbaldeston resulted in his capturing thirty-six prisoners, six machine guns, and one trench mortar, and enabled the whole line to continue its advance.

Supplement to the London Gazette, September 14, 1917.

His Majesty the King, etc. :—

No. 16. No. 6895 Sergeant (acting Company Sergeant-Major) JOHN SKINNER, King's Own Scottish Borderers. (Pollokshields, Glasgow.)

For most conspicuous gallantry and good leading. Whilst his company was attacking, machine-gun fire opened on the left flank, delaying the advance. Although Company Sergeant-Major Skinner was wounded in the head he collected six men, and with great courage and determination worked round the left flank of three blockhouses from which the machine-gun fire was coming and succeeded in bombing and taking the first blockhouse single-handed ; then, leading his six men towards the other two blockhouses, he skilfully cleared them, taking sixty prisoners, three machine guns, and two trench mortars.

The dash and gallantry displayed by this warrant officer enabled the objective to be reached and consolidated.

Supplement to the London Gazette, November 26, 1917.

His Majesty the King, etc. :—

No. 17. No. 10605 Sergeant JAMES OCKENDEN, Royal Dublin Fusiliers. (Southsea.)

For most conspicuous bravery in attack. When acting as Company Sergeant-Major, and seeing the platoon on the right held up by an enemy machine gun, he immediately rushed the machine gun, regardless of his personal safety, and captured it. He killed the crew with the exception of one man who made his escape. Sergeant Ockenden, however, followed him, and when well in front of the whole line killed him and returned to his company.

He then led a section to the attack on a farm. Under very heavy fire, he rushed forward and called upon the garrison to surrender. As the enemy continued to fire on him, he opened fire, killing four, where-upon the remainder, sixteen in number, surrendered.

Supplement to the London Gazette, November 26, 1917.

HIS Majesty the King, etc. :—

> No. 18.   No. 1817 Sergeant JOHN MOLYNEUX, Royal Fusiliers.
> (St. Helens.)

For most conspicuous bravery and devotion to duty. During an attack, which was held up by machine-gun fire, which caused many casualties, Sergeant Molyneux instantly organized a bombing paity to clear the trench in front of a house. Many of the enemy were killed and a machine gun was captured.

Having cleared this obstacle, he immediately jumped out of the trench and called for some one to follow him, and rushed for the house. By the time the men arrived he was in the thick of a hand-to-hand fight ; this only lasted a short time, and the enemy surrendered, and in addition to the dead and wounded, between twenty and thirty prisoners were taken.

Apart from the personal bravery of this N.C.O., his initiative and dash prevented a slight check from becoming a serious block in the advance, and undoubtedly prevented many casualties.

Supplement to the London Gazette, November 26, 1917.

HIS Majesty the King, etc. :—

> No. 19.   No. 8133 Sergeant JOSEPH LISTER, Lancashire Fusiliers.
> (Reddish, Stockport.)

For most conspicuous bravery in attack. When advancing to the first objective, his company came under machine-gun fire from the direction of two " pill-boxes." Seeing that the galling fire would hold up our advance and prevent our troops keeping up with the barrage, Sergeant Lister dashed ahead of his men and found a machine gun firing from a shell-hole in front of the " pill-box." He shot two of the enemy gunners, and the remainder surrendered to him. He then went to the pill-box and shouted to the occupants to surrender. They did so with the exception of one man, whom Sergeant Lister shot dead ; whereupon 110 of the enemy emerged from shell-holes farther to the rear and surrendered.

This N.C.O.'s prompt act of courage enabled our line to advance with hardly a check and to keep up with the barrage, the loss of which might have jeopardized the whole course of the local battle.

Supplement to the London Gazette, November 26, 1917.

His Majesty the King, etc. :—

> No. 20. No. 21654 Private FREDERICK GEORGE DANCOX,
> Worcester Regiment. (Worcester.)

For most conspicuous bravery and devotion to duty in attack. After the first objective had been captured and consolidation had been started, work was considerably hampered and numerous casualties were caused by an enemy machine gun firing from a concrete emplacement situated on the edge of our protective barrage.

Private Dancox was one of a party of about ten men detailed as moppers-up. Owing to the position of the machine-gun emplacement it was extremely difficult to work round a flank. However, this man with great gallantry worked his way round through the barrage, and entered the pill-box from the rear, threatening the garrison with a Mills bomb. Shortly afterwards he re-appeared with a machine gun under his arm, followed by about forty of the enemy.

The machine gun was brought back to our position by Private Dancox, and he kept it in action throughout the day.

By his resolution, absolute disregard of danger, and cheerful disposition, the *morale* of his comrades was maintained at a very high standard under extremely trying circumstances.

Supplement to the London Gazette, January 11, 1918.

His Majesty the King, etc. :—

> No. 21. Major (acting Lieutenant-Colonel) J. SHERWOOD-KELLY,
> C.M.G., D.S.O., Norfolk Regiment, Commanding
> a Battalion Royal Inniskilling Fusiliers.

For most conspicuous bravery and fearless leading when a party of men of another unit detailed to cover the passage of the canal by his battalion were held up on the near side of the canal by heavy rifle fire directed on the bridge. Lieutenant-Colonel Sherwood-Kelly at once ordered covering fire, and personally led the leading company of his battalion across the canal, and after crossing, reconnoitred under heavy rifle and machine-gun fire the high ground held by the enemy. The left flank of his battalion advancing to the assault of this objective was held up by a thick belt of wire, whereupon he then crossed to that flank, and with a Lewis gun team forced his way under heavy fire through the obstacles, got the gun into position on the far side, and covered the advance of his battalion through the wire, thereby enabling them to capture the position.

Later, he personally led a charge against some pits from which a heavy fire was being directed on his men, captured the pits, together with five machine guns and forty-six prisoners, and killed a large number of the enemy.

The great gallantry displayed by this officer throughout the day inspired the greatest confidence in his men, and it was mainly due to his example and devotion to duty that his battalion was enabled to capture and hold their objective.

Supplement to the London Gazette, January 11, 1918.

His Majesty the King, etc. :—

> No. 22. No. 9522 Sergeant CHARLES EDWARD SPACKMAN, Border Regiment. (Fulham.)

For most conspicuous bravery when, in action, the leading company was checked by the heavy fire of a machine gun mounted in a position which covered the approaches. The ground was absolutely devoid of cover of any description. Sergeant Spackman, realizing the position and seeing that it would be impossible for troops to advance, went through the fire to attack the gun. Working forward gradually, he succeeded in killing all but one of the gun crew. He then rushed the gun and captured it single-handed, thereby enabling the company to advance.

The behaviour of this N.C.O. was gallant in the extreme, and he set a fine example of courage and devotion to his men.

Supplement to the London Gazette, January 11, 1918.

His Majesty the King, etc. :—

> No. 23. Lieutenant (Temporary Captain) ROBERT GEE, M.C., Royal Fusiliers.

For most conspicuous bravery, initiative, and determination when an attack by a strong enemy force pierced our line and captured a brigade headquarters and ammunition dump. Captain Gee, finding himself a prisoner, killed one of the enemy with his spiked stick, and succeeded in escaping. He then organized a party of the brigade staff with which he attacked the enemy fiercely, closely followed and supported by two companies of infantry. By his own personal bravery and prompt action he, aided by his orderlies, cleared the locality.

Captain Gee established a defensive flank on the outskirts of the village ; then, finding that an enemy machine gun was still in action, with a revolver in each hand and followed by one man, he rushed and captured the gun, killing eight of the crew.

At this time he was wounded, but refused to have the wound dressed until he was satisfied that the defence was organized.

Supplement to the London Gazette, May 22, 1918.

HIS Majesty the King, etc. :—

> No. 24. Captain (Acting Lieutenant-Colonel) JAMES FORBES-ROBERTSON, D.S.O., M.C., Border Regiment.

For most conspicuous bravery whilst commanding his battalion during the heavy fighting.

Through his quick judgment, resource, untiring energy, and magnificent example Lieutenant-Colonel Forbes-Robertson on four separate occasions saved the line from breaking, and averted a situation which might have had the most serious and far-reaching results.

On the first occasion, when troops in front were falling back, he made a rapid reconnaissance on horseback, in full view of the enemy under heavy machine-gun and close range shell fire. He then organized and, still mounted, led a counter-attack which was completely successful in re-establishing our line. When his horse was shot under him, he continued on foot.

Later on the same day, when troops to the left of his line were giving way, he went to that flank and checked and steadied the line, inspiring confidence by his splendid coolness and disregard of personal danger. His horse was wounded three times and he was thrown five times.

The following day, when the troops on both his flanks were forced to retire, he formed a post at battalion headquarters and with his battalion still held his ground, thereby covering the retreat of troops on his flanks. Under the heaviest fire this gallant officer fearlessly exposed himself when collecting parties, organizing and encouraging.

On a subsequent occasion, when troops were retiring on his left and the condition of things on his right were (*sic*) obscure, he again saved the situation by his magnificent example of cool judgment. Losing a second horse, he continued alone on foot until he had established a line to which his own troops could withdraw and so conform to the general situation.

Supplement to the London Gazette, December 26, 1918.

HIS Majesty the King, etc. :—

> No. 25. No. 4119 Sergeant JOHN O'NIELL, M.M., 2nd Battalion Leinster Regiment. (Glenboig.)

For most conspicuous bravery and devotion to duty near Moorsele on October 14, 1918, when the advance of his company was checked by two machine guns and an enemy field battery firing over open sights. At the head of eleven men only he charged the battery, capturing four field guns, two machine guns, and sixteen prisoners.

Again, on the morning of October 20, 1918, Sergeant O'Niell, with one man, rushed an enemy machine-gun position, routing about one hundred of the enemy, and causing many casualties. Throughout the operations he displayed the most remarkable courage and power of leadership.

No. 26.   No. 18321 Private MARTIN MOFFAT, 2nd Leinster Regiment. (Sligo.)

For most conspicuous bravery and devotion to duty on October 14, 1918, near Ledeghem, when, advancing with five comrades across the open, the party suddenly came under heavy rifle fire at close range from a strongly held house.

Rushing towards the house through a hail of bullets, Private Moffat threw bombs, and then working to the back of the house, rushed the door single-handed, killing two and capturing thirty of the enemy. He displayed the greatest valour and initiative throughout.

Supplement to the London Gazette, December 14, 1918.

HIS Majesty the King, etc. :—

No. 27.   Lieutenant DAVID STUART McGREGOR, late 6th Battalion Royal Scots (T.F.), and 29th Battalion Machine Gun Corps.

For most conspicuous bravery and devotion to duty near Hoogmolen on October 22, 1918, when in command of machine guns attached to the right flank platoon of the assaulting battalion.

Immediately the troops advanced, they were subjected to intense enfilade fire from Hill 66 on the right flank. Lieutenant McGregor fearlessly went forward and located the enemy guns, and realized that it was impossible to get his guns carried forward either by pack or by hand without great delay, as the ground was absolutely bare and fire-swept. Ordering his men to follow by a more covered route, he mounted the limber and galloped forward under intense fire for about 600 yards to cover.

The driver, horses, and limber were all hit, but Lieutenant McGregor succeeded in getting the guns into action, effectively engaging the enemy, subduing their fire, and enabling the advance to be resumed. With the utmost gallantry he continued to expose himself in order to direct and control the fire of his guns until, about an hour later, he was killed. His great gallantry and supreme devotion to duty were the admiration of all ranks.

APPENDIX II

SECTION I.—RELIEFS

I.

BEAUMONT HAMEL, 1916.

Date and hour when 29th Division took over front.	2nd April, at 9 a.m.
Division relieved . . .	31st (92nd and part of 93rd Infantry Brigades).
Position on Corps front .	Right.
Corps and Army. . . .	VIII. Corps, Fourth Army.
Divisional front	700 yards north-west of Hamel to Watling Street.
Formation on the right. .	36th Division, X. Corps.
Formation on the left . .	31st Division, VIII. Corps.
Remarks	In the middle of June the 36th and 4th Divisions relieved the right and left of the 29th in readiness for the Battle of Albert, 1916. During and after this battle further alterations in the front took place.
Date and hour of handing over front	25th July, at 9 a.m.
Relieving Division . . .	25th.

2.

YPRES, 1916.

Date and hour when 29th Division took over front.	31st July, at 2.30 p.m.
Division relieved . . .	6th.
Position on the Corps front	Right.
Corps and Army . . .	VIII. Corps, Second Army.
Divisional front	Bellewaardebeek to north of Wieltje.
Formation on the right. .	3rd Canadian Division, Canadian Corps.

Formation on the left . . 38th Division, VIII. Corps.
Remarks . . . . . .

Date and hour of handing
   over front . . . . . 5th October, at 2 p.m.
Relieving Division . . . 55th.

3.
GUEUDECOURT, 1916.

Date and hour when 29th
   Division took over front. 19th October, at 5 p.m.
Division relieved . . . 12th.
Position on the Corps front Right.
Corps and Army . . . XV. Corps, Fourth Army.
Formation on the right. . 8th Division was relieving 6th in XIV.
   Corps.
Formation on the left . . 30th Division, XV. Corps.
Remarks . . . . . . On 9th October the 88th Infantry
   Brigade came under 12th Division and
   relieved the 37th Infantry Brigade in
   the right sub-sector on 10.10.16. When
   the 29th came in on 19th October the
   86th relieved the 35th Infantry Brigade
   in the left sub-sector and the 88th
   Infantry Brigade reverted to 29th
   Division.
Divisional Front . . . East-north-east of Gueudecourt to the
   Flers–Ligny–Thilloy road.

Date and hour of handing
   over front . . . . . 30th October, at 9 a.m.
Relieving Division . . . 1st Australian.

4.
LESBŒUFS, 1916.

Date and hour when 29th
   Division took over front. 18th November, at 10 a.m.
Division relieved . . . 8th.
Position on Corps front . Right.
Corps and Army . . . XIV. Corps, Fourth Army.
Divisional front . . . East of Lesbœufs.
Formation on the right. . 152nd French Division, IX. French Corps.
Formation on the left . . Guards Division, XIV. Corps.
Remarks . . . . . . 87th and 88th Infantry Brigades in line.

Date and hour of handing
   over front . . . . . 12th December, at 10 a.m.
Relieving Division . . . 20th.

5.

MORVAL, 1917.

Date and hour when 29th Division took over front.	16th January, at 10 a.m.
Division relieved . . .	17th.
Position on Corps front .	Left.
Corps and Army . . .	XIV. Corps, Fourth Army.
Divisional front	1,000 yards north of Sailly–Saillisel to 1,000 yards north-east of Lesbœufs.
Formation on the right .	20th Division, XIV. Corps.
Formation on the left . .	5th Australian Division, I. Anzac Corps.
Remarks	————
Date and hour of handing over front	9th February, at 10 a.m.
Relieving Division . . .	20th.

6.

SAILLISEL, 1917.

Date and hour when 29th Division took over front.	21st February, at 10 a.m.
Division relieved . . .	17th.
Position on Corps front .	Centre.
Corps and Army . . .	XIV. Corps, Fourth Army.
Divisional front	Rancourt–Saillisel road (incl.) to 1,000 yards north of Sailly–Saillisel.
Formation on the right .	Guards Division, XIV. Corps.
Formation on the left . .	20th Division, XIV. Corps.
Remarks	————
Date and hour of handing over front	4th March, at 10 a.m.
Relieving Division . . .	Guards Division relieved right brigade and part of left brigade, while the 20th Division relieved the balance of the left brigade.

7.

MONCHY LE PREUX, April 1917.

Date and hour when 29th Division took over front.	13th April, at 9 a.m.
Division relieved . . .	12th.
Position on Corps front .	Centre.
Corps and Army . . .	VI. Corps, Third Army.
Divisional front	South of Arras–Cambrai road to north of Monchy le Preux.

Formation on the right   . 3rd Division, VI. Corps.
Formation on the left . . 17th Division, VI. Corps.
Remarks . . . . . . On 14th April, at 6 a.m., 29th Division relieved the 3rd. This relief brought the right flank of the 29th Division to the Cojeul River. The VI. Corps had now only two divisions in line—29th on right, 17th on left. At 3 a.m. on 20th April the 15th Division relieved the right brigade of the 29th Division, thus giving the VI. Corps a three-division front again.

Date of handing over front . . . . 25th April.
Relieving Division . . . 3rd.

8.

MONCHY LE PREUX, May 1917.

Date and hour when 29th Division took over front. 15th May, at 10 a.m.
Division relieved . . . 3rd.
Position on Corps front . Centre.
Corps and Army . . . VI. Corps, Third Army.
Divisional front . . . . 1,200 yards south-east of Monchy to track Monchy–Pelves.
Formation on the right . 56th Division, VI. Corps.
Formation on the left . . 12th Division, VI. Corps.
Remarks . . . . . . The dispositions shown above were soon changed, for on 17th May, at 9 a.m., the 29th Division relieved the 12th Division to the left of the VI. Corps front (River Scarpe). The formation on the left was now the 51st Division of XVII. Corps.

Date and hour of handing over front . . . . 3rd June, at 10 a.m.
Relieving Division . . . 3rd.

9.

YPRES, July 1917.

Date and hour when 29th Division took over front. 29th June, at 9 a.m.

Division relieved . . .	38th.
Position on Corps front .	Right.
Corps and Army . . .	XIV. Corps, Fifth Army.
Divisional front	Essen Farm to Farm 14.
Formation on the right .	153rd Infantry Brigade (51st Division) acting under 39th Division, XVIII. Corps.
Formation on the left . .	Guards Division, XIV. Corps.
Remarks	———
Date and hour of handing over front	21st July, at 10 a.m.
Relieving Division . . .	38th.

10.
YPRES, August 1917.

Date and hour when 29th Division took over front.	8th August, at 10 a.m.
Division relieved . . .	Guards.
Position on Corps front .	Left.
Corps and Army . . .	XIV. Corps, Fifth Army.
Divisional front	Ypres–Staden railway to 400 yards south-south-west of point where Langemarck–Bixschoote road crosses the Hannebeek.
Formation on the right .	20th Division, XIV. Corps.
Formation on the left . .	2nd French Division, I. French Corps.
Remarks	———
Date and hour of handing over front	29th August, at 10 a.m.
Relieving Division . . .	Guards.

11.
LANGEMARCK, September–October 1917.

Date and hour when 29th Division took over front.	22nd September, at 9 a.m.
Division relieved . . .	Guards.
Position on Corps front .	Left.
Corps and Army . . .	XIV. Corps, Fifth Army.
Divisional front	Ypres–Staden railway to south of Ney Copse.
Formation on the right .	20th Division, XIV. Corps.
Formation on the left .	French Division, XXXVI. French Corps.

APPENDIX II

Remarks	On 29th September the 29th extended to the right, relieving the left brigade of the 20th Division. On 6th October the Guards Division relieved the 87th Infantry Brigade on the left of the 29th front. Command passed at 10 a.m., making 29th the centre division of XIV. Corps.
Date and hour of handing over front	11th October, at 10 a.m.
Relieving Division . . .	17th.

12.

CAMBRAI, 1917.

Date and hour when 29th Division took over front.	20th November. Exact hour when 29th took over not known. Forward move commenced at 10.15 a.m.
Position on Corps front .	Left centre.
Corps and Army . . .	III. Corps, Third Army.
Formation on the right .	20th Division, III. Corps.
Formation on the left . .	6th Division, III. Corps.
Remarks	
Date of handing over front	4th December 1917.
Relieving Division . . .	16th Infantry Brigade, 6th Division, relieved part of the 87th Infantry Brigade on 2nd December, and the 108th Infantry Brigade, 36th Division, relieved 88th Infantry Brigade and 1st K.O.S.B. on 4th December.

13.

PASSCHENDAELE, January 1918.

Date and hour when 29th Division took over front.	19th January, at noon.
Division relieved . . .	8th.
Position on Corps front .	Left.
Corps and Army . . .	VIII. Corps, Fourth Army.
Divisional front	North of Mosselmarkt–Goudberg.
Formation on the right .	33rd Division, VIII. Corps.

Formation on the left .   .   35th Division relieving 39th Division, II. Corps.

Remarks .   .   .   .   .   .

Date and hour of handing
    over front .   .   .   .   .   12th February, at 10 a.m.

Relieving Division .   .   .   8th.

14.

PASSCHENDAELE, March 1918.

Date and hour when 29th
    Division took over front .   8th March, at 10 a.m.

Division relieved .   .   .   8th.

Position on the Corps front   Left.

Corps and Army .   .   .   VIII. Corps, Fourth Army.

Divisional front .   .   .   .   North of Passchendaele.

Formation on the right .   33rd Division, VIII. Corps.

Formation on the left .   .   1st Division, II. Corps.

Remarks .   .   .   .   .   .   On 4th April the 86th Infantry Brigade relieved the left brigade of 33rd Division on the right.   All three brigades of the 29th were now in line—86th, right ; 87th, centre ; 88th, left.

Relief from this front .   .   On 8th April, at 10 a.m., the 122nd Infantry Brigade, 41st Division, relieved the 86th Infantry Brigade.
On 9th April, the 124th Infantry Brigade relieved the 87th Infantry Brigade.
On 10th April, the 123rd Infantry Brigade relieved the 88th Infantry Brigade.

Date and hour of change of command uncertain : 29th Division records say 10th April, at 10 a.m. ; 41st Division say 9th April, at 7 p.m.

15.

NEUF BERQUIN, 1918.

The information about this tour in line is not given in the same way as the others, as the information available is not so complete, and the whole situation was constantly fluctuating.

On 10th April the 86th and 87th Infantry Brigades arrived in the Neuf Berquin area under the XV. Corps.   The 88th Infantry Brigade, on this day, went to the IX. Corps, and a brief account of their doings is given in the *History of the 34th Division*, one of the sources of the account given in the text of this story.

During the day the 86th and 87th Brigades took up reserve positions behind the 50th Division south-east of Doulieu.

On 11th April remnants of the 50th Division passed through the 29th, and the latter appears to have taken over the front about noon. The 31st Division was on the left, and the 149th Infantry Brigade on the right.

The next two days were spent in heavy fighting, during which the division gradually fell back in a north-westerly direction on Merris.

The 1st Australian Division had now prepared a position behind the 29th and 31st Divisions, and during the night 13th–14th April the two latter divisions fell back through the Australians, who took over the front.

16.

VIEUX BERQUIN, 1918.

Date and hour when 29th Division took over front.	28th April, at 10 a.m.
Division relieved . . .	31st.
Position on Corps front .	Right.
Corps and Army . . .	XV. Corps, Second Army.
Divisional front	Caudescure to Hazebrouck-Armentières railway.
Formation on the right. .	5th Division, XI. Corps.
Formation on the left . .	1st Australian Division, XV. Corps.
Remarks	
Date and hour of handing over front	22nd June, at 10 a.m.
Relieving Division . . .	31st.

17.

STRAZEELE, 1918.

Date and hour when 29th Division took over front.	3rd August, at 10 a.m.
Division relieved . . .	1st Australian.
Position on the Corps front	Centre.
Corps and Army . . .	XV. Corps, Second Army.
Divisional front	South of Hazebrouck–Armentières railway to south of Meteren Beek.
Formation on the right. .	31st Division, XV. Corps.
Formation on the left . .	9th Division, XV. Corps.

Remarks . . . . . . After the middle of August the division pushed eastwards, and when relieved in September was just west of Ploegsteert Wood.

Date and hour of handing
over front . . . . . 6th September, at 9 a.m.
Relieving Division . . . 31st. (This Division had already relieved the right brigade of the 29th on 4th September, at 9 a.m.)

18.
YPRES, 1918.

Date and hour when 29th
Division took over front. 20th September, at 10 a.m.
Division relieved . . . 41st Infantry Brigade, 14th Division.
Position on Corps front . Right.
Corps and Army . . . II. Corps, Second Army.
Divisional front . . . . Zillebeke Lake to Menin Road.
Formation on the right. . 35th Division, XIX. Corps.
Formation on the left . . 9th Division relieving the other brigade of the 14th Division, II. Corps.
Remarks . . . . . . The battle of Ypres, 1918, opened on 28th September.

Date and hour of handing
over front . . . . . 4th October, at 6 a.m.
Relieving Division . . . 41st.

19.
LEDEGHEM, 1918.

Date and hour when 29th
Division took over front. 6th October, at 6 a.m.
Division relieved . . . Parts of 36th and 9th.
Position on Corps front . Centre.
Corps and Army . . . II. Corps, Second Army.
Divisional front . . . . West of Menin–Roulers railway, opposite Ledeghem.
Formation on the right. . 36th Division, II. Corps.
Formation on the left . . 9th Division, II. Corps.
Remarks . . . . . . During this tour a considerable advance took place.

Date and hour of handing
over front . . . . . 24th October, at 3 a.m.
Relieving Division . . . 41st.

20.

SCHELDT, 1918.

Date and hour when 29th
   Division took over front. 8th November. (Hour not known.)
Division relieved . . . 89th Infantry Brigade, 30th Division,
                    and 41st Infantry Brigade, 14th Division.
Position on Corps front . Right.
Corps and Army . . . X. Corps, Second Army.
Formation on the right. . 14th Division, XV. Corps.
Formation on the left . . 30th Division, X. Corps.
Divisional front . . . . Along the Scheldt from north of Helchin
                    to Bossuyt.

(From here the division advanced to the " Armistice Line.")

SECTION II.—MOVEMENTS

General Guide to the Movements of the 29th Division
when out of line, 1916–1918.

1916.

March 29......... Concentration of division completed after move from Egypt. Area, Long–Domqueur–Surchamps.
March 30......... Commenced move towards the line.
April 1............ Divisional Headquarters at Beauquesne.
April 4............ Relieved 31st Division (see No. 1, page 242).
July 25 .... Relieved by 25th Division. To Amplier-Beauval area.
July 27–28....... Moved by train to Flanders. Entraining stations, Doullens and Candas.
July 29............ In Poperinghe area.
July 31 .... Relieved 6th Division (see No. 2, page 242).
October 5 .... Relieved by 55th Division. To Wormhoudt–Poperinghe area.
Oct. 7–8 .... Moved by train to the Corbie–Allonville–Daours area.
October 9 .... 88th Infantry Brigade forward to 12th Division.
October 10....... To Ribemont–Buire–Dernancourt area.
October 13....... To Fricourt–Mametz area.
October 19....... Relieved 12th Division (see No. 3, page 243).
October 30....... Relieved by 1st Australian Division. To Corbie–Mericourt–Mametz area.

Nov. 14–15...... Concentrated in Albert area.

November 18 ... Relieved 8th Division (see No. 4, page 243).

December 12.... Relieved by 20th Division. To Corbie (Divisional Headquarters), Meaulte (86th), Citadel (87th), and Ville (88th).

December 13..... To Cavillon (Divisional Headquarters), Picquigny (86th), Soues (87th).

December 14..... 88th Infantry Brigade to Molliens Vidame.

1917.

January 10...... Return to line commenced, when the 86th Infantry Brigade moved to Corbie.

January 13 ...... Division in the Carnoy–Corbie area.

January 16 ...... Relieved 17th Division (see No. 5, page 244).

February 9...... Relieved by 20th Division. To Meaulte–Heilly–Bussy–Rainneville areas.

February 21 ..... Relieved 17th Division (see No. 6, page 244).

March 4........... Relieved by Guards and 20th Divisions. To Meaulte–Bussy–Ville.

March 20......... 87th and 88th Infantry Brigades to Cavillon area.

March 21......... 86th Infantry Brigade to Cavillon area.

March 31......... Division in the Vignaucourt area.

April 1............ To Beauval area.

April 2............ To Lucheux area.

April 5............ To Le Cauroy area.

April 7............ To Couturelle area.

April 8............ Bavincourt (86th), Monchiet (87th), Couturelle (88th).

April 13 .... To line (see No. 7, page 244).

April 25 .... Relieved. To Couin area.

May 2............. Moved to Arras for exploitation of attack on 3rd May; but as this attack failed, the division was not used, and it remained in, and to the west of, Arras until

May 15........... when it went into line (see No. 8, page 245).

June 3............. Relieved. To Canaples area.

June 26–27 ...... The division moved by train to the Proven area.

June 29........... To line (see No. 9, pages 245–6).

July 21........... Relieved. To Proven area, with one brigade back at Herzeele.

July 31 .... To Forest area.

August 8 .... To line (see No. 10, page 246).

August 29........ Relieved. To Proven area, with one brigade at Herzeele.

September 22 ... To line (see No. 11, page 246).

October 11....... Relieved. To Proven area.

Oct. 15–17....... Moved by train to the Basseux area.

November 17.... To Haut Allaines–Moislains area.

November 18.... After dark to the Fins–Sorel–Equancourt area.

November 20.... Battle of Cambrai, 1917. After relief from this battle the division moved by train to the Le Cauroy area.
Dec. 16–18....... To Fruges area.
    1918.
Jan. 3–4.......... Division moved to Tilques–Wizernes area.
January 19 ...... To line (see No. 13, page 247).
February 12..... Relieved. To Steenvoorde area.
March 8 .... To line (see No. 14, page 248).
April 10 .... Relieved. Division moved to Lys battles (see No. 15, page 248).
April 14 .... After withdrawing through 1st Australian Division, the 29th Division went to St. Sylvestre. Here a composite brigade was formed for counter-attack on the XV. Corps front.
April 18–19...... The division moved to the Hondeghem, and was reorganized.
April 28 .... To line (see No. 16, page 249).
June 22........... Relieved. Dispositions : Divisional Headquarters. Wardrecques; 86th, Lumbres; 87th, Racquinghem; 88th, west of the Hazebrouck–Morbecque road. Several small changes took place in the dispositions, the more important being as follows :—
    June 27. 86th Infantry Brigade moved forward in support of the 31st Division during that division's attack on 28th June. The brigade was not required, and returned to Blairinghem on 29th June.
    July 14–19. The 87th Infantry Brigade went forward in support of the 1st Australian Division in readiness for an anticipated enemy attack. This attack did not materialize.
July 19 .... The division was in the Blairinghem area.
July 22 .... To Bavinchove area.
August 3 .... To line (see No. 17, page 249).
September 6..... Relieved. To Hazebrouck area.
Sept. 16–17...... To Proven area.
September 20 ... To line (see No. 18, page 250).
October 4 .... Relieved. To Ypres area.
October 6 .... To line (see No. 19, page 250).
October 24....... Relieved. To Harlebeke–Cuerne area.
October 28....... Division to Mouveaux–Croix–St. Andre–Bondues area.
November 7 ..... To Rolleghem area.
November 8..... To line (see No. 20, page 251).
    (N.B.—The figures in brackets after each mention of entry into line refer to the numbers dealing with the reliefs.)

SECTION III.—ORDER OF BATTLE, ETC.

(*a*) Pre-war stations of the original regular battalions of the 29th Division.

86th Infantry Brigade.

2nd Royal Fusiliers. . . . . . Calcutta
1st Lancashire Fusiliers . . . . Karachi
1st Royal Munster Fusiliers . . . Rangoon
1st Royal Dublin Fusiliers. . . . Madras

87th Infantry Brigade.

2nd South Wales Borderers . . . Tientsin
1st King's Own Scottish Borderers . Lucknow
1st Royal Inniskilling Fusiliers . . Trimulgherry
1st Border Regiment . . . . . Maymyo

88th Infantry Brigade.

4th Worcestershire Regiment . . . Meiktila, Burma
2nd Hampshire Regiment . . . . Mhow
1st Essex Regiment. . . . . . Mauritius

(*b*) Order of Battle of the 29th Division in March 1915.

86th Infantry Brigade.
2nd Royal Fusiliers.
1st Lancashire Fusiliers.
1st Royal Munster Fusiliers.
1st Royal Dublin Fusiliers.

87th Infantry Brigade.
2nd South Wales Borderers.
1st King's Own Scottish Borderers.
1st Royal Inniskilling Fusiliers.
1st Border Regiment.

88th Infantry Brigade.
4th Worcestershire Regiment.
2nd Hampshire Regiment.
1st Essex Regiment.
1/5th Royal Scots.

Divisional Troops.
Artillery.
15th Brigade R.H.A. (B, L, and Y Batteries R.H.A.).
17th Brigade R.F.A. (13th, 26th, and 92nd Batteries R.F.A.).
147th Brigade R.F.A. (10th, 97th, and 368th Batteries R.F.A.).
4th Highland Mountain Brigade R.G.A. (T.F.) Argyllshire and Ross Mountain Batteries R.G.A. (T.F.)].
460th (Howitzer) Battery R.F.A.
14th Siege Battery R.G.A. (6-inch howitzers.)
90th Heavy Battery R.G.A. (60-pounders.)

Engineers.
    1/1st West Riding Field Company R.E. (T.F.).
    1/2nd Lowland Field Company R.E. (T.F.).
    1/2nd London Field Company R.E. (T.F.).
    2nd London Divisional Signal Company R.E. (T.F.).

    (c) Order of Battle of the 29th Division
            in November 1918.

86th Infantry Brigade.   *87th Infantry Brigade.*
2nd Royal Fusiliers.   2nd South Wales Borderers.
1st Lancashire Fusiliers.   1st King's Own Scottish Borderers.
1st Royal Dublin Fusiliers.   1st Border Regiment.
86th Light Trench Mortar Battery.   87th Light Trench Mortar Battery.

            88th Infantry Brigade.
        4th Worcestershire Regiment.
        2nd Hampshire Regiment.
        2nd Leinster Regiment.
        88th Light Trench Mortar Battery.

            Divisional Troops.
Artillery.
    15th Brigade R.H.A. (B, L, and 1st Warwick Batteries R.H.A.).
        X/29th Trench Mortar Battery.
    17th Brigade R.F.A. (13th, 26th, 460th, and D 17th Batteries
        R.F.A.).   Y/29th Trench Mortar Battery.
    29th D.A.C.
Engineers.
    455th (West Riding) Field Company R.E.
    497th (Kent) Field Company R.E.
    510th (London) Field Company R.E.
    29th Divisional Signal Company R.E.
Pioneers.
    1/2nd Monmouth Regiment.
Machine-Gun Corps.
    29th Battalion Machine-Gun Corps.
Army Service Corps.
    29th Divisional Train A.S.C.
Medical.
    87th, 88th, and 89th Field Ambulances R.A.M.C.
Veterinary.
    17th Mobile Veterinary Section A.V.C.
Employment.
    213th (226th) Employment Company Labour Corps.
        (The titles of units are given as they were at this date.)

(d) Order of Battle of Infantry Brigades with changes.

86th Infantry Brigade.

2nd Royal Fusiliers.	Remained throughout.
1st Lancashire Fusiliers	Remained throughout.
1st Royal Munster Fusiliers	Went to 16th Division in April 1916.
1st Royal Dublin Fusiliers.	To 16th Division, October 19, 1917.
16th Middlesex Regiment .	Joined division on April 26, 1916, in place of 1st Royal Munster Fusiliers. Disbanded February 1918.
1st Royal Guernsey L. I.	Joined division apparently in summer of 1917, and left towards the end of April 1918, in consequence of heavy losses in the Lys Battle.
1st Royal Dublin Fusiliers.	Came back to the division from 16th Division on April 26, 1918, in place of the Royal Guernsey Light Infantry.

Note from *History of the 1st Royal Dublin Fusiliers* :—" After the landing on Gallipoli the 86th Infantry Brigade was temporarily broken up (May 4, 1915). The Royal Dublin Fusiliers and Royal Munster Fusiliers formed a composite battalion called the ' Dubsters,' which was posted to the 87th Brigade. The Royal Fusiliers and Lancashire Fusiliers went to the 88th Brigade. On 19th May the Royal Munster Fusiliers and the Royal Dublin Fusiliers re-formed."

87th Infantry Brigade.

2nd South Wales Borderers	Remained throughout.
1st King's Own Scottish Borderers	Remained throughout.
1st Royal Inniskilling Fusiliers	To 36th Division, February 19, 1918.
1st Border Regiment	Remained throughout.

88th Infantry Brigade.

4th Worcestershire Regiment .	Remained throughout.
2nd Hampshire Regiment .	Remained throughout.
1st Essex Regiment.	To 37th Division, February 4, 1918.
1/5th Royal Scots	Left division in September 1915.
1st Royal Newfoundland Reg. .	Joined Division in September 1915, in place of 1/5th Royal Scots. The battalion went to line of communications, April 1918.
2nd Leinster Regiment .	From 16th Division, 23rd April 1918, in place of Royal Newfoundland Regiment.

(e) Notes on the Organization of a Division in the Great War (France and Flanders).

1. *Infantry.*

An infantry brigade was composed of four battalions, until February 1918, when it was reduced to three. The fourth battalions were disposed of as follows : The 16th Middlesex Regiment was disbanded. The 1st Royal Inniskilling Fusiliers and the 1st Essex Regiment went to the 36th and 37th Divisions respectively.

2. *Royal Artillery.*

When the 29th Division arrived in France a divisional artillery was organized in most divisions as follows :—

> Three brigades, each of three 18-pounder batteries and one 4.5 howitzer battery.
> One brigade of three 18-pounder batteries.
> (All batteries had four pieces.)

In May 1916 the brigade ammunition columns were absorbed by the divisional ammunition column.

In September 1916 the brigade of three 18-pounder batteries was broken, and its guns were sent to the other three brigades to bring the 18-pounder batteries up to six-gun units.

In January 1917 further reorganization was carried out : a divisional artillery was now fixed at two brigades, each of three six-gun 18-pounder batteries and one 4.5 howitzer battery of six howitzers. To conform to this organization the howitzer batteries were made up to six pieces.

Each division now had one spare brigade ; these spare brigades were formed into army field artillery, and were used according to the situation. In a battle a C.R.A. might have three Army Field Artillery Brigades to look after, in addition to his own two brigades.

No further important changes were carried out.

For details regarding the 29th Divisional Artillery see Brigadier-General Marr Johnson's History.

3. *Trench Mortars.*

The first trench mortars were hurriedly improvised from old pieces of ordnance (the 5th Division had some dating back to the Crimea) in the winter of 1914–15. Gradual improvement and standardization took place, and by the spring of 1916 the trench mortars available in a division were as follows :—

Each infantry brigade had a Light Trench Mortar Battery of eight 3-inch Stokes mortars. This unit was manned by personnel drawn from the battalions of the brigade, and was numbered with the number of the brigade.

(2,655)

Next there were three Medium Trench Mortar Batteries, each of four 2-inch mortars. These batteries were designated X, Y, and Z, followed by the number of the division.

Later in 1916 each division was given a battery of two 9.45-inch mortars, designated V battery. The Medium and Heavy Trench Mortar Batteries were manned by R.A. personnel.

Taking the 7th Division as an example, this division, at the end of 1916, had the following Trench Mortar Batteries :—

> 20th, 22nd, and 91st Light Trench Mortar Batteries.
> X/7th, Y/7th, and Z/7th Medium Trench Mortar Batteries.
> V/7th Heavy Trench Mortar Battery.

In February 1918 the Trench Mortar organization was changed. The Medium Batteries were reorganized into two batteries (X and Y) and re-armed with 6-inch Newton Trench Mortars, while the Heavy batteries left their divisions and became corps troops.

4. *Machine Guns.*

In March 1916 the battalion machine-gun sections (4 Vickers) were formed into Brigade Machine-Gun Companies of the Machine-Gun Corps, bearing the same number as that of the infantry brigade to which they were attached. In 1917 another company was added to each division as Divisional Machine-Gun Company. In the spring of 1918 these companies were combined into a Machine-Gun Battalion.

When the Vickers guns left the battalions, each battalion had four Lewis guns. For the Somme battles a battalion had 8 Lewis guns ; for the 1917 offensive, 16 ; and by 1918 a battalion had 32 Lewis, plus 2 for anti-aircraft.

5. *Pioneers.*

Originally the British Expeditionary Force had no Pioneer Battalions, but each division received one during 1915 and 1916.

In February 1918 a Pioneer Battalion was reorganized on a three-company basis.

6. *Signal Service.*

The Signal organization was very intricate, and many important changes took place. This branch is beyond an ordinary divisional history.

The increase in establishment is interesting : in 1914 a Divisional Signalling Company had 7 officers and 170 other ranks ; in 1918, 15 officers and 400 other ranks.

One of the most important changes took place in the spring of 1917, when the signals of the divisional artillery came under the Divisional Signal Company.

APPENDIX III

RED-LETTER DAYS

(Compiled by Captain Maurice Healy, M.C.)

JANUARY.

1916.   8th.—Evacuation of Cape Helles.

1917.   27.—Capture of Le Transloy by the 1st Border Regiment and 1st Inniskilling Fusiliers, 87th Brigade. A brilliant local operation, resulting in the capture of over 400 prisoners and a considerable amount of the line.

FEBRUARY.

1917.   28th.—Capture of Sailly-Saillisel by the 2nd Royal Fusiliers and 1st Royal Dublin Fusiliers, 86th Brigade. This was a development of the success gained at Le Transloy, but proved a more costly operation. The ground gained was held against many counter-attacks.

MARCH.

1919.   15.—The division was finally disbanded, and its place was taken by the Southern Division of the Rhine Army.

APRIL.

1915.   25th.—The division, in the teeth of the strongest defence and in spite of appalling obstacles, made good a landing at Cape Helles. This day, upon which the division first went into action, must always remain the most memorable of its title to immortality.

1917.   14th.—An attack from Monchy-le-Preux by the 88th Brigade coincided with a German attack upon the village. The brigade suffered heavy losses, which fell chiefly upon the 1st Essex Regiment and the Newfoundland Regiment, which took the full brunt of the attack, while the other regiments organized a defence. Subsequently, all attacks having been beaten off, the brigade advanced and gained ground.

23rd.—A hotly contested action east of Monchy-le-Preux, in which the division succeeded in making good its objectives, although flanking units were held up.

1918.   10th to 13th.—Battle of the Lys. The 88th Brigade, attached to the 34th Division, fought a splendid rear-guard action south-east of Bailleul. The other brigades, going into action near Estaires, although repeatedly out-flanked and thus compelled to give ground, succeeded in holding up the German attack until a complete line of defence, which the Germans never penetrated, had been completed behind them.

MAY.
1915.   1st.—A very powerful night attack by the Turks broke through the lines of the Senegalese, the Royal Munster Fusiliers, and the Royal Dublin Fusiliers, but was repulsed by the R.A., Worcestershire Regiment, 2nd Royal Fusiliers, 1st Essex Regiment, and 5th Royal Scots.
          6th.—Attack by all three brigades from the Eski line towards Krithia. A gain of 800 yards upon a wide front.

JUNE.
1915.   4th.—The division, formed into two brigade groups in conjunction with the 42nd Division, attacked towards Krithia, capturing several lines of trenches and many prisoners.
          28th.—Battle of Gully ravine, in the course of which the Turkish defences were pierced. With a fresh brigade for pursuit, the course of the campaign might have been very different.

JULY.
1916.   1st.—Opening of the Battle of the Somme. The division lost more than 50 per cent. of its battle strength in gallant but unsuccessful efforts to carry Beaumont Hamel and Beaucourt.

AUGUST.
1917.   16th.—Battle of Langemarck. The division success-fully attained all its objectives.

1918.   18th.—Capture of the Outersteen ridge by the 86th and 87th Brigades.

SEPTEMBER.
1918.   4th.—Capture of Ploegsteert and Hill 63 by the 86th and 88th Brigades.
          28th.—Under the supreme command of the King of the Belgians the Second Army attacked the Germans east of Ypres, and drove them back several miles upon a wide front. The division attacked towards Menin. The 86th and 87th Brigades carried Hooge and the high ground on the Menin road, and the 88th Brigade, passing through them, captured Gheluvelt, and continued the advance as far as Kruiseke.

OCTOBER.
1916.   12th.—The 88th Brigade, in conjunction with the 12th Division, attacked from Gueudecourt. The 1st Essex Regiment and the Newfoundland Regiment, which were the attack battalions, carried all their objectives, and inflicted very heavy losses on the enemy.

18th.—On a day upon which no success was attained in any other part of the attack, the 4th Worcesters and 2nd Hampshires carried and held all their objectives in spite of heavy counter-attacks.

1917.   4th.—Battle of Broodseinde. On the northern flank of the British attack the 1st Royal Dublin Fusiliers, as a farewell to the 29th, in co-operation with 87th Brigade troops, made a most brilliant attack.

9th.—Battle of Poelcappelle. Three battalions of the 86th and three battalions of the 88th gained all objectives in scheduled time, inflicting heavy losses on the enemy, and beating off several counter-attacks.

1918.   14th to 16th.—Starting from Ledeghem, the division fought a three-days' battle which brought them to the Lys near Courtrai.

20th.—The 88th Brigade forced the passage of the Lys below Courtrai and advanced two miles beyond the river. The 86th Brigade " leapfrogged," and advanced to the high ground near St. Louis.

NOVEMBER.
1917.   20th and 21st.—Surprise attack by the Third Army towards Cambrai. The division was not in the first line of attack, but passed through and exploited the success already gained, advancing beyond the Scheldt Canal.

30th.—The German counter-attack having broken through between two of the divisions on the right of the 29th Division, the latter was placed in a position of great peril. Its three infantry brigades were turned, its guns were all but overrun by enemy infantry, and its divisional headquarters was actually carried by the enemy. With the exception of this incident and the capture of a small portion of Les Rues Vertes, which also was recaptured immediately, the division lost no inch of ground committed to its care. The 1st Lancashire Fusiliers, after repelling nine attacks, counter-attacked and improved their line. The gap in the British line was rendered useless to the enemy by this superb feat of arms, in which all units of the division covered themselves with honour. The special thanks of the Corps Commander, Army Commander, and Commander-in-Chief were conveyed to all ranks of the division by Special Orders of the Day.

1918.   11th.—Armistice Day. Brilliant exploit of G.O.C. 88th Brigade, who, attended by one or two staff officers and the attached cavalry, rode into Lessines at 10.55, just in time to prevent the destruction of the bridges over the river Dendre.   One hundred and three prisoners captured.

22nd.—Re-entry of the King of the Belgians into Brussels.   The 29th Division, represented by a detachment from each unit, took part in the ceremony.

DECEMBER.

1915.   19th.—Evacuation of Suvla Bay.   The division covered the operation, which was successfully carried through.

1918.   4th.—The division crossed the German frontier at Malmedy.

13th.—The division marched across the Rhine, the salute being taken by General Plumer at the foot of the Kaiser statues on the Hohenzollern Bridge.

APPENDIX IV

THE SONG OF THE 29TH DIVISION

From the border vales and the northern dales,
   From the rolling wave-beat coast,
From south to north the lads stream forth,
   Oh ! we are the army's boast !
And where there's a bitter fight to wage
   On a field all rent and gory,
The whole world knows there the Red Sign goes,
   Well famed in Britain's story.

     Oh, this is the song of the Twenty-ninth,
       In the east and the west you'll find it ;
     There's never a fight where the Red Sign goes
       But it leaves its mark behind it.

In desert sands of alien lands
   Sleep our bravest and our best ;
There's a Turkish hill where the flowers wave still
   O'er the graves where our dear lads rest.
And wherever the red war trail's agleam,
   And the battle thunders waken,
There's a tale to be told of a soul of gold
   Who trod Death's path unshaken.

     (Refrain as above.)

With a roll of drum the divisions come
   Hotfoot to the battle's blast ;
When the good Red Sign swings into the line,
   Oh ! there they'll fight to the last !
And the souls of those from the east and west,
   Well famed in Britain's story,
March at our head with silent tread
   To honour and to glory.

     Oh, this is the song of the Twenty-ninth,
       On every field you'll find it ;
     For wherever the Red Triangle went
       It left its mark behind it.

LANCELOT CAYLEY SHADWELL.

INDEX

INDEX

PRINTED AND BOUND IN GREAT BRITAIN BY INTYPE LONDON LTD.

LIEUT.-GENERAL SIR AYLMER HUNTER-WESTON
K.C.B., D.S.O., M.P., OF HUNTERSTON

7839972R10199

Printed in Great Britain
by Amazon.co.uk, Ltd.,
Marston Gate.